ABOUT ISLAND PRESS

Island Press is the only nonprofit organization in the United States whose principal purpose is the publication of books on environmental issues and natural resource management. We provide solutions-oriented information to professionals, public officials, business and community leaders, and concerned citizens who are shaping responses to environmental problems.

In 2000, Island Press celebrates its sixteenth anniversary as the leading provider of timely and practical books that take a multidisciplinary approach to critical environmental concerns. Our growing list of titles reflects our commitment to bringing the best of an expanding body of literature to the environmental community throughout North America and the world.

Support for Island Press is provided by The Jenifer Altman Foundation, The Bullitt Foundation, The Mary Flagler Cary Charitable Trust, The Nathan Cummings Foundation, The Geraldine R. Dodge Foundation, The Charles Engelhard Foundation, The Ford Foundation, The German Marshall Fund of the United States, The George Gund Foundation, The Vira I. Heinz Endowment, The William and Flora Hewlett Foundation, The W. Alton Jones Foundation, The John D. and Catherine T. MacArthur Foundation, The Andrew W. Mellon Foundation, The Charles Stewart Mott Foundation, The Curtis and Edith Munson Foundation, The National Fish and Wildlife Foundation, The New-Land Foundation, The Oak Foundation, The Overbrook Foundation, The David and Lucile Packard Foundation, The Pew Charitable Trusts, The Rockefeller Brothers Fund, Rockefeller Financial Services, The Winslow Foundation, and individual donors.

National Parks
and Rural
Development

NATIONAL PARKS
AND RURAL
DEVELOPMENT
Practice and Policy in the United States

Edited by
GARY E. MACHLIS and DONALD R. FIELD

ISLAND PRESS
Washington, D.C. ◆ Covelo, California

ISLAND PRESS is a trademark of The Center for Resource Economics.

All photos courtesy of the National Park Service.

Library of Congress Cataloging-in-Publication Data

National parks and rural development : practice and policy in the United States / edited by Gary E. Machlis and Donald R. Field.
    p. cm.
Includes bibliographical references and index.
    ISBN 1-55963-814-1 (cloth : acid-free paper) — ISBN 1-55963-815-X (paper : acid-free paper)
    1. National parks and reserves—United States—Management. 2. Rural development—United States. 3. Land use, Rural—United States—Planning. I. Machlis, Gary E. II. Field, Donald R.
    SB482.A4 N37425 2000
    333.78'0973—dc21
                                        00-010476

Printed on recycled, acid-free paper

Manufactured in the United States of America
10 9 8 7 6 5 4 3 2 1

Contents

Acknowledgments

Edited volumes are always the result of collective effort and dedication, and this book is no exception. Our initial proposal for preparing a book on national parks and rural development was enthusiastically supported by Walt Gardiner of the Economic Research Service (ERS) of the U.S. Department of Agriculture. The ERS provided funding for the project under Cooperative Agreement No. 43-3AEN-6-80096. Walt challenged us to provide a book that bridged the research literatures on national parks and rural development, and provided numerous and useful insights. Mary Ahearn of the ERS continued that support with patience and interest.

Nina Chambers, research associate with the National Park Service Social Science Program, was an indispensable and invaluable colleague. Nina assisted in preparing the introduction, conclusion, and other editorial material. She coauthored a critical and comprehensive appendix on federal programs. She corresponded with authors, managed the preliminary review of the chapters, cajoled authors for revisions, typed and retyped versions of the manuscript, and otherwise moved the project forward—all with good cheer and professionalism; we are deeply grateful to her.

Others provided important assistance. The 1998 International Symposium on Society and Resource Management in Columbia, Missouri, provided an important venue for authors to come together and discuss their preliminary approaches to the issue of national parks and rural development.

A large and talented set of reviewers helped improve earlier drafts of the chapters: Arnold Alanen, Michael Bell, Steven Brechin, Matt Carroll, Tim Clark, Hannah Cortner, Sam Ham, Lori Hunter, Richard Krannich, Walter Kuentzel, Patrick West, and Erv Zube. Jean McKendry prepared the case study maps with a cartographer's eye for clarity and grace. Todd Baldwin of Island Press provided able and efficient editorial assistance.

We, of course, are indebted to the authors whose work is collected in this volume. Their willingness to participate and contribute is testament to the importance of national parks and rural development.

Gary E. Machlis
Donald R. Field
January 2000

Foreword

It is not what we have that will make us a great nation; it is the
way in which we use it.

—President Theodore Roosevelt, July 4, 1886

Beginning with President Roosevelt and Yellowstone National Park in 1872,
Americans have placed a unique priority on preserving and protecting our
nation's natural and cultural heritage. One could argue that on that same day,
Roosevelt formed the first "gateway" community—a neighboring town or village, often rural—that is adjacent to a national park and provides much of the
needed infrastructure and services for the park itself. Today, as much as any, the
complex relationship between specially protected areas and the people who live
and work in cities and towns around them has become a central policy question
engaging park superintendents, politicians, and the public.

Much has changed since Roosevelt spoke eloquently and often about the
need to conserve, maintain, and develop our natural resources. From biotech-
nology opportunities to recreation, or questions over boundaries and access, the
people designated to manage our parks have faced many pressing issues with
some success, and some confrontation. These decisions need always be made
with the knowledge that a distinct symbiosis exists between the parks and their
adjacent communities.

America's National Park System has set an impressive standard for environmental stewardship, but the relationship between park and small business, or
park and homeowner, has never been as clear. As we progress in a new century,
the challenge to maintain the complex economies of the West, while nurturing
an appreciation for our natural and historic heritage, becomes even greater.
Careful analysis and debate that intersects with public determination will yield
the results we need to insure both goals of healthy parks and vibrant economies.

The authors of *National Parks and Rural Development* seek to capture and
explain their views as to how we best sustain this ongoing relationship and

develop solutions to the debates that exist between local communities and parks. Most importantly, each scholar offers a number of ideas, analyses, and new questions in search of answers—valuable contributions if we are determined to keep both Roosevelt's charge alive and our rural economies growing.

Senator Craig Thomas (Wyoming)

Introduction

This is a book about national parks and rural development and the connection between them. The central thesis is that national parks and rural development in the United States have been, are, and will continue to be intertwined. The thesis has three main elements. First, national parks play an important role in regional rural development, and a critical role in gateway communities. Second, regional rural development and the growth or change of gateway communities have a powerful influence on national parks—their resources, management, and visitors' experience. Third, this relationship has implications for policy, management, and research relevant to both national park and rural development decision makers, as well as those interested in parks and the citizens of rural areas.

All who visit a Yellowstone, Denali, Bryce Canyon, or Yosemite National Park (NP) quickly recognize the park's importance in the local economy and region. Visitors (and employees) need access, food, fuel, and housing, in addition to environmental education, recreational opportunities, and the inspiration found in these special places. Parks create transportation routes, energy grids, water and waste systems, housing needs, and business opportunities—all of which provide varying contributions to rural development. At the regional level, such a contribution can be significant to modest—Yosemite NP is an economic engine for several California counties, yet has a minor role in the immense California economy. For gateway communities—the towns and cities that border public lands—national parks can often be *the* economic engine, and play a dominant role in all aspects of community life. For the community of West Yellowstone and many other gateway communities, the role of national parks in their future is significant, critical, and enduring.

At the same time, rural development and the growth of gateway communities have immense impacts on the national parks. Development, such as that occurring in the city of Gatlinburg outside Great Smoky Mountains NP or in communities on Mount Desert Island adjacent to Acadia NP, increases demand for natural resources. Water is a prime example, and the demands for water in South Florida are both critical to the fate of Everglades NP and a warning of future crises. Development requires infrastructure to deliver resources and distribute waste products, garbage, and sewer effluent. The pipelines, roads, leach fields, and transmission cables outside Mount Rainier NP, or in Tusayan near Grand Canyon NP, are testimony to the engineering requirements of rural development.

Development leads to increased population, which leads to increased housing, and in turn to habitat fragmentation in often critical landscapes adjacent to park boundaries. Saguaro National Monument (NM), once outside the city of Tucson and now surrounded by the modern Tucson metro area, is an example at the extreme—with wildlife, water, habitat, vegetation, air, noise, and light pollution impacts from rapid development atypical for even the rural West. Development increases visitation by making parks more accessible. Yellowstone

NP in winter requires the special staging grounds and infrastructure of the few gateway communities prepared for winter recreation. The town of Cruz Bay, where available land for a school or playground is scarce, serves as the sole staging area for many tourists to Virgin Islands NP. Civil War battlefields are encroached on by rural development in Virginia; Denver's immense population growth and urban expansion has had its impacts on Rocky Mountain NP.

Emerging economic alternatives (such as cottage industries spawned by the electronic revolution), along with the quality-of-life attractions of national park areas, lead to increasing numbers of year-round and/or seasonal residents. These residents take advantage of proximity to park resources and increase the number, diversity, and demand of needed visitor services. The attraction of suburbia (and subsequent real estate values) adjacent to Santa Monica Mountains National Recreational Area (NRA) is testimony to the importance of parks as a quality-of-life amenity. Corporate location in rural America has its developmental impacts as well. When the Sony Corporation invests in facilities near Springfield, Oregon (a gateway to Crater Lake NP), or US West locates in Boulder, Colorado (near Rocky Mountain NP), the impacts are felt in the rural regions near parks. The result is that park management, of everything from fees to fires, must respond to rural development occurring outside park boundaries.

The relationship between rural development and national parks has significant implications for policy, in the fields of both rural development and park management. Policymakers interested in rural development—at the local, state, and regional levels—ignore the role of national parks and historic sites only at the peril of their strategies' success. Tribal governments, from those representing the Ute near Mesa Verde NP, to the Navajo at Canyon de Chelly NM, to the Miccosukee in Everglades NP, must deal with parks and protected areas as part of the landscape of development, or be unlikely to succeed in improving the quality of life of tribal members. And federal policymakers for the national parks—the current administration, Departments of the Interior, Agriculture, and Commerce (all concerned with rural development), Congress, the National Park Service (NPS) director, regional administrators, park superintendents, and park advocates—all must consider and decide park policy in light of rural development adjacent to the parks.

Hence, national parks and rural development are intertwined, and it is the purpose of this book to explore and assess this relationship.

Definitions

Throughout this book, the term "national parks" is used in a general sense, referring to all units within the National Park System. The system contains national parks, monuments, recreation areas, historic sites, historical parks, battlefields, lakeshores, seashores, and others. The book will employ the acronyms used by the NPS to designate national parks (NP), national monuments (NM), and the twenty-seven other kinds of NPS units (for a list of these abbreviations and acronyms, see appendix I). While each designation implies variation in how the unit was established, or in legal statutes, regulation, and policy, all are commonly managed by the NPS under its authority and mission. The mission of the NPS is derived from its Organic Act of 1916:

> To conserve the scenery and the natural and historic objects and the wild life therein and to provide for the enjoyment of the same in such a manner and by such means as will leave them unimpaired for the enjoyment of future generations (16 U.S.C. Sec. 1).

Importantly, rural development issues are as relevant to NPS recreation areas, historic sites, seashores, and other designations as they are to the traditionally defined national parks.

Rural development, a core concept in this book, can carry many different meanings. While chapter 1 provides an extensive discussion of various definitions, rural development as referred to in this book is defined as *economic prosperity, diversification, and sustainable community development that expands local opportunities and does not compromise quality of life or environmental protection.*

Hence, rural development encompasses economic development in the traditional sense of job and wealth creation, but extends further to include issues of quality of life and conservation of resources.

Change at a Critical Time

This book is prepared at a critical time. National parks in the United States, for all their supposed permanence, are changing in significant ways, as are the rural regions of the country. A general overview of conditions may be useful in providing a context for the chapters that follow.

Some of these changes are social and economic in nature. Rural economies across the United States are in flux, powered by a decade of national prosperity and their share of the capital investment and discretionary wealth. Rural regions and communities are less isolated than they used to be, and they are increasingly affected by regional and national economic shifts—from manufacturing to service, from postwar family agriculture to modern large-scale agribusiness, from analog to digital communication, from railroad station to airport as core transportation hub, and so forth.

In rural America, many extraction-based economies (such as timber, mining, and fishing) are being replaced by more service-oriented economies, such as tourism. No longer isolated from global markets, now connected by information technology, business firms are seeking (in addition to profitability) rural environments that provide amenities to support the workplace and excellent living conditions for employees and their families. For some towns, such as Leavenworth, Washington, near North Cascades NP, the shift is all-significant (covering everything from jobs to architecture) and reasonably successful. For other communities, such as the northern Minnesota towns near Voyageurs NP, the transformation is minimal, the frustrated expectations disheartening.

Migration of people to amenity-rich regions adjacent to parks is one reason for these economic changes. Counties adjacent to Yellowstone NP are growing at rates much faster than the rest of rural America; the same pattern holds for counties adjacent to wilderness areas. Many people moving to rural areas near parks migrate with their own businesses or work as telecommuters. Others are retirees, whose transfer payments in the form of investments, social security payments, and savings can represent a significant economic flow for small, rural communities. Communities such as Estes Park, Colorado (near Rocky Mountain NP), and St. George, Utah (near Zion NP), have experienced significant increases in retirees making these communities their home.

This in-migration to rural regions can have modestly transforming effects. For gateway communities such as Moab, Utah, near Canyonlands NP and Arches NP, in-migration can dramatically change the local population mix and demographic characteristics of the community. Citizens' reactions to the social and economic issues confronting a gateway community—such as growth planning, environmental restrictions, and provision of services—can sometimes be divided by "old-timers" vs. "newcomers," creating the continuing need to perceive these communities not as monolithic cultures but as often-fractured and competing interests.

These social and economic changes contribute to regional environmental changes in the rural landscape surrounding parks. Economically sound, environmentally sustainable, productive, rural industry is well practiced in rural America—examples of sustainable fishing, ranching, mining, agriculture, forestry, and other traditionally rural enterprises are often the norm, not the exception, and these patterns have long had a profound effect on rural landscapes and the environmental context of contemporary rural development. Examples of short-term outlook and poor practices are unfortunately also common—witness Forks, Washington, and its historical struggle with federal land management near Olympic NP. The result is that policies that protect fisheries from overexploitation, endangered species from extinction, and old-growth forests from unnecessary harvest have had a role in the changing rural landscape perhaps as much as the unsustainable nature of these abuses themselves.

Rural development, population growth, and habitat loss are often linked in cycles of land conversion. As rural populations grow (almost entirely from in-migration), land-use practices near parks are subject to significant change. Traditional large farms and ranches are subdivided to create more real estate for development. Five- and one-acre "ranchettes" replace larger holdings, making land management actions from weed control to groundwater protection more difficult. Scarce acreage for commercial development is pressured to absorb additional service businesses, further threatening traditional land use. This conversion of land use can cause the loss of wildlife habitat and environmental buffers that provide protection to water sources and forests. Often the conversion has impacts inside the parks—examples include the expansion of Jackson Hole adjacent to Grand Teton NP, or the growth of Miami and Dade County near Everglades NP.

This is a critical time for changes within parks as well. Partly as a function of the external pressures described above, significant biophysical and ecosystem-level changes are occurring inside the national parks. Air quality is degraded at numerous national parks (Grand Canyon NP and Great Smoky Mountains NP are prime examples), and water quality problems can be particularly damaging to plant and animal species (such as mining-related pollution on the Yellowstone River in Yellowstone NP).

Hence, development is an issue of concern *within* as well as outside parks. Increasing infrastructure and demand for visitor services within parks can create some of the same problems as development adjacent to parks—sewage discharge, lowered water quality, air pollution, overtaxed transportation systems, and more. Yosemite Valley in Yosemite NP confronts infrastructure and population pressures equivalent to a moderately sized city. Noise pollution (such as that from personal watercraft) can be disturbing to both wildlife and human populations; helicopter overflights in Grand Canyon NP have significant visitor impacts. Light pollution (from house lights, commercial lighting, and industry) can degrade night skies inside parks—Saguaro NM and surrounding Tucson, Arizona, is an emerging example.

In numerous cases, the NPS both attempts to ameliorate such problems (its laudable sustainable-design program) and contributes to their spread—maintaining antiquated sewer systems, running unnecessary noisemaking machines, installing lighting without light shields, and more. Importantly, rural development is both the large-scale conversion of arable land and the small-scale use of gas-powered leaf blowers. The changes wrought on park environments are both widespread and obvious, and localized and subtle. Responsibility for these pressures is widely shared.

One of the most significant changes inside national parks is the sheer increase in their popularity and use. Visits to national parks increased by more than 66 million people from 1980 to 1998, a 30 percent increase. These increases are not spread evenly throughout the National Park System. Some parks, such as Chattahoochee River NRA, have experienced significant increases (for Chattahoochee, more than 2.5 million *additional* annual visits) since 1980. Other parks, such as Cape Cod NS, have seen visitation levels remain constant, or like North Cascades NP, modestly decline.

In addition, the demographic character of the visitor population is changing, with park managers greeting a new clientele. While the "average visitor" has never existed, the diversity of visitors is likely to increase further in the next decade. The potential mix of visitors is changing. Ethnic minority populations are increasing (with Hispanic Americans overtaking African Americans as the largest minority group), and these increases are often localized in regions of the country with numerous national parks (such as Arches NP, Canyonlands NP, and others in the Southwest, or Everglades NP and Biscayne NP in South Florida). Hence, the ethnic diversity of visitors is likely to expand, bringing new recreation styles, uses, and needs to national parks and their gateway communities.

As the baby boomers age, and the ranks of the retired, affluent, healthy, and mobile senior citizenry expand, the national parks are likely to be attractive targets for their attention and visitation. An aging park-going population will create new challenges for park managers, as they move to provide services (such as interpretation and facilities) relevant to and required by seniors. Increased international tourism, encouraged by economic development in other countries, ever-expansive jet travel, and the realization that foreign visitors can mean high profits for the U.S. tourism industry, will also alter the mix of visitors, and the nature of rural development in parks and gateway communities. Those affected will not only be the obvious international "favorites" such as Grand Canyon NP, Mesa Verde NP, or Yellowstone NP, but other National Park System areas near international entry points—for example, foreign visitation originating at Miami International Airport contributing to a change in visitors to Big Cypress National Preserve (NPres).

The result is not only a change in visitors, but changed visitor experiences. Many visitor experiences in the National Park System have surprising stability. Viewing the Grand Canyon, climbing the Statue of Liberty, walking the fields of Gettysburg, and hiking in the North Cascades remain largely similar experiences year after year. Yet rural development adjacent to parks has the potential to alter the visitor experience.

A visit to a national park is not merely the actual park visit alone. Travel to the region, staging activities in the gateway community (such as eating, spending the night, shopping, and sightseeing), and travel to the park itself are all part of the visitor's experience. It is no surprise that visitor experiences can be affected by the character of the communities surrounding parks. The impacts can be positive, due to amenities or charm of traditional towns (Fredericksburg, Virginia, and its efforts to serve as an effective gateway for four Civil War battlefields), or negative in cases of poorly planned, overly developed, and ill-functioning "tourist traps" (Pigeon Forge, near Great Smoky Mountains NP, is often used as a classic example).

The changes that have been occurring are not limited to broad social or environmental trends. New forms of management are emerging. In recent years, more dialogue and collaboration is occurring between the communities and parks—or more precisely between community leaders, citizens, and park managers. One example is the Canyon Country Partnership, which includes Arches NP and Canyonlands NP, Bureau of Land Management officials, advocacy interest groups, the private sector, and county representatives. Other examples include the Cuyahoga Valley Communities Council (Cuyahoga Valley NRA), the Teton County Economic Development Council (Grand Teton NP), and the Greater Yellowstone Coalition (Yellowstone NP and Grand Teton NP). Park managers are becoming more active (with some controversy) regarding development in lands surrounding the parks, for they realize that such development will affect park management.

Similarly, citizens and gateway communities are increasingly demanding participation in decision making. A new association for gateway communities has recently been formed, the National Alliance of Gateway Communities. The group's mission, as stated in its brochure, is "to support policies and programs that enable gateway communities to achieve essential economic growth and vitality while maintaining and preserving the social, cultural, and environmental values of their citizens." Its establishment is indicative of the importance gateway communities place on public participation in park management.

In addition, there is a significant and growing relationship between national parks and other units of natural resource management. National parks, wildlife refuges, state forests, national forests, public and private reserves, tribal lands, and others are all part of a continuum of resource preservation critical to our nation's quality of life. The result is that new management strategies are emerging that create alliances between local communities, the NPS, and other federal agencies.

Innovation is increasing. Land trusts (such as the Aspen Valley Land Trust), comanagement of adjacent lands (such as the use of Regional Advisory Councils in Alaska), and new cooperative agreements involving a range of federal, state, and private partners are being used to permit collaboration in order to promote preservation. At this important juncture in the history of rural development and national parks, there is a real sense that invention—or in the language of the Clinton administration, "reinvention"—of government bureaucracy and methods is both possible and encouraged.

Why This Book Now

If, as we have argued, this is a critical time of change for national parks and rural development, why this book now? The answer lies, in part, in the current state of knowledge provided by the research and policy communities.

As several of the following chapters describe, the role of U.S. national parks in rural development has yet to be systematically defined or fully examined, and the impact of rural development on national parks has yet to be comprehensively explored. It *is* true that a significant research and policy literature on economic development in rural America currently exists. However, this literature largely ignores parks and other protected areas as engines of change in local economies or as elements of rural development strategies. Given the importance of both parks and rural development, this reflects a surprising lack of attention.

Likewise, the research and policy literature on threats to parks, environmental crises, and issues of species or ecosystem preservation is almost exclusively devoted to individual threats or stresses on specific areas. The focus is local, the causes often narrowly defined. The impacts described are rarely treated as a comprehensive package of environmental or socioeconomic consequences, and even more rarely linked to the forces and strategies of rural development. The present book attempts to redress this lack of attention and provide an introduction to important issues of concern.

Ironically, the majority of research and policy literature that *does* link rural development and parks comes from outside the United States. In particular, researchers and policymakers working in Latin America, parts of Asia, Europe, and West and East Africa have been active in describing the relationship between national parks and rural development. There, the interplay of national parks and protected areas with neighboring landscapes or regions has been more thoroughly discussed than in the United States. Policies acknowledging the corelationship of conservation and development have been developed, and management strategies (not always successful) have been implemented on the ground.

Often, however, there is an unwillingness within the U.S. policy and park management community to fully learn from or apply this international literature. Sometimes, cultural differences create barriers to embracing lessons learned from other countries. And it is often difficult to discern what lessons can be directly transplanted into the U.S. context—with its emphasis on private property rights and profit, democratic traditions veering toward special-interest politics, a tendency toward litigation, and significant federal ownership of public lands. It may be equally unwise not to accept any of the available international lessons as it would be to embrace them all. There needs to be a sorting of ideas and critical analysis of opportunities, conducted through the lens of conditions and interests unique to the United States. Hence, an indigenous analysis of the link between rural development and national parks in the United States is a worthwhile step—and we think timely.

About This Book

The primary purpose of this book is to assess the relationship of national parks and rural development. Of special importance is an understanding of the role of

U.S. national parks in rural development, and how that role can be most effectively managed. As described above, the book is focused on U.S. parks and development policies. The book brings together available theory, methods, findings, case studies, and policy implications. As an edited volume, it provides a wide range of authors' perspectives. The thinking and views of economists, historians, rural sociologists, recreation researchers, park managers, and others are collected in its pages.

The book has several intended audiences. An obvious audience is those NPS managers charged with the stewardship of the National Park System. These professionals face the challenge of implementing a complex mission (provide for current enjoyment *and* preserve unimpaired for future generations, all at the same time) in an era of critical change (see the earlier discussion). Park superintendents, in particular, may find the book contains useable knowledge as they grapple with issues of preservation and seek partnership with local communities. Importantly, the NPS is more than a collection of park managers, and the professionals involved in its many technical assistance programs may also gain benefit from the book. Beyond NPS managers, the book should be useful to federal, tribal, state, and local resource managers charged with management of parks, wildlife refuges, and other protected areas. Some of the same issues concerning conservation and rural development confront these managers, and the national parks can provide telling examples and insights.

Managers of other federal agencies with land-use, environmental regulation, and rural development responsibilities—such as the Environmental Protection Agency, the USDA's Economic Research Service, the U.S. Forest Service, and the Natural Resources Conservation Service—may find the book useful. Policymakers in Congress, and the staff they rely on for background as new federal laws, policies, and budgets are debated, authorized, and appropriated, may find several of the chapters enlightening.

And while the focus of the book is on national protected areas, similar issues often confront state and federal forests, public grazing lands, and other resource "commons." Managers of these areas can benefit from increased understanding of the relationship between public lands and rural development.

In addition, the book should be useful to local decision makers attempting to guide and direct rural development in ways that benefit local people, cultures, economies, and environments. Community leaders, state legislators, rural development specialists, business leaders, and residents can benefit from a broader understanding of rural development affecting communities and regions tied to national parks. Those whose livelihood is linked to tourism may find much that is of concern, or at least of interest.

Researchers interested in issues of national park management and rural development may find the book a useful summary of current perspectives, understanding that its focus is clearly not a discourse on contemporary rural sociology, economic development, or community theory (though some theory appears), or an analysis of empirical research data (though much is provided and interpreted). It might serve as a companion text or supplemental reading for courses in park management, rural development, community forestry, regional planning, tourism, landscape architecture, and conservation. Graduate students in the fields of park management, rural sociology, resource economics, tourism, and rural development may find it an efficient introduction and a starting point for their own investigations.

The book is organized into three parts, each with a different purpose and strategy. Each part begins with a brief editors' introduction, and ends with a brief editors' discussion. Their purpose is to place individual articles in context and point out areas of similarity and divergence among the chapters. Part One, "Theory, Concepts, and Contributions," includes a series of chapters that provide a wide-ranging review of the literature on rural development and national parks. Collectively, the authors demonstrate that national parks have historically been linked to rural development, and that contemporary strategies are being expanded to embrace preservation, protection of ecosystem services, and tourism as alternate engines of rural development.

Part Two is based on the assumption that the case study approach has significant value in examining the role of national parks in rural development. The individual chapters explore a varied set of examples—from the Pacific Northwest, the Southwest, Alaska, Cape Cod, and Yellowstone. Lessons learned, principles applied, mistakes committed, and advances made—all related to national parks and rural development—are identified in these carefully drawn cases.

Part Three shifts from comprehensive review and careful case study to strongly held opinion. This portion of the book includes personal essays from several key leaders in the field of national park management. While each essay differs from the others in tone, focus, and viewpoint, they collectively suggest that the role of national parks in rural development is controversial, evolving, and open to creative problem solving.

A detailed conclusion is provided and summarizes the policy implications of the preceding chapters and includes specific recommendations for improving rural development and park management policies. The conclusion is followed by several appendices, including an important guide that inventories current federal programs useful to rural development and gateway communities.

The central thesis of this book is that national parks and rural development in the United States have been, are, and will continue to be intertwined. If the book succeeds in describing and examining this relationship, in ways useful to its intended audiences, it is possible that both parks and the rural regions that surround them will benefit.

Part One

THEORY, CONCEPTS, AND CONTRIBUTIONS

A traditional view of parks as vignettes of nature, cultural heritage, and historical events neglects the role of protected lands within their larger sociocultural context. Parks are not isolated icons of nature. They are interdependent with other natural resources and are integral elements of a landscape mosaic; lands and waters inseparable from human communities and their economic enterprises. This broad perspective is critical to understanding the relationship between national parks and rural development. In this first section, the authors review our collective knowledge about rural development in general, and rural development associated with tourism and recreation specifically. This is followed by a brief history of the role of national parks in rural development, and a review of social science research associated with parks and adjacent communities.

Gene Summers and Don Field, in the opening chapter of this book, introduce the concept of rural development and trace its many interpretations. Rural development is a *goal,* not a *theory.* It is a process in which a community considers a range of options for economic and social well-being and applies them to a strategy for change. The chapter is an overview of this rural development process. There is a growing recognition that rural development is no longer created by local areas alone, but occurs in the context of regional, state, and federal guidelines and is influenced by state, federal, and international actions. The authors introduce us to four factors influencing rural development: macropolicies, sectoral policies, territory policies, and human resources—each of which can pose barriers or create opportunities for rural development strategies. It is clear from their review that these strategies must be pursued through a partnership of mutual respect and understanding between parks and local communities.

In the next chapter, Dave Marcouiller and Gary Green help build a knowledge base through what Summers and Field call *sectoral analysis.* Marcouiller and Green suggest rural development be viewed through the lens of the economic sector, and express a growing need for tourism and recreation to be integrated into rural development. The authors acknowledge and review trends in rural economies shifting from dependence on extractive and manufacturing industries to service-based economies. They argue that tourism is one of many economic development strategies to enrich economies of communities adjacent to national parks. Recreation and tourism can contribute to the diversity and complexity of economic life in a community, making it less vulnerable to employment downturns, contributing to population growth, and changing the structure and social organization of the community.

At the same time, they acknowledge the pitfalls of tourism as a dominant source of employment, and the differential impact tourism may have on segments of the population. Tourism can lead to overdependence and economic fragility. The authors recognize parks and other public lands as the natural resources that can drive the recreation and tourism economy. Linking these natural resources with sustainable economic development strategies will require greater collaboration between park managers and local community decision makers.

While the first two chapters provide an overview of the role of rural development and tourism in economic development, the next two chapters focus attention on national parks. Hal Rothman describes the historical role of national parks in rural development. Rothman provides a historical sketch of the emergence of national parks, and the evolutionary way rural development arises and matures. His description implies an informal process by which park and community come together in development. Rothman notes the unevenness of development. It is clear the establishment of a park will alter the local and regional social and economic structure, but the results have not always been the same. His spatially linear development scenario suggests development is clustered along travel routes rather than broadly developed across the region surrounding a park. A series of historical examples illustrates the themes of development raised in earlier chapters.

While Rothman describes the historical and cumulative relationship of national parks and rural regions, Francis Achana and Joseph O'Leary review the contemporary social science literature pertaining to the relationship between parks, local communities, and rural development. While some research exists to document the relationship between parks and local communities, few studies have been conducted in the United States. Economic impact assessments are an example—not widely done, complex in method, and variable in results. And as the authors note, the interests of local people have not always been seriously considered by the NPS. This overview of social science research describes the varying roles of national parks in local communities, and emphasizes that a park is a social invention—with ties to local communities and cultures—as much as it is a natural area or a cultural site.

Chapter 1

Rural Development: Meaning and Practice in the United States

Gene F. Summers and Donald R. Field

The primary objective of this book is to consider the role of U.S. national parks in rural development. It is timely to do so. The relationship of federal public land management agencies with communities in the shadow of parks, forests, and refuges has been unclear, inconsistent, and unorganized. In part, this ill-defined relationship can be understood by the narrow mandates of the federal agencies, which focus on their national-interest lands and not landscapes or regions in which the public lands are located. While it is true public land managers have ventured into local community assistance, a consistent national policy or strategy toward local communities has not been executed over time.

With the emergence of ecosystem management strategies, including local community participation in planning and management of local natural resources, a new national policy on the role of public land management in rural development is appropriate to consider. Therefore it is the aim of this chapter to provide an introduction to rural development from a community perspective, review different dimensions of rural development, and explore one rural development strategy in some depth. We emphasize the economic aspects of rural development as the thread to community change while noting the linkages to other institutional sectors of community.

What Is Meant by "Rural Development"?

To address this question, it is helpful to step back to the 1880s. As industrial capitalism made its great surge, urban America quickly surpassed earlier achievements of European nations. To many urbanites, the evidence clearly supported their undaunted optimism and faith in evolutionary progress from a stagnant agrarian society to dynamic urbanism. Yet, in the midst of obviously rising national affluence there existed rural-urban inequality. America was not an equally good and just society for all; being "left behind" in the rural hinterland conferred significant disadvantages on rural people and their communities.

In 1900, the nation held a vivid recollection of the radical agrarian mood of the Populist Party, which had grown increasingly ugly in response to the escalating farm crisis of the last quarter of the nineteenth century (Goodwyn 1978). Although William Jennings Bryan was defeated in 1896 as the Populist candidate for the presidency, the political unrest in the countryside continued to be a serious concern of urban industrial interests who depended on farmers to supply cheap food for the growing army of industrial workers. At the same time, projections of agricultural output fell far short of expected population growth. There was a sense that something had to be done about "farm and rural problems." Thus, rural development became an important feature of the public policy landscape of American society.

There are various definitions and interpretations of rural development. [*Edi-*

tors' Note: For additional discussion, see chapters 5 and 10.] Rural development, for example, could simply be defined as a process of expanding the range of opportunities economically, culturally, and socially for rural people. It is a multifaceted set of policy objectives and processes. Rural development, for example, often includes discussion of local infrastructure improvements; enhancement of human capital such as education, training, job skills, and leadership skills; and enhancement of community organization, civic responsibility, and collective action toward common goals. As Rogers et al. (1988:324) note, "rural development is organized efforts to improve the quality of life in rural areas." Nevertheless, rural development has traditionally begun with the economic institutional structure as the entry point for advancing community growth and expansion of opportunities for people. Ron Shaffer places this notion of economic development within a rural development context in the following way when he notes:

> economic development is the sustained, progressive attempt to attain individual and group interests through expanded, intensified and adjusted use of resources. Important elements in development include: (1) setting goals, (2) identification of individuals and groups and inter-relationships, (3) understanding of the present and future effect of decisions made now, (4) the attempt to form new combinations of existing resources or the pursuit of new resources. Economic development can also be defined as those activities which lead to greater resource productivity, a wider range of real choices for consumers and producers, and broader clientele participation in policy formation. Economic development is goal oriented change, not change for the purposes of change (Shaffer 1989:7).

Jim Christianson builds on Shaffer's point on social change. He suggests, "community development is concerned with the process of change and how people affect and are affected by change" (Christianson 1982:266).

Beyond Definitions: Focusing the Debate on Rural Development

Rural development above all, then, is a process, a predetermined emphasis on change, a focus on people and social goals rather than solely on community as place. A summary statement written by James Copp in 1972 provides ample guidance to contemporary thinking. He said, "Rural development is not a theoretical concept; rather, it is a policy goal. It is a target justified . . . by normative arguments" (Copp 1972:518).

For some policy architects the normative argument is based on equity considerations—all Americans should have equal access to necessary goods and services such as education, employment, an adequate income, housing, health care, and other aspects of an acceptable quality of life regardless of their place of residence and work. Therefore, the argument continues, investments should be made and programs established to reduce place differentials in quality-of-life indicators. [Existing federal programs are described in appendix II.]

For others, the normative argument is rooted in the notion of efficiency. In reality, there are two very different versions of the efficiency argument that lead to diametrically opposite conclusions. One accepts the policy goal of improving the quality of life in rural places and states that this goal can best be achieved by making structural changes in the organizations and institutions of rural communities and industries. As Hobbs (1980:14) points out, "It [efficiency] has been foremost among criteria involved in structural changes in agriculture in the United States and in the move toward extensive consolidation of rural schools and other rural services institutions."

The other version of the efficiency argument arrives at a conclusion that rural America should *not* be developed or preserved. The neoclassical economic position is more likely to hold that resources (labor and capital) are often "trapped" in underproductive rural areas, and that rural development further compounds the problem, reducing efficiency and national economic growth (Drabenstott et al. 1987).

It would appear there is considerable agreement that rural development means creating policies (public and private) that are intended to produce greater equality of living conditions among places, especially when rural and urban residents are compared. This involves attention to the consequences of economic change and to the processes by which the change occurs. It has both a macroorientation and a local orientation. Since the rural segment of society has an inevitable interdependence with the rest of society, policies to improve rural conditions must consider the well-being of society. At the same time, rural development policies are implemented by actions in communities, a reality that dictates attention to local conditions, processes, and outcomes. In other words, national policies without local imperatives remain incomplete.

Therefore, this chapter considers several critical elements of a national rural development policy along with a comprehensive community economic development strategy. An effective rural development policy must integrate macro, sectoral, territorial, and human resource policies to create a positive and supportive environment for communities. Local leaders must design and implement a comprehensive community economic development strategy, but with an eye to national and regional policies that can enhance or constrain community success.

National Rural Development Policy

While local officials and community leaders have some degrees of freedom to take actions that affect their economic future, there are "city limits," as Paul Peterson (1981) has argued. Local initiatives are more likely to be successful when they are embraced by supportive federal and state policy environments. However, there is not a consensus about the most appropriate elements for a rural economic development policy (Swanson 1990). This situation seems to derive from the diversity and specialization of rural economies (Deavers 1988a, 1988b; Pulver and Summers 1992) and from differences in theoretical orientations toward economic development (Eisinger 1988; Shaffer 1989).

Since the end of World War II, rural America has ceased being dominated by agriculture and other natural resource–based industries. Rural America has become quite diverse in its economic structure; not dramatically different from urban America in the aggregate. Rural people are employed in a wide range of industries and occupations, with manufacturing, trade, and services dominating (Brown et al. 1988; Drabenstott and Gibson 1988). Thus, the rural economy of the United States is exposed to a much wider range of external factors than was previously the case (Deavers 1988a, 1988b). A farm policy will no longer suffice as an economic development policy for all of rural America; nor will any other policy that is focused on a single industry sector. Diversity in the aggregate has rendered obsolete the notion that one policy will fit all situations. A national tourism policy espoused by land management agencies focusing only on tourism and recreation with gateway communities will suffer a similar fate.

At the same time that rural America has become more diverse in the aggregate, there has been an increase in economic specialization by communities and regions. Where once nearly all rural communities were specialized in agriculture or other natural resource exploitation, there now exist many other types of economic specialization: manufacturing, education, health services, retirement centers, destination tourism and recreation, information technology, government administration, and military installations. Consequently, there is now a wide range of "single-industry" communities in rural America. Faced with this situation, Deavers (1988a, 1988b) argues that a rural development policy should consist of four complementary elements: macropolicy, sectoral policy, territorial policy, and human resource policy.

Macropolicies

Because the rural economy is now an integral part of the national and global economies, macropolicies that achieve national goals will have significant impacts on the performance of local rural economies. Fiscal, monetary, transportation, tariff and trade, and other macropolicies may affect rural areas differentially, depending on their particular economic base, but no rural area will escape macropolicy impacts. Therefore, rural interests need to be given recognition in the shaping of these macropolicies.

Sectoral Policies

Although sectoral policies are being roundly criticized—particularly farm policy—they cannot be abandoned entirely. Even under the conditions of free trade, with its consequent shifting of resources from declining to growing sectors, there is a need for sectoral policies to cushion industries against the shocks of transition. In some instances, this may mean public investments to accelerate expansion in growing industries. At other times, it may require short-term support for declining industries and the people and places that depend on them. There will be much debate about which sectors to support, at what level of subsidization, and for how long, but sectoral policies continue to be important to rural development.

Territorial Policies

Territorial, or place-oriented, policies that facilitate the process of rural institutional capacity building are an important element in rural development. Formerly, such policies were based primarily on an efficiency argument that maintained that it was more efficient to assist rural communities through support of infrastructure building than to encourage out-migration of the population. While equity arguments have been offered for their political value, they seldom have been determinant in the targeting of programs. The infrastructure-building approach of past place-oriented policies was aimed at making "backward areas" more attractive to goods-producing industries. Today there is little optimism about goods-producing industries as a source of job growth, and "future rural infrastructure needs are more likely to be for facilities that reduce rural disadvantage in access to information (and communication)" (Deavers 1988b:389–90). Rowley and Porterfield (1993) note, however, that information and communication technology should be viewed as a necessary but not sufficient condition for rural development.

Human Resource Policies

The fourth requirement for rural development is a human resource policy. Much of the burden of economic adjustment falls on human resources—displaced workers, farmers, business owners, and members of their families and households. Public investment in the education of children and youth, as well as adult retraining, is essential to rural development and can be supported by both efficiency and equity arguments (Fox and Murray 1993). Human resource policies that equip people for employment and major changes in employment are critical. One may add health services to the educational component of human resource policy, as does Swanson (1990).

Were a national rural development policy to be adopted, there would be great uncertainty about its impact on any particular community. National policy merely sets some aspects of the environments in which communities exist. The tasks of adapting to changing internal and external conditions still fall to the actors within the community. Each community must devise its own strategy for enhancing its economic future. It would seem to us that once national policies associated with land management agencies and communities are formulated it is in the arena of local-oriented actions where national parks and park managers have the greatest potential for playing a role (or roles) in rural development.

Local Economic Engine of Change

Given the awareness of the four elements of national policies that influence local options, it may be argued that it is the local economy that serves as the engine of community development and it is there that land managers and community leaders will initially focus their attention. Therefore, it would be helpful to describe a fundamental dimension of local economic structure, namely, export base theory, which serves as the conceptual guide for most local and regional economic development efforts. Conceptually it is quite simple. A local or regional economy is divided into two parts. One part of the economy consists of all the economic activities within the boundaries of the local community or region that bring a flow of money into the local economy. These activities are the "export" sector. Typically, one thinks of exports as things being shipped to other places. But in reality, it is the flow of money into the local economy that denotes the export sector. Shipping raw materials and manufactured goods presumably generates a flow of money into the local economy. But the export sector also includes the selling of services outside the local community, such as workers who sell their labor to employers in neighboring communities or states and bring their earnings back to the community. Similarly, the export sector may consist of buyers of services who come into the community to purchase health care or an education, or to engage in recreation. It is equally appropriate to regard retirees as an export industry if they move into the community and bring their passive incomes with them (pensions and investment returns).

The other part of the local or regional economy is known as the secondary sector and consists of all the economic activities within the bounded area that provide goods and services to local consumers (e.g., individuals, households, businesses, government). The theory presumes that activity in the export sector drives the secondary sector. As money comes into the local economy, some portion of it is spent locally for goods and services required by the export sector. This local spending of export-generated money creates jobs and income in the secondary sector of the local economy. Therefore, if one wishes to stimulate the local economy, the place to begin is with the export sector. As export-generated money is spent locally for goods and services, the providers of those goods and services also become purchasers of additional goods and services, some of which may be purchased locally. Thus, a portion of the export-generated money is spent and respent in the local economy, creating what is known as a positive multiplier effect. Every 100 jobs created in the export sector are expected to generate additional jobs as these workers in the export sector spend their earnings in local goods and services markets. Thus, community and regional economic development (rural development) are driven by the challenge to find ways to create jobs in the export sector and generate additional income for individuals, households, businesses, and governments in the area while sustaining the natural resources on which they depend. To do so requires a comprehensive game plan in which economic growth is placed in the context of development and conservation goals of both communities and public land management agencies.

A Comprehensive Community Economic Development Strategy

In this section, we outline one approach to rural development planning in which the NPS could participate in concert with local communities, blending the desire for community sustainability to be compatible with the natural environment, which both seek to protect. In 1979, Glen Pulver published a theoretical framework for the analysis of community economic development policy options that provides a comprehensive strategy to guide local initiatives (Pulver 1979). He argued that reliance on increased productivity in agriculture, greater exploitation of natural resources, and attraction of new manufacturing industries is too narrow as a strategy for community economic development. This vision of the export sector is needlessly restrictive, and if followed exclusively would doom rural development in contemporary society. Additional options are needed to complement these traditional export-oriented economic activities, which focused almost exclusively on goods production for external markets. With this premise in one hand and the export base theory in the other, Pulver described five elements of a comprehensive strategy, which are discussed in the paragraphs that follow. Summers has added two additional elements that are explicitly more social than economic, but that have important consequences for long-term economic development. A community economic development strategy should be constructed keeping in mind the four elements of national or regional policies.

Strategic Community Audit

Every community has basic resources that can be used to create jobs and improve incomes. They should be identified through a strategic community audit. While there are many basic resources, they can be arranged under the broad categories of natural resources, labor, capital, technology, and institutions. The amounts and qualities of these resources need to be ascertained; then their current and potential uses in a comprehensive plan of development can be analyzed. It is through efficient and effective use of basic resources that more jobs and income may be added to the community, but maximum utilization of resources depends first on a thorough awareness and understanding of them. The audit of local resources juxtaposed with all four of the national elements would provide a measure of strength for the community to interact with regional and national directions in the design of a local development initiative. The NPS should likewise complete an audit of the human and capital resources it can contribute to the rural development effort.

Community Needs Assessment

Alongside the strategic community audit of basic resources, there ought to be an assessment of what the citizens feel are the needs and desired goals for their community. Such needs assessment is grassroots democracy at work. It permits planning to proceed in ways that assure citizens their needs are being heard and incorporated. Moreover, it helps to avoid the possibility of misplaced priorities. Sometimes, it is not what we don't know that is a problem; it is what we "know" that is wrong. Accurate knowledge of expressed needs of various groups within the community permits the designing of a more rational comprehensive community economic development strategy (Johnson et al. 1987). The NPS must also be clear when outlining its needs such that the process for building consensus on directions are mutually beneficial.

New Basic Employers

First, communities may seek to attract new basic employers. No community is economically self-sufficient, and a viable export sector is essential for economic growth and development. However, the concept of exports must be broadened to include economic activities beyond natural resource–based extractive industries and the goods-producing sectors. For many years, these have been the standard bearers of the export sector. During the 1970s, a national policy of rural industrialization was pursued on the premise that manufacturing activities could be used as an instrument for expanding local export activities. However, the success of this policy was minimal and rather short-lived (Barkley 1993; Summers et al. 1976). More recently, efforts have been made to use high-tech manufacturing decentralization as a source of new basic employment for rural areas, but these also have produced limited benefits. As Glasmeier concludes, "Given the emphasis on technology in industry, our rural areas are more vulnerable now than ever" (1993:181).

One alternative to the low-tech, high-tech manufacturing solution to expanding the export base of rural economies is to broaden the concept of an export base. Any activity that generates a flow of money into the local economy is a legitimate component of the export sector. This includes a wide range of ser-vice-producing industries as well as destination tourism and even the passive incomes of the elderly and retirees.

Smith (1984, 1993) and Smith and Pulver (1981) have shown that service-producing businesses can generate significant amounts of export activities for rural communities. However, many rural service businesses are household ori-ented and primarily driven by local consumer demands. Therefore, business-ori-ented services, which have a greater potential for export, are those to be targeted as basic employers. For the most geographically remote and physically isolated rural areas, business-oriented services may prove to be quite elusive.

One of the potential roles of the rural countryside is that of playground for urban residents. The natural and cultural features of the rural landscape are val-ued highly by millions who are willing to spend huge sums of money for the pleasure they receive, if only for a few hours or days. Recreation and tourism are big business, but it is only recently that their overlap with economic develop-ment potentials of rural areas has been recognized. For some rural communities and regions, recreation and tourism may be important items on the menu of development options. [*Editors' Note:* For additional discussion on the impacts of tourism on rural communities, see chapters 2 and 4.]

Research shows that passive income (investment returns, pensions, retire-ment payments) to rural community residents also has the ability to generate jobs in local labor market areas (Hirschl and Summers 1982; Reeder et al. 1993). In many rural communities, passive income is more than half the total personal income and provides a potentially strong source of increased consumer goods and services demand as well as a source for development capital (Summers and Hirschl 1985). Reeder et al. (1993) have demonstrated that attracting retirees is a viable development option for communities with attractive climate and amenities.

The list of nontraditional rural economic activities that have a potential for generating a flow of money into the local economy is quite large. The range of possibilities has not been fully explored but surely includes medical centers that serve a nonlocal clientele, universities and colleges, recreation and tourism, research and development laboratories, military installations, regional offices of federal and state governments, and a variety of export-oriented business and consumer services.

Business Retention and Expansion

The retention and expansion of existing businesses is a major source of employ-ment growth. The vast majority of jobs created in any given year come from the expansion of existing firms. Therefore, Pulver (1979) quite reasonably argues that a comprehensive strategy of community economic development should include attending to the requirements of businesses that already exist in the local economy.

If existing businesses remain competitive, they continue to provide income and employment. When the profits of existing firms are reinvested in the community, further benefits to the community result. Therefore, communities ought to consider possible actions that may improve the efficiency of existing employers, assist them in identifying market expansion opportunities, minimize constraints on their growth potentials, and enhance the employers' sense of community citizenship.

A recent study of efforts to assist rural economies concludes that "trying to get industry relocations and trying to attract branch plants can still be an important economic development strategy in the more rural areas, but it is not nearly as important as strategies that deal with retentions, start-ups, and expansions" (Sidor 1990:75). While there are limits to which communities can, or should, subsidize existing employers through retention and expansion programs (Peterson 1981), attending to their needs is an important element in a comprehensive strategy.

Import Substitution

Steps may be taken to improve the ability of the local economy to capture monies generated within the community and to acquire monies generated in other places. All of the income that flows into the local economy, or is generated locally and expended within the community, adds to employment and income benefits. Therefore, it is reasonable to consider ways and means of producing locally those goods and services that are being purchased outside the local economy (Pulver 1979).

While no community is able to capture all its existing income, the larger the percentage spent locally, the better will be the economic well-being of the community. There may be an inclination to interpret this strategy element as a main-street merchants' "buy at home" campaign. But it should not be so limited. It has been demonstrated empirically in several recent studies that import substitution is not limited to household-oriented goods and services. Smith (1993) has provided evidence of situations in which imported business-oriented goods and services also may be produced locally.

New Business Formation

Communities may encourage new business formation as another element in a comprehensive community strategy (Pulver 1979). In dynamic international, national, regional, and local economies there are opportunities for the creation of new businesses to meet growing and shifting demands for goods and services. Moreover, existing demands sometimes are being met by a nonlocal supplier which could be supplied by the creation of a local business. All these forces indicate opportunities for new business formations for at least some communities.

Throughout rural America, the decline of agriculture as a source of employment has community leaders seeking ways to diversify their economies. Clearly,
the structure of agriculture has shifted toward larger and more capital-intensive
farms, which has resulted in nearly two-thirds of farm households, mainly those
with small acreage, depending on off-farm income. In this situation, it is tempt-
ing to think only of nonfarm enterprises as new sources of employment for the
decanted farmers and farm workers. However, in many instances the natural
resource base and the agricultural experience of workers may be efficiently and
profitably redirected to the creation of nontraditional agricultural enterprises.
The opportunities include industrial crops, fresh vegetables and specialty crops,
aquaculture, fee hunting and fishing, and others.

Many communities also are experimenting with a variety of programs to
encourage and assist the start-up of new businesses. One of the most popular has
been the creation of "business incubators" that lease space to tenants at below-
market rents and provide shared overhead services, as well as technical and
financial consultative services and training programs. Some communities also
have established enterprise free zones and grant regulatory relief for newly established companies. In addition, there are programs that provide subsidized financial assistance through community development corporations (CDCs), loan
pools, and other schemes.

Recapture Taxes Paid to Nonlocal Governments

Finally, communities may seek to increase aid received from senior units of government (Pulver 1979). This should not be misconstrued as "welfare hunting"
or creating "welfare magnets." All communities contribute taxes to nonlocal
units of government that are spent on a great variety of programs for which local
governments, businesses, and individuals may be eligible recipients. Without
judging the cost-effectiveness of the various programs, it is reasonable from a
community's perspective to capture the income provided through such programs.

Public expenditures in a community by broader units of government, which
are respent locally by recipients, have employment and income-generating
effects similar to other flows of money into the local economy. Therefore, it is
to the economic advantage of a community to reacquire funds taxed away by
broader governmental units, at least in the short term.

In summary, the exercise of each of these options within the comprehensive
strategy of community economic development will be enhanced by the collective actions of local organizations (Esman and Uphoff 1984; Rubin 1986; Schell
and Davig 1981). This means that community economic viability demands a
broad base of citizen participation in examining the goals, needs, resources, and
market conditions of the local community (Johnson et al. 1987). By involving
people from all corners of the community, leaders have access to more complete

information about resources and needs. Citizen participation also may develop future leaders and a stronger commitment of citizens to projects.

Moreover, community economic viability requires leadership in both the public and private sectors, active local organizations, and supportive community institutions (John et al. 1988; Shaffer 1989; Sokolow 1990; Sokolow and Spezia 1989). Leadership and organization are the engines of community economic development and, therefore, are basic resources for economic development. Often we fail to think of them as being vital in the same way as land, capital, labor, or natural resources. Yet a community with a variety of active citizen groups and associations is wealthy because these organizations are the incubators for leadership and organizational skills so essential to community economic development.

Rural development is above all defined as a process by which the range of opportunities for people and their communities is enhanced.

Conclusion

In this chapter we have outlined the meanings and fundamental dimensions of rural development and emphasized economic structure as the entry point for rural development partnerships between land management agencies and leaders of rural communities. Further, the link between national rural policy and local action cannot be ignored. National elements such as macro, sectoral, territorial, and human resource policies provide the context and sideboards within which communities operate individually and collectively. The NPS should interpret its place in these national policies for local communities. Once community assets are accumulated and needs expressed within a comprehensive community development strategy, the execution will depend on local leaders. In short, it is people, not necessarily the place where people live, that will determine a successful outcome.

The future of rural America is in the balance. While change is the one constant in history, the recent past has been one of dramatic transitions for most rural communities and people. Agrarian dominance has given way to economic diversity in the aggregate, while at the same time, some localities have become more specialized as centers of manufacturing, education, health care, regional trade, business services, retirement residences, government installations, or destination tourism.

As manufacturing and the various service industries become more significant elements in local economies, the conditions and organization of work associated with them come to play a greater role in shaping the conditions and performance of local markets of all types. For example, rural areas with a greater reliance on manufacturing are more exposed to the consequences of shifts in national and international economies than they were previously, which makes them more sensitive to macroeconomic policies, business cycles, and global competition in product markets.

These shifts also signal the increasing relevance and necessity for theories of economics, politics, and sociology that treat rural phenomena as integral elements in the fabric of national society and international relations. Rural areas and economies are no longer isolated from the mainstream processes of the economy, politics, or society. Consequently, theories and social policy planning that treat rural areas as "ghetto" phenomena are largely undermined and irrelevant.

The context for rural policies has been dramatically altered socially, economically, and politically. Where once rural policies could be aligned closely with agricultural policy, the options are now far more diverse and complex. Single sectoral policies, such as agricultural policy, cannot properly address the concerns of all (or even many) rural communities. Similarly, the economic diversity of localities within regions undermines the utility of regional policies. This suggests the need for greater local involvement in the creation of development policies and strategies that can be tailored to the requirements of the local economy. But localities are limited in the range of relevant factors they can influence.

Effective policy options for the future will require a greater partnership between local and national architects of policies and programs than has been characteristic of the past. This is where the NPS can play an important role. For example, rural areas need to improve labor quality, through public education and training, throughout the lifetime careers of workers. Localities must invest in upgrading their human resources or they will be destined to receive the least attractive of the economic activities. But inasmuch as workers are geographically mobile, a large share of the costs for human capital development and maintenance must be a national responsibility. An equitable partnership is essential.

But the partnership involves more than cost sharing. It also requires a division of labor and coordination. Macroeconomic and sectoral policies almost surely will remain the responsibility of the national government. But their formulation and administration could be more sensitive to their impacts on local economies, which seems reasonable inasmuch as the national economy is a federation of local economies. A new partnership could identify the distributive effects of macro and sectoral policies and provide instruments to cushion the inevitable hardships of transition.

So long as the United States operates within the system of market-oriented competition among communities, local agencies (public and private) will remain critical actors in determining each community's economic viability. Functionaries of local government and organizations have a heavy responsibility that could be lightened somewhat by the adoption of a partnership model of local, state, and national relations. Even so, some areas will be more successful than others, but small towns and rural America might move in the direction of having fewer extreme losers.

References

Barkley, David L. 1993. Manufacturing decentralization: Has the filtering down process fizzled out? In *Economic Adaptation: Alternatives for Non-Metropolitan Areas,* ed. David L. Barkley, 21–48. Boulder, CO: Westview Press.

Brown, David L., J. Norman Reid, Herman Bluestone, David A. McGranahan, and Sara Mills Mazie, eds. 1988. *Rural Economic Development in the 1980s: Prospects for the Future.* Rural Development Research Report Number 69. Washington, DC: United States Department of Agriculture, Economic Research Service.

Christianson, James A. 1982. Community development. In *Rural Sociology in the U.S. Issues for the 1980s,* ed. Don A. Dillman and Daryl J. Hobbs, 264–72. Boulder, CO: Westview Press.

Copp, James H. 1972. Rural sociology and rural development. *Rural Sociology* 37: 515–33.

Deavers, Kenneth L. 1988a. Rural economic conditions and rural development policy for the 1980s and 1990s. In *Agriculture and Beyond: Rural Economic Development,* ed. Gene F. Summers, John Bryden, Kenneth L. Deavers, Howard Newby, and Susan Sechler, 113–23. Madison: University of Wisconsin, College of Agricultural and Life Sciences.

———. 1988b. Choosing a rural policy for the 1980s and 1990s. In *Rural Economic Development in the 1980s: Prospects for the Future,* ed. David L. Brown, J. Norman Reid, Herman Bluestone, David. A. McGranahan, and Sara Mills Mazie, 377–95. Rural Development Research Report Number 69. Washington, DC: United States Department of Agriculture, Economic Research Service.

Drabenstott, Mark, and L. Gibson, eds. 1988. *Rural America in Transition.* Kansas City, MO: Federal Reserve Bank of Kansas City.

Drabenstott, Mark, Mark S. Henry, and L. Gibson. 1987. The rural economic policy choice. *Economic Review* October: 41–58.

Eisinger, Peter K. 1988. *The Rise of the Entrepreneurial State: State and Local Economic Development Policy in the U.S.* Madison: University of Wisconsin Press.

Esman, Milton J., and Norman T. Uphoff. 1984. *Local Organizations: Intermediaries in Rural Development.* Ithaca, NY: Cornell University Press.

Fox, William F., and Matthew N. Murray. 1993. State and local government policies. In *Economic Adaptation: Alternatives for Non-Metropolitan Areas,* ed. David L. Barkley, 223–46. Boulder, CO: Westview Press.

Glasmeier, Amy K. 1993. High-tech manufacturing: Problems and prospects. In *Economic Adaptation: Alternatives for Non-Metropolitan Areas,* ed. David L. Barkley, 165–184. Boulder, CO: Westview Press.

Goodwyn, Lawrence. 1978. *The Populist Movement: A Short History of the Agrarian Revolt in America.* New York: Oxford Press.

Hirschl, Thomas A., and Gene Summers. 1982. Cash transfers and the export base of small communities. *Rural Sociology* 47: 295–316.

Hobbs, Daryl J. 1980. Rural development: Intentions and consequences. *Rural Sociology* 45: 7–25.

John, DeWitt, Sandra S. Batie, and K. Norris. 1988. *Brighter Future for Rural America? Strategies for Communities and States.* Washington, DC: National Governors Association.

Johnson, Donald E., Lorna R. Meiller, and Gene Summers, eds. 1987. *Needs Assessment: Theory and Methods.* Ames: Iowa State University Press.

Peterson, Paul E. 1981. *City Limits.* Chicago: University of Chicago Press.

Pulver, Glen C. 1979. A theoretical framework for the analysis of community economic development policy options. In *Non-Metropolitan Industrial Growth and Community Change,* ed. Gene F. Summers and Arne Selvik, 105–17. Lexington, ME: D. C. Heath.

Pulver, Glen C., and Gene Summers. 1992. *A Jobs Program for Rural Areas.* Washington, DC: The Urban Institute.

Reeder, Richard J., Mary Jo Schneider, and Bernal L. Green. 1993. Attracting retirees as a development strategy. In *Economic Adaptation: Alternatives for Non-Metropolitan Areas,* ed. David L. Barkley, 127–44. Boulder, CO: Westview Press.

Rogers, Everett M., Rabel J. Burge, Peter F. Gorsching, and Joseph F. Donnermeyer. 1988. *Social Change in Rural Societies: An Introduction to Rural Sociology.* Englewood Cliffs, NJ: Prentice-Hall.

Rowley, Thomas D., and Shirley L. Porterfield. 1993. Removing rural development barriers through telecommunications: Illusion or reality? In *Economic Adaptation: Alternatives for Non-Metropolitan Areas,* ed. David L. Barkley, 247–64. Boulder, CO: Westview Press.

Rubin, Herbert J. 1986. Local economic development organizations and the activities of small cities in encouraging economic growth. *Policy Studies Journal* 14(3): 363–88.

Schell, Douglas W., and William Davig. 1981. The community infrastructure of entrepreneurship: A sociological analysis. In *Frontiers of Entrepeneurship Research,* ed. Karl H. Vesper, 563–90. Babson Park, MA: Babson Center for Entrepreneurial Studies.

Shaffer, Ron E. 1989. *Community Economics: Economic Structure and Change in Smaller Communities.* Ames: Iowa State University Press.

Sidor, John. 1990. *Assisting Rural Economies: The Role of the State Community Development Block Grant Program in Rural Economic Development.* Washington, DC: Council of State Community Affairs Agencies.

Smith, Stephen M. 1984. Export orientation of non-manufacturing businesses in non-metropolitan communities. *American Journal of Agricultural Economics* 66(2): 145–55.

———. 1993. Service industries in the rural economy: The role and potential contributions. *Economic Adaptation: Alternatives for Non-Metropolitan Areas,* ed. David L. Barkley, 105–26. Boulder, CO: Westview Press.

Smith, Stephen M., and Glen C. Pulver. 1981. Non-manufacturing business as a growth alternative in non-metropolitan areas. *Journal of the Community Development Society* 12(1): 33–47.

Sokolow, Alvin D. 1990. Leadership and implementation in rural economic development. In *American Rural Communities,* ed. A. E. Luloff and Louis E. Swanson, 203–13. Boulder, CO: Westview Press.

Sokolow, Alvin D., and J. Spezia. 1989. *Political Leaders as Entrepreneurs? Economic Development in Small Communities.* Report presented to the Economic Research Service. Washington, DC: United States Department of Agriculture, Economic Research Service.

Summers, Gene F., Sharon D. Evans, Frank Clemente, E. M. Beck, and Jon Minkoff. 1976. *Industrial Invasion of Non-Metropolitan America: A Quarter Century of Experience.* New York: Praeger.

Summers, Gene F., and Thomas A. Hirschl. 1985. Retirees as a growth industry. *Rural Development Perspectives* 1(1): 13–26.

Swanson, Louis E. 1990. Dilemmas confronting rural policies in the U.S. In *National Rural Studies Committee: A Proceedings,* ed. Emery Castle and Barbara Baldwin, 21–29. Corvallis, OR: Western Rural Development Center.

Chapter 2

Outdoor Recreation and Rural Development

David W. Marcouiller and Gary Paul Green

Outdoor recreation and nature-based tourism have become important development issues in many rural areas today. Most rural areas are no longer limited to agriculture, forestry, and mining as their primary economic base. As a strategic component of rural development, the recreational use of open space is on the rise because of increasing recreational demand, infrastructure development, tourism's apparent ease in creating jobs and income, its relatively low capital requirements for starting businesses, and other community development benefits (Frederick 1993). Outdoor recreation and nature-based tourism also are perceived as being more "environmentally friendly" than many other economic development activities.

The rural development literature suggests there are costs to tourism development as well. There are numerous examples of how unfettered tourism growth has had detrimental impacts on the sociocultural values of local residents (de Kadt 1976; Jordon 1980) and economic diversity and development (Becker and Bradbury 1994; Britton 1977; Fritz 1982). In addition, many of tourism's effects on rural communities are complex and as yet unknown. [*Editors' Note:* For additional discussion of these effects, see chapter 4.]

In this chapter, we evaluate several questions regarding outdoor recreation and tourism as a rural development strategy. What social and economic theories are at our disposal to address tourism within a rural development context? What do we know about the social and economic effects of tourism? What are the key elements of an integrative approach to rural tourism development? We discuss these issues in this chapter and then turn to outlining a research agenda on tourism development research.

Rural Development Research

Rural America continues to lag behind urban areas in several important development dimensions. These include socioeconomic disparities in household incomes, levels of educational attainment, rates of poverty incidence, and access to health care and other social services. Many rural areas, especially in the Great Plains, continue to lose population to urban areas. Depopulation leads to lower levels of public services, higher tax burdens, and fewer economic opportunities for residents who remain.

Historically, rural development theory has focused on these problems and has assessed strategies for generating employment opportunities in lagging regions. Yet in many rural areas today the problems are quite different. Many rural communities, especially those in the urban-rural fringe and those that have become retirement destinations, are facing problems associated with rapid growth. [*Editors' Note:* For example, see chapter 8.] These developments raise new issues for rural development theory. Although job creation and income generation are still important issues in many rural localities, land-use planning, skills matching, and conservation of natural resources have become much higher priorities for many communities.

In this section, we discuss some of the traditional and more contemporary issues in rural development theory and provide an outline of the contemporary social science literature on rural development. For decades, much of the focus of rural development theory has directed attention to generating jobs and creating income in rural areas, while ignoring the importance of the natural environment and its management. More recent work, however, has emphasized the importance of natural resources to the development of rural communities. We identify the primary obstacles rural communities face and the various strategies that have been used for promoting development. Throughout this paper we use the term "development" rather than "growth." In the context of our discussion, growth usually refers to more jobs and income, while development implies institutional and structural changes in the economy that lead to higher levels of living and changes in the distribution of income. Finally, we explore some of the recent work on rural sustainability, and pay special attention to problems related to land-based recreational use, natural resource management, and tourism development, suggesting that interests between development and maintenance of natural resources are more compatible than is commonly believed.

Key Obstacles to Development in Rural Areas

Social science research on rural development has emphasized several obstacles facing communities in rural areas. Next, we briefly discuss problems related to dependency, scale, and space. Much of the work on rural development has focused on strategies for increasing the economic base of regions. Increasingly, rural areas are being viewed not only as a source of natural resource commodities for production of raw materials, but also for their recreational values and aesthetic worth. Maintaining the aesthetic quality of rural areas has an increasingly important economic dimension as well. Thus, we need to examine how job creation and income generation are linked to broader, more holistic approaches to resource management and environmental sustainability.

Resource Dependency and Economic Diversity

Rural communities are frequently dependent on industries that are vulnerable to wide fluctuations in prices, especially those industries based in natural resource extraction (Freudenburg 1992) or manufacturing industries late in the product or profit cycle (Markusen 1985). Historically, most rural communities have been dependent on agriculture, forestry, fishing, or mining. In the case of manufacturing employment, rural areas are primarily recipients of low-wage, low-skilled jobs. Employment in natural resource industries and low-wage manufacturing industries tends to be unstable because of high levels of competition from countries overseas and the tendency for overproduction in these industries. Dependence on these types of industries also tends to produce lower-paying jobs that provide few opportunities for occupational mobility as compared to the industrial structures associated with more diverse economies found in urban areas.

Rural communities typically suffer from a lack of diversity in their economic structure, which means they are highly dependent on a few employers for use of locally available land, labor, and natural resource endowments. Market changes in the industries in which these employers are located can lead to rapid changes in employment. Not only are rural communities dependent on a few major employers, other businesses in the community tend to be linked to these businesses as suppliers, which also makes them vulnerable to fluctuations in the activities of base firms.

Finally, rural communities are frequently dependent on external, rather than local, sources of financial capital. Globalization and economic restructuring have produced changes in the spatial organization of production and increased absentee ownership of economic activity in rural America. Although rural communities have never been entirely independent from these processes, they are much more closely linked to international markets than ever before. These processes tend to move the location of decision making outside the local community, making it more difficult for communities to play a role in developing strategic policies that affect their social and economic well-being.

Rural communities have been encouraged to diversify their economies in response to these structural problems. Rural development strategies often emphasize the importance of attracting nontraditional firms to the community and promoting the retail and service sectors of the local economy. Retail and service sectors have been shown to create a large number of jobs, while maintaining much of the social surplus in the local community. In more recent years, rural development theory has debated the importance of promoting small businesses in rural areas as a method for reducing dependency on large employers in small communities (Green 1994). It should be pointed out, however, that often there is not consensus in the literature on the benefits of diversification. Some critics have argued that it is more beneficial to recruit and retain large firms that provide better wages and benefits.

Scale of Rural Communities

The small size of rural communities also presents obstacles in providing public services. Because of low population densities in rural communities, the cost of providing education, health care, transportation systems, water and sewage/septic, and other services is higher than in larger, more densely populated communities. Because of these relatively high costs, rural communities may not be able to afford to provide the level of services demanded by residents or may have to generate higher revenues through taxes to pay for the services. Economic theory suggests that residents may move to locations where there is a better match between the quality and level of services offered and the services demanded by residents.

Scale also is an important issue for the development of new businesses in rural areas. Most small businesses need access to business services and professional services that may only be available in larger communities. As the economy shifts to the retail and service sectors from an agricultural and manufacturing economy, rural communities are at a disadvantage because they lack the supporting businesses that are essential to the creation, expansion, and retention of new businesses. Examples of these supporting businesses include professional services such as insurance, accounting, and technical support firms.

Federal and state governments have attempted to address many of these problems of scale by providing resources through grants and loans to rural communities. [Appendix II describes some of these programs.] More recently, rural development strategies have included multicommunity efforts at collaboration that bring together several communities to gain economies of scale in providing services to residents (North Central Regional Center for Rural Development 1992). Multicommunity collaboration may offer benefits to rural communities that lack resources, but there remain several social and political obstacles to implementing these strategies in most communities. For example, tax laws make it difficult to share revenues across several different municipalities.

Space and Distance

Spatial considerations are essential to rural development. First, rural areas are usually the location for space-using production and consumption activities. Agricultural and silvicultural commodity production are two important space-using activities that have typically accounted for much of the demand for land in rural areas, although technological change is tempering much of that demand. On the urban-rural fringe, the growth of megastores, such as Wal-Mart and Home Depot, as well as encroaching residential developments are increasing the demand for land. Clearly, the growth of outdoor recreation and urban sprawl is increasing and changing the demand for land in many rural areas. The value of open space in these areas often provides greater economic return than commodity production. As we will discuss below, there is a growing conflict in many rural communities between open space values and use values associated with commodity production.

A second way in which space affects rural development is through the costs of distance. Castle (1983:15) reminds us of the need to distinguish between geographic and economic distance: ". . . financial costs associated with overcoming space are no longer a linear function of geographic distance, if they ever were."

Rural areas tend to be more isolated in terms of transportation, which adds to the cost of economic activities.

Rural development strategies have primarily addressed the latter spatial effect rather than the former. Strategies for reducing the economic cost of space include improved transportation systems and telecommunication systems. For decades, analysts have predicted that technological change would eliminate the spatial barriers of rural communities, as telecommuting makes it more possible to live and work in rural communities. Although these technological changes have made it possible for a small number of workers to reduce the barriers of distance, it is unlikely to have a major impact on the location of work in the near future.

Rural Development and Community Sustainability

Research on rural sustainability has focused primarily on the ecological critique of economic growth and development (Mitlin 1992; Rees 1995). Sustainability refers to the extent to which development is either self-undermining or self-renewing. Most of the literature has focused on whether and how economic development can generate a sustainable environment. At their core, most threats to environmental sustainability are driven by economic development concerns. We believe it is important to take a broader perspective on sustainability in rural communities. To create sustainable economies, communities need to develop long-term strategies for the viable use of financial, human, and social resources, as well as environmental resources. Although most rural communities continue to work toward attracting new capital as part of their development strategies, a few localities are employing community-based strategies to generate jobs and income. These strategies attempt to minimize dependence on external actors and organizations by promoting local ownership and control of resources (especially land, labor, and capital). These efforts are creating demand among extralocal actors, which produces benefits and returns surplus created to the community. They emphasize a decentralized and more egalitarian social order based on ecological principles.

Economic sustainability relies on development of community-based strategies that are compatible with the comparative advantage of local productive resources. Traditional rural development strategies often focused attention on the productivity of labor and capital resources. Rural areas often struggle to generate comparative advantage in these two factors of production. Factor productivity is hindered by a lack of diversity, economic scale, and distance. Land, and the associated natural resource base, however, provides an all-too-often overlooked factor of production that rural areas enjoy as compared to more densely populated urban areas.

Community-based strategies include the development of land-based recreational opportunities that rely on natural amenities, thus building on the comparative advantage of rural regions. These strategies contribute to economic development through nature-based tourism businesses and their supporting supply structure. In recent studies of community-based strategies it has been found that a disproportionate number of communities engaged in these home-grown development activities are involved in tourism (Green et al. 1994). Many of the communities turn to tourism-related activities because other strategies have failed or because of the relatively low cost of initiating these activities. Often these failures were the result of an emphasis on stimulating factor resources in which rural areas suffer from a comparative disadvantage. Rural tourism is unique in building from a resource base in abundant supply—land and the natural amenities that exist in rural regions.

The relevant linkage of outdoor recreation to community development often remains within the activities of tourism-sector businesses and their suppliers. Thus, we now turn our attention to the literature on tourism as a strategy for community development. In the following section, we briefly summarize some of the major research findings about the consequences of tourism on rural communities.

Rural Tourism and Community Development

Tourism's success as a community-based development strategy often hinges on how it affects the wide array of rural interest groups. Contemporary public policies that address tourism development often focus solely on supporting tourism-sector interests without considering the broader community development issues. In the United States, public tourism policies at all levels of government are dominated by marketing and promotional activities that result in increased tourist visits intended to provide expanded opportunities for tourism-sector businesses. There is a need to extend policies beyond this myopic focus to more effectively account for broader linkages to environmental, social, and economic sustainability of communities (Marcouiller 1997).

This section focuses on two aspects of the increasingly prominent tourism phenomenon: (1) how tourism generates and distributes income, and (2) fiscal elements of tourism for rural communities. The ability of tourism to generate jobs and income is often a leading reason for promoting tourism as a development strategy. Simple measures of job creation or income generation, however, mask important distributional implications of tourism in rural communities. Indeed, tourism may not create benefits that are distributed in an equitable fashion.

The ability of local units of government to generate revenue is an important impact of tourism on rural communities. Simple assessments of revenues generated, however, are incomplete without also discussing the costs of public service provision. Significant costs and externalities often are found to offset revenues from tourism. These assessment issues leave little in the way of clear indications on which to generalize the efficacy of tourism as a community-based strategy for rural development. The effects of tourism depend on several factors including the resource base upon which tourism produces outputs and specific community attributes, such as the manner in which the variety of stakeholders are included in the planning process.

Income Generation and Distribution

Tourism in rural communities often is encouraged for its ability to create jobs and income for local households. We begin by discussing the ill-defined nature of tourism from a supply-side, or economic-sector, perspective. Relative to most industries, tourism is very poorly defined. Most would agree, however, that the core economic sectors associated with tourism are classified in the service (hotels, amusement, and recreation) and retail (restaurants, miscellaneous retail) categories. Indeed, these are the sectors used by many analysts to assess tourism in rural communities (Brown and Connelly 1986, Johnson and Thomas 1990). Broader definitions would include construction and real estate sectors, as well as those involved in transportation and public utilities. Regardless of the way in which tourism is defined, the question then turns to how these businesses create employment opportunities and how this employment leads to income for rural households.

In the broadest sense, employment requires an assessment of returns to the spectrum of factors used in production. These include employment of labor, capital, and land. For purposes of this discussion on tourism, we can limit our focus on labor and capital resources. Land, and issues of natural resources, will be discussed later.

Relative to other industries, tourism is considered to be highly labor intensive (Bull 1991). Certainly, variation exists among different tourism types. For instance, capital-intensive tourism types (firms requiring large capital investments) are found when tourism includes higher-end hotels or large-scale amusement sites. Land-intensive tourism is typically found where land prices are very high or where vast expanses of privately owned land resources are required.

Because of the unique nature of labor intensity in tourism, jobs-based measures of economic contributions provide biased assessments of tourism relative to other sectors. Although commonly used, these aggregate assessments of jobs and income are insufficient criteria on which to evaluate the effectiveness of tourism in fostering economic development. The development implications of tourism in rural communities require a more focused assessment on the types of jobs created, their match with local labor markets, the effect these jobs have on income distribution, and the returns to other factors of production; namely land and capital returns. Focusing solely on the number of jobs created demonstrates the simple fact that aggregate assessments of a single factor used in production provide insufficient and biased measures of development contributions among different economic sectors.

Two aspects of labor use in tourism need to be taken into account in more objective assessments: the seasonality of labor use and the wage rate structure of tourism jobs. Tourism is a highly seasonal phenomenon (Stynes and Pigozzi 1983; Sutcliffe and Sinclair 1980). The seasonality of labor use in tourism regions has important implications for rural income generation, transfers of income among regions, complementarity of labor pools, availability of afford-able rural housing, and general rural migratory patterns. Little effort has been made to assess the types of jobs created by tourism, their match with regional employment goals, and the integration of tourism with broader development planning that occurs in rural regions.

There is a growing body of evidence that suggests the growth of tourism in rural communities can lead to greater income inequality. Critics of tourism development argue that jobs in tourism businesses create a situation whereby rural residents are placed in a subservient role catering to wealthy tourists (Ashworth 1992). Others suggest that tourism subjects income-poor local residents, disproportionally represented by female-headed households, to persistent poverty (Smith 1989). Yet others argue that a broader approach to tourism def-initions is required to fully evaluate the economic role tourism development plays in the distribution of benefits to rural residents (Rudzitis 1996).

Recent work on aggregate comparisons among rural economic sectors sup-ports some of these distributional concerns (Wagner 1997; Zhou et al. 1997). Differences in the use of factor inputs by economic sector leads to differential impacts by income group. In an examination of a rural region of southwestern Wisconsin (Leatherman and Marcouiller 1996), five alternative development strategies, ranging from agriculture and forestry production to tourism, were assessed for their effects on the distribution of income. Tourism was shown to create a "hollowing out" of the income accruing to middle-class households, thus supporting some of the arguments of Ashworth (1992) and Smith (1989). Tourism businesses often are owned by and provide returns to relatively wealth-ier entrepreneurs, while the people employed by these firms are paid low wages and hold predominantly part-time or seasonal jobs. Traditional agricultural and forestry development alternatives, on the other hand, tended to create more evenly distributed income impacts.

Equity in benefits and costs is an important aspect of rural development planning. Whereas certain planning arenas account for and target effects to spe-cific income groups implicitly (e.g., housing policy, social services), current rural tourism development planning, as tracked in the tourism literature, is generally satisfied with aggregate analysis that identifies gross benefits of industry growth on regional economic structures (Kottke 1988; Fletcher 1989; Johnson and

Moore 1993). Recently, there has been growing interest in research that accounts for differential impacts of alternative policies (Kamas and Salehi-Esfahani 1992) and addresses the continuing need to more accurately assess who benefits from various alternatives (Thraen et al. 1989; Smith 1987; Stoll et al. 1987; Eadington and Redman 1991). Although distributional (or class) arguments for differentiating tourism impacts by income category have been made (de Kadt 1976; Farrell 1979; Britton 1982), their integration into tourism development planning is lacking.

Furthermore, disaggregating tourism impacts based on other demographic characteristics such as race and gender (Smith 1989) would, most probably, explain many important stakeholder perceptions of tourism. Assessing the distribution of income and jobs generated by tourism development and taking actions to ameliorate negative results are fundamental to sustainable community development using tourism.

Fiscal Aspects

One of the driving forces behind tourism's development appeal is the notion that visitors provide a flexible mechanism for rural communities to shift the incidence of local revenue generation onto nonresidents. Typically, sales and use taxes are the primary mechanisms for generating revenue from tourism. These ad valorem taxes are paid for retail goods (restaurants and merchandise) and services (amusements). One negative aspect of ad valorem taxes on locally purchased goods or services is that the taxes are equally burdensome to local residents. These regressive local revenue mechanisms shift the proportional influence of the tax onto lower-income resident households. One type of ad valorem tax that effectively shifts the incidence onto incoming tourists is the hotel (or room) tax common throughout the United States. Initially developed for metropolitan regions and larger cities, room taxes have become commonplace in smaller communities and rural areas. Although some question the impact of room taxes on the vitality of local accommodations firms (Hiemstra and Ismail 1993; Hultkrantz 1994), such taxation mechanisms are effective in generating revenue for local units of government from nonresident tourists (Weston 1983).

Ad valorem taxes are certainly not the only means by which local units of government generate revenue from nonresident visitors. Property taxes paid by nonresidents are increasingly understood to be important for local units of government. Amenity-rich rural regions have witnessed dramatic increases in the in-migration of recreational homeowners (Moss 1994). These trends will most probably continue, particularly given the increased level of telecommuting and the continued demand for amenity locations. Recreational homes in rural regions have been shown to be significant net revenue generators for local units of government (Deller et al. 1997; Fritz 1982).

Tourism places demands on local goods and services, particularly infrastructure and public services. Heavy seasonal tourism demands for roads, water, police, and fire protection create very real costs to local units of government in rural communities. These public services are often difficult to provide because of the limited revenue generated from local year-round resident populations. A recent study has shown that as the level of tourism dependence increases, so does the level of public expenditure (Wong 1996). Seasonal demands on local public goods and services provide justification for revenue-generating mechanisms that shift incidence of tax receipts to travelers (such as the room tax). Often, local debate is polarized between those who advocate general revenue fund use of tourism taxes and those who favor earmarking these funds to further tourism promotional uses. Specific fiscal issues for rural communities relate to the limits of tax base expansion, taxation incidence, and burdens on local governments resulting from highly seasonal tourism demands. These issues require thorough examination, particularly with respect to tourism-related sales taxes and property taxes paid by nonresident second homeowners.

A broader development approach to tourism in rural communities is needed that extends public policy beyond the current narrowly defined realm of tourism promotion and marketing. Increasingly, rural communities face difficult extralocal questions that deal with more than maintenance and further attraction of visitors. This issue is particularly evident when we begin to examine linkage issues associated with land-based recreation and tourism incidence. The next section develops a social science research agenda that intends to inform a more integrative approach to rural tourism development planning.

Toward an Integrative Rural Policy on Tourism Development

To further our understanding of how parks and natural areas contribute to community development in rural regions, we must study a number of other issues in greater depth. Next we briefly outline further needs for research on tourism and outdoor recreation in rural areas. These topics fall within three broad categories: (1) linking the resource base with recreational use, (2) compatibility of alternative uses and resource management, and (3) rural tourism impacts on community structure.

Recreational Use and the Resource Base

The linkages between local resources, recreational use, and tourism are not well understood. The underlying motivations for visitors who support local tourism businesses are a function of both physical tourism developments (e.g., hotels, amusements) and the natural resource base. Motivations of outdoor recreationists to visit amenity-rich rural regions are influenced by the quality and quantity of naturally occurring resources such as forests, lakes, and mountains. What relationships exist between land-based resources present in local regions, demands for recreational use, and the influence of natural resources on surrounding tourism businesses? We manage natural resources for a variety of uses, with an increasing emphasis on recreation. Federal, state, and local units of government "package" natural resources for recreational use in parklands, trail developments, and open-access permission for wildland recreation. Businesses in surrounding communities respond to increased recreational use of this resource base through development of supporting retail and service activities (restaurants, overnight accommodations, and amusements).

Significant levels of public funding continue to be spent on providing the "resource infrastructure," or supply of recreational opportunities. Yet we have only recently undertaken studies that assess the effects of natural resources on tourism, amenity-related attributes, and local transmission of economic effect. Recent examinations linking resources to rural economic activities have attempted to develop typologies of amenity-based rural economies (e.g., Kusmin et al. 1996) and more closely specify the effects of natural areas on rural economic conditions (Duffy-Deno 1998; English et al. 2000).

A host of rural development and resource management questions remain. What are the elements that bind nature-based tourism regions together? How important is the natural resource base in attracting visitors? What aspects of the natural resource base help define tourism regions? How does natural resource management affect tourism? Environmental resources such as forests, mountains, and water bodies provide nonpriced open space inputs into the tourism production process (Marcouiller 1998). These latent inputs appear critical to rural nature-based tourism, yet resource managers have only anecdotal information on which to tailor their development activities. The assessment of linkages is needed to better inform decision making in resource management and community development.

Compatibility of Recreational Use with Traditional Extractive Resource Use

Traditionally, rural amenity-rich regions have been dependent on extractive resource use that has been both renewable (timber production and grazing) and nonrenewable (mining). There is a general perception that resource extraction and recreational use of a resource base are mutually exclusive; specifically, that resource planners and community development practitioners must recognize a trade-off between the two and plan accordingly. If recreational use and its linkage to tourism development requires "pristine" environmental conditions and extractive industries require wood, minerals, and livestock, what is to be done? Do we trade off output of commodity production for output of tourism, or are there interrelationships that, when understood, combined, and nurtured, enable development of a complementary association? Arguments for the latter tend to be cast aside by an oversimplistic approach to development issues. Good examples are policy analysis reports and critiques of the Federal Resources Planning Act (RPA) that sport such titles as "Recreation or Timber: Which Brings More Economic Benefit?" (Schallau et al. 1995). Regional analysis often pits alternative resource uses against each other and fails to address the core issues of compatibility between uses. In reality, more compatible forms of land use may serve as a better mechanism for economic development.

A host of land-use compatibility issues require further theoretical and empirical study. The conceptual framework for assessing land-use compatibility dates back to the work of Marion Clawson during the late 1960s and early 1970s (Clawson 1974, 1975). One particularly interesting aspect of Clawson's work is his comprehensive assessment of forest-use compatibilities. During the latter portion of his career, Clawson attempted to qualitatively assess the compatibility of alternative forest uses. Some forms of forest use have been described as clearly compatible (e.g., aesthetics and wilderness or water quality and wildlife production), while others are completely incompatible or inimical (wood production and wilderness use). Perhaps more importantly, Clawson observes that many uses are compatible if certain management controls are applied (wood production and wildlife or wood production and recreational use). Thus, Clawson has identified the basis for management interaction—management should be applied to control uses such that relative compatibility is maximized. Compatibility of land uses has provided an important goal behind contemporary resource management policy, yet further development of underlying theory and empirical support of Clawson's early work remains to be done.

Development of Rural Communities

Resource-based recreation and rural tourism need to be placed within a broader, more integrative context of regional development. Many local residents of rural communities have questioned the efficacy of tourism as a major development component simply because of the low-wage, seasonal nature of employment opportunities that are created by tourism businesses. Rural residents have a critical stake in development options that provide for household income sustenance. As social scientists, we need to make progress in regional analysis of economic structure to focus on the more important aspects of matching labor supply with labor demand. Some would characterize this need as a shift in emphasis from aggregate measures of rural economic growth to the richer, more complex analysis of economic development. A development context would necessarily shift from the traditional focus on markets for goods and services to an objective assessment of factor resources available locally. A more comprehensive assessment of local factor resources that address supply-and-demand conditions for labor, land, and capital assets present in rural communities could inform community development planning.

There are various components associated with factor resource assessments.

Skills matching and job access provide important issues that arise with rural tourism. Addressing these issues requires a shift away from aggregate measures of job growth to the more immediate need for employment opportunities that provide liveable wages for rural residents. Thus, the significant question that needs to be addressed deals with the types of jobs created by tourism and their match with the needs of rural households. What are the elements that we include in assessment of benefits and costs of a recreation-based development strategy? What are the distributional implications of tourism in rural regions?

Another important set of research issues concerns more permanent seasonal or amenity-based homeowners. This issue is particularly important given recent migratory trends of people seeking real estate in amenity-rich rural regions. How does the continuing flow of amenity migrants affect rural household income generation and its distribution? Of particular interest are assessments that sort out the benefits and costs of recreation and tourism among different socioeconomic groups. In-migrants tend to arrive in rural regions with significantly higher valued labor resources and larger capital endowments as compared to original longer-term residents of rural communities. Conflicts arise as higher-income residents begin to demand a different mix of services than lower-income residents. The more general aspect of equity in assessing benefits and costs of recreation-based strategies needs to be assessed. Issues of class, gender, race, residency-status, and fiscal issues will tend to dictate the effectiveness of tourism in meeting local development needs. A more integrative approach can capture these issues and better inform community-based development strategies in rural communities.

Conclusions

In this chapter, we have attempted to outline social science issues associated with community development focusing on smaller rural communities and their surrounding resource bases. In particular, we developed discussion around rural tourism development and a more integrative approach to development planning that viewed tourism within the broader context of community sustainability. Parks and natural areas in rural regions provide an important component of attraction and vitality within rural communities. They provide an opportunity for viable and sustainable development in these communities. As demands on natural resources increase in rural amenity-rich regions, more holistic approaches to community development and resource management must be developed that explicitly link the resource bases within surrounding communities. This more human dimension of natural resources remains a critical issue that deserves much more research attention.

We believe that a more holistic approach to managing the natural resource base requires a greater emphasis on community-based decision making. Public natural resource assets have not traditionally been managed by rural communities, but instead by state and federal officials. Linking the natural resource base with sustainable forms of economic development will require greater input from local communities. Management decisions based on this local knowledge will contribute to sustainability and will provide the "buy-in" among local residents that is sorely needed in many rural communities.

References

Ashworth, G. I. 1992. Planning for sustainable tourism. *Town Planning Review* 63: 325–29.

Becker, Barbara, and Susan L. Bradbury. 1994. Feedback on tourism and community development: The downside of a booming tourist economy. *Community Development Journal* 29: 268–76.

Britton, Robert A. 1977. Making tourism more supportive of small state development: The case of St. Vincent. *Annals of Tourism Research* 4(5): 268–78.

Britton, Stephen G. 1982. The political economy of tourism in the third world. *Annals of Tourism Research* 9: 331–58.

Brown, Tommy L., and Nancy A. Connelly. 1986. Tourism and employment in the Adirondack Park. *Annals of Tourism Research* 13: 481–89.

Bull, Adrian. 1991. *The Economics of Travel and Tourism.* Melbourne, Australia: Pitman.

Castle, Emery. 1983. Policy options for rural development in a restructured rural economy: An international perspective. In *Agriculture and Beyond,* ed. Gene F. Summers, John Bryden, Kenneth Deavers, Howard Newby, and Susan Sechler, 11–27. Madison: University of Wisconsin, College of Agriculture and Life Sciences.

Clawson, Marion. 1974. Conflicts, strategies, and possibilities for consensus in forest land use and management. In *Forest Policy for the Future: Conflict, Compromise, Consensus,* ed. M. Clawson, 101–91. Working Paper LW.1. Washington, DC: Resources for the Future.

———. 1975. *Forests for Whom and for What?* Washington, DC: Resources for the Future.

de Kadt, Emanuel. 1976. *Tourism: Passport to Development? Perspectives on the Social and Cultural Effects of Tourism on Developing Countries.* Washington, DC: The World Bank.

Deller, Steven C., David W. Marcouiller, and Gary P. Green. 1997. The influence of recreational housing development on local government finances. *Annals of Tourism Research* 24: 687–705.

Duffy-Deno, Kevin. 1998. The effect of federal wilderness on county growth in the intermountain western United States. *Journal of Regional Science* 38: 109–36.

Eadington, William R., and Milton Redman. 1991. Economics and tourism. *Annals of Tourism Research* 18: 41–56.

English, Donald B. K., David W. Marcouiller, and H. Ken Cordell. 2000. Linking local amenities with rural tourism incidence: Estimates and effects. *Society and Natural Resources* 13: 185–202.

Farrell, Brian H. 1979. Tourism's human conflicts: Cases from the Pacific. *Annals of Tourism Research* 6: 122–36.

Fletcher, John E. 1989. Input-output analysis and tourism impact studies. *Annals of Tourism Research* 16: 514–29.

Frederick, Martha. 1993. Rural tourism and economic development. *Economic Development Quarterly* 7: 215–24.

Freudenburg, William R. 1992. Addictive economies: Extractive industries and vulnerable localities in a changing world economy. *Rural Sociology* 57: 305–32.

Fritz, Richard G. 1982. Tourism, vacation home development and residential tax burden. *American Journal of Economics and Sociology* 41: 375–85.

Green, Gary P. 1994. Is small beautiful? Small business development in rural areas. *Journal of the Community Development Society* 25: 229–45.

———. 1997. Self-development as a strategy for rural sustainability. In *Rural Sustainable Development in America,* ed. Ivonne Audirac, 175–89. New York: John Wiley.

Green, Gary P., Jan L. Flora, Cornelia B. Flora, and Fred E. Schmidt. 1994. Community-based economic development projects are small but valuable. *Rural Development Perspectives* 8: 8–15.

Hiemstra, Stephen J., and Joseph A. Ismail. 1993. Incidence of the impacts of room tax on the lodging industry. *Journal of Travel Research* 31: 22–26.

Hultkrantz, Lars. 1994. Incidence of the impacts of room taxes on the lodging industry: Comment. *Journal of Travel Research* 33: 57.

Johnson, Peter, and Barry Thomas. 1990. Employment in tourism: A review. *Industrial Relations Journal* 21: 36–48.

Johnson, Rebecca L., and Eric Moore. 1993. Tourism impact estimation. *Annals of Tourism Research* 20: 279–88.

Jordan, James William. 1980. The summer people and the natives: Some effects of tourism in a Vermont vacation village. *Annals of Tourism Research* 7: 34–55.

Kamas, Michael, and Haideh Salehi-Esfahani. 1992. Tourism and export-led growth: The case of Cyprus, 1976–1988. *Journal of Developing Areas* 26: 489–504.

Kottke, Marvin. 1988. Estimating economic impacts of tourism. *Annals of Tourism Research* 15: 122–33.

Kusmin, Lorin, John M. Redman, and David W. Sears. 1996. *Factors Associated with Rural Economic Growth.* USDA ERS Technical Bulletin Number 1850. Washington, DC: United States Department of Agriculture, Economic Research Service.

Leatherman, John, and David W. Marcouiller. 1996. Income distribution characteristics of rural economic sectors: Implications for local development policy. *Growth and Change* 27: 434–59.

Marcouiller, David W. 1997. Toward integrative tourism planning in rural America. *Journal of Planning Literature* 11: 337–57.

———. 1998. Environmental resources as latent primary factors of production in tourism: The case of forest-based commercial recreation. *Tourism Economics* 4(2): 131–45.

Markusen, Ann R. 1985. *Profit Cycles, Oligopoly and Regional Development.* Cambridge, MA: MIT Press.

Mitlin, D. 1992. Sustainable development: A guide to the literature. *Environment and Urbanization* 4: 111–23.

Moss, Lawrence A. G. 1994. Beyond tourism: The amenity migrants. In *Coherence and Chaos in Our Uncommon Futures: Visions, Means, and Actions,* ed. Mannermaa, M., S. Inayatullah, and R. Slaughter, 121–28. Turku, Finland: Turku School of Economics and Business.

North Central Regional Center for Rural Development (NCRCRD). 1992. *Rural Development News* (special issue—multicommunity collaboration) 16(1): 1–35.

Rees, W. 1995. Achieving sustainability: Reform or transformation? *Journal of Planning Literature* 9: 343–61.

Rudzitis, Gundars. 1996. *Wilderness and the Changing American West.* New York: John Wiley.

Schallau, C., W. Maki, and W. McKillop. 1995. *Recreation or Timber: Which Brings More Economic Benefit? A Critique and Alternative Socioeconomic Analysis of the 1995 Draft RPA Program.* Unpublished report available from Con Shallau, 1435 Northwood Drive, No. 39, Moscow, ID 83843-1456.

Smith, Michal. 1989. *Behind the Glitter: The Impact of Tourism on Rural Women in the Southeast.* Lexington, KY: Southeast Women's Employment Coalition.

Smith, V. Kerry. 1987. Benefit estimation and recreation policy. *Policy Studies Review* 7: 432–42.

Stoll, John R., John B. Loomis, and John C. Bergstrom. 1987. A framework for identifying economic benefits and beneficiaries of outdoor recreation. *Policy Studies Review* 7: 443–52.

Stynes, Barbara White, and Bruce William Pigozzi. 1983. A tool for investigating tourism-related seasonal employment. *Journal of Travel Research* 21: 19–24.

Sutcliffe, C. M. S., and M. T. Sinclair. 1980. The measurement of seasonality within the tourist industry: An application to tourist arrivals in Spain. *Applied Economics* 12: 429–41.

Thraen, Cameron S., Ted L. Napier, and Stephen L. McClaskie. 1989. Factors influencing attitudes toward the commitment of economic resources to outdoor recreation development. *Journal of the Community Development Society* 20: 19–36.

Wagner, John. 1997. Estimating the economic impacts of tourism. *Annals of Tourism Research* 24(3): 592–608.

Weston, Rae. 1983. The ubiquity of room taxes. *Tourism Management* 4: 194–98.

Wong, John D. 1996. The impact of tourism on local government expenditures. *Growth and Change* 27: 313–26.

Zhou, D., J. Yaniagida, U. Chakravorty, and P. Leung. 1997. Estimating the economic impacts of tourism. *Annals of Tourism Research* 24(1): 76–89.

Chapter 3

A History of U.S. National Parks and Economic Development

Hal K. Rothman

Since the establishment of Yellowstone NP in 1872, national parks have served as an important catalyst for local and regional economic development. During the twentieth century in particular, the national parks—a rubric that includes all the variously named areas of the National Park System—played a transformative role in rural areas and small-town settings. Throughout the century, they offered an economic boost that has been widely regarded as a shadow economy, but has often been critically important as historical patterns of economic endeavor cease to sustain communities. In changing circumstances, national parks function as anchors, sources of employment and revenue that keep communities and regions afloat. Some regions view their parks as a transitional strategy; others embrace their parks wholeheartedly as the next phase in their existence. In these latter circumstances, national parks play a pivotal role in regulating change. They function as a way to standardize tourism, to hold it to a national idea of visitor service and maintain, wherever possible, existing relationships. In this sense, national parks protect the fabric of community from wholesale change, mitigating the impacts felt in unregulated tourist destinations.

Often national parks function as a replacement for declining sectors of the existing economy. This is particularly apparent in rural areas where agriculture and ranching have toppled from the precipice, near or on Native American reservations, in the vicinity of defunct mining towns, and in other similar contexts. National parks bring paychecks, employment opportunities, start-up and other entrepreneurial options, and often better infrastructure and connections to the outside world. Especially on reservations, where the cultural change that accompanies tourism can be particularly dislocating, national parks can serve as shields to guard against the consequences of comprehensive transformation, welcomed way stations between the traditional world and the onrushing outside that swoops down on destinations that catch the interest of the public.

Like any other economic engine, national parks create corridors of influence both in their immediate vicinity and along the routes to them. Within this sphere of influence, change happens more rapidly, and economic opportunities abound. These service areas require restaurants and hotels, service stations, and souvenir shops—the entire range of amenities to which the American traveling public is accustomed. The money spent at these often small-scale enterprises ripples outward through communities, infusing regions with a fresh source of capital that can often be used to sustain other, less economically viable practices with significant social meaning. In this, national parks serve as a hedge against dislocating social change, against the full-scale and seemingly pointless transformation that often accompanies tourist development.

National park areas are almost never conceived as economic development entities, but only in rare circumstances do they not serve in this capacity. Their proclamation usually stems from one of two major sources: places that have special resonance as a result of their history, cultural features, or natural attributes are often touted as candidates for inclusion in the National Park System. More common in recent years has been the elevation of places for distinctly political reasons—called "park barreling" and perfected by U.S. Representative A. Philip Burton of California during the 1970s. As a result, the economic development that often accompanies national parks is often an afterthought, clearly made possible by the creation of units that attract a national public, but often largely unrelated to the forces that created the park.

There were both regional variations and changes throughout the course of the twentieth century in the use of national parks for the goals of economic development. Typically, the differences were between places with developed economies and those without a solid economic structure or in serious decline as a result of a changing economic climate. In the former, national park areas served as an important add-on to existing economic circumstances; in the latter, especially in declining rural areas, national parks often became the linchpins of local and sometimes regional economies, offering the clearest road to prosperity in the middle of otherwise dislocating change.

During the twentieth century, the creation of a national park area most often provided a guiding force, allowing communities and regions to reach toward much-welcomed prosperity at the same time the park mitigated the impact of transformative change. In a variety of settings, this purpose manifested itself in valuable local relationships, economic sustenance for communities and individuals, and greater local control of sociocultural change than in parallel private-sector tourist development. Locales and regions fortunate enough to acquire a national park area received an economic base from which to build. They retained more input into the mechanisms of change and greater social cohesion than their unregulated peers, cushioning the impact of the transition to a service economy. Throughout the century, a national park area was a valuable economic asset for healthy and moribund communities alike.

Rural development and national parks have always been tied together, although, especially in the nineteenth century, the tie was often more a hope than a reality. From the beginning of national park history, economic development accompanied their formation. A national designation provided something special that people in any region expected would attract visitors, who would spend dollars, which would in turn promote new businesses and local growth. While in some instances, such as Yosemite NP, expectations were realized, mostly the economic lift from nineteenth-century national parks was confined to fortunate individuals who purveyed goods to visitors instead of communities and regions that surrounded them. Until Stephen T. Mather assumed responsibility for the national parks in 1915, becoming the first director of the NPS in 1916, development was haphazard at best. A few companies offered facilities at more than one park, but a relatively small number of visitors meant that whatever economic boost was received was minimal.

Mather's National Park Service worked on a series of specific principles, one of which was that high-quality service should be standardized, especially in the large national parks. A graduate of the University of California who made his fortune in public relations and marketing, Mather favored national companies over local ones. His sentiments institutionalized a pattern in national parks that meant that the broader the reach of the company, the more successful it would become at securing national park contracts. This made local development a double-edged business. On one hand, national companies offered the opportunity to work for wages in many places where such opportunity was fleeting. On the other, the situation meant that power and the decisions that came from it usually were located far from the region.

By the end of the 1920s, the pattern had been established. Entities such as the Harvey Company or the Curry Company held lucrative contracts throughout the National Park System, and local economic development coincided with corporate need for local labor. In many places, ancillary businesses in or near national parks—souvenir shops, motels and motor courts, gasoline stations, auto repair shops, guide services, and other activities—provided an entrepreneurial dimension to the local market. Communities could supplement their economies with the revenue from the growing number of automobile travelers.

The Great Depression and the New Deal enhanced the role of national parks in local and regional economies. The depression killed industry all over the nation, and people were forced to look for new ways to make a living. The federal government became a haven, especially after the creation of the New Deal in 1933. National park areas provided not only opportunities to provide services for visitors; under New Deal efforts such as the Emergency Conservation Work (ECW) program, which included the Civilian Conservation Corps (CCC), young men were employed to build facilities, clear roads and trails, and engage in an entire array of physical development activities not only in national park areas but on nearly all federal lands. Paid a dollar a day, of which all but five dollars a month was sent home for their families, these workers provided a crucial boost to moribund regional economies throughout the nation. Such work primed the pump of the American economy during a desperate time, adding another, but situationally specific and not exclusive, economic impact for national parks.

Although national park areas played almost no part in World War II–era economic development, in the aftermath of the war they developed even greater significance. An American population wealthy from wartime work and filled with pent-up desire—both to purchase and to travel—that had been impossible to fulfill during the war came in ever-increasing numbers, and each and every one of the visitors needed services and amenities. The result was a rapid and often uncontrolled proliferation of economic concerns, mostly in addition to the ones sanctioned in concession contracts. The places later labeled "gateway communities" began to take shape as the entryways to national parks, and became crowded with local concerns competing for the visitor dollar.

The expansion in size, reach, and range of the traveling public made national parks almost a sure bet. By the 1960s, with the politicization of the process of park creation, local communities and their congressional representatives became more aware of the benefits of national park areas. Congressional representatives such as Winfield K. Denton of Indiana, who shepherded the George Rogers Clark National Historical Park in Vincennes, Indiana, into the National Park System, or Joe Skubits of Kansas, responsible for the creation of Fort Scott National Historic Site (NHS), recognized that such areas conveyed not only an increased sense of patriotism or regional identity, but also economic benefits.

Since 1970, this pattern has held. National park areas are established first with an eye to national values, but the economic possibilities of their creation are an integral part of most proclamation strategies. This clear pattern suggests that national park areas have significant value to communities, especially rural areas in which declining opportunities hamper the basis for the regional economy. In places that have lost their way as a result of the change from industrial to postindustrial economy or for those that have never found it, national park areas serve as an important component of regional growth. This situation, the result of more than a century of development associated with national park areas, can be illustrated with three prominent examples: Carlsbad Caverns NP, Navajo NM, and Grand Teton NP. These three areas reveal the traits of economic development associated with parks as well as the way the NPS functions in small towns and on Indian reservations that depend on it. These capsule histories reveal both the significance and value of national parks in a changing rural America.

For two generations of Americans, Carlsbad Caverns NP was part of the constellation of the spectacular that everyone had to see. Located about 20 miles from the town of Carlsbad in southeastern New Mexico, which topped a population of 20,000 for the first time during the 1960s, the caverns had been "discovered" by a cowboy named Jim White around 1900. In the subsequent twenty years, they had been mined for their bat guano, still in use as an agricultural fertilizer. During the 1920s, a U.S. Geological Survey inspector reported on the caves, and a presidential proclamation established Carlsbad Cave NM. The new park quickly became the center of a budding local tourist industry, led by the intrepid Jim White and the Carlsbad Chamber of Commerce. After 1,280 visitors came to Carlsbad Cave NM during the years 1923–1924, the first year following its October 1923 establishment, the number rapidly rose to 76,822 in the years 1928–1929. When Carlsbad Cave NM became Carlsbad Caverns NP in 1930, the growth of tourism continued despite the depression (Ise 1961; Rothman 1989).

In a region previously known for its guano and irrigated agriculture, tourism meant a plethora of economic opportunities. Not only did the park benefit Jim White, who served as a ranger for the NPS, many others also found opportunity. Hotels sprang up in Carlsbad, photographers came to take pictures of the caves, guide services began, and other businesses opened, offering local and regional residents a more varied economy. Efforts to pave the road from El Paso to Carlsbad began in earnest, ensuring a supply of secondary jobs for many of the ranch families whose homes dotted the battered old stage route that served as a road, and providing a new transportation route for area farmers and ranchers. In the depressed agricultural economy of the 1920s and depression-ridden 1930s, these kinds of opportunities became a lifeline (Rothman 1998).

The NPS also let contracts for a range of services within the park. Road construction offered one kind of opportunity that put many local men to work. Sewer lines and houses were built, as were water lines, power stations, and other similar necessities of modern life. All required labor, a commodity easily found in a depressed part of the West. During the New Deal, CCC camps provided the resources for capital improvement projects at the park as well as in other federal and state endeavors in the region. One level of opportunity the national park provided helped the least skilled workers in the community.

Visitor services within the park also provided economic advantages to the local community. In 1928 the Cavern Supply Company, a Carlsbad-based concern, opened a lunchroom in the caverns, 750 feet below ground, near the elevator to the top. Advertisements touted the prospect of eating so close to the center of the earth, ensuring an ongoing tourist trade. The lunchroom also created employment opportunities, most of them seasonal in nature—a hallmark of national parks—and a smaller number that lasted throughout the year. Generations of Carlsbad natives worked at the lunchroom during "the season," and some made careers of it or other aspects of the visitor service industry (Demaray 1927; Rothman 1989).

Such endeavors showed how the NPS embarked on the long and often intricate process of developing the park without alienating the people of the area. Even in the 1920s, the NPS preferred to separate visitor services from the features of the national parks, to contract them out to responsible operators such as the ones Stephen T. Mather, the first director of the agency, favored. Typically these were established and run by members of the same class as Mather and his second in command, Horace M. Albright (Shankland 1970; Catton 1996). In this case, the agency consented to having a commercial operation located in the heart of the attraction as part of its habit of accommodating local economic needs. The lunchroom became a staple and an essential cog in the mythology of the caverns. It also became an important economic activity that linked the community of Carlsbad, about 20 miles away, with the park, for it became a source of seasonal employment for local youth, a tradition through which young people passed on their way to adulthood.

In this respect, the lunchroom in Carlsbad Caverns served a function that communities expected from their national parks. Almost every community near a national park came to count on it for seasonal and sometimes year-round employment. Young adults in southern Utah worked at the national parks of the area. Cedar City, a small university town along Interstate 15, provided a constant stream of youthful workers for the parks, most of whom were employed in concessions at Zion NP or Bryce Canyon NP. Those of a generation ago fondly recalled meeting the trains that came to Bryce Canyon. The few from smaller communities gravitated to national monuments such as Cedar Breaks or to more remote national parks such as Capitol Reef. The parks provided socialization as well as employment opportunities for the rural young, not only supplementing their experiences but enlarging the pool of marriageable partners. The pattern of seasonal migration to tourist destinations became characteristic of the region, articulated in the complicated embrace and disavowal of the Grand Staircase-Escalante NM, established in 1996 by southern Utahans. People who favored mining and other extractive development found the monument a threat; the small towns in southern Utah that already depended on the parks recognized opportunity inherent in the new monument, even if it was managed by the Bureau of Land Management (Truman 1996; Scrattish 1985; Sproul 1998).

Outside park boundaries, economic development followed the growth of services at the park. At Carlsbad Caverns NP by 1927, an unregulated, privately owned visitor service industry sat astride the entrance at the intersection with the main highway. Named White's City for C. L. "Charlie" White, who homesteaded the tract, it provided gasoline, food, and a place to sleep. When White arrived in southeast New Mexico from Kentucky in 1909, the approach road to the cavern entrance served only the guano industry. In a chance meeting in 1926, he encountered Jim White, and on hearing of the caverns and White's promotional efforts, Charlie White rushed to Carlsbad to file a homestead claim on one half section, 320 acres, that straddled the road at the turnoff. He had never even seen the land (Ripp 1984; Jones 1967).

In 1926 automobile visitors had only begun to reach the caverns in huge numbers, but White, a seasoned entrepreneur with successes and failures behind him, anticipated that a deluge would ensue. White built a Texaco station and a little cafe, and put up ten tents. Despite a struggle to acquire water, White found himself in control of a precious resource, the only stop with food, gasoline, and overnight accommodations between the town of Carlsbad, 20 miles down the road, and the caverns. A tireless worker, White developed the area; by 1940, not only did White's City sport a post office, it offered more than 300 rooms that were typically filled each night during the summer season. The operation required significant numbers of workers, again mostly seasonal and a smaller number full-time throughout the year (Ripp 1984; Bryant 1985). In another way, the national park served as a catalyst for job creation that injected much needed income into a region in transition.

Under different circumstances, and with a great deal more resistance from some sectors of the local community, a similar situation accompanied the establishment of Grand Teton NP in 1929. In this instance, the creation of the national park not only furthered the economic goals of much of the region, it also played a role in healing social division caused by the remote location and limited agricultural and animal husbandry opportunities available to settlers. Although the reconciliation took time, without the national park it never could have occurred.

Jackson, Wyoming, the town that became the gateway to the new park, had already become a destination for tourists by the 1920s. As was true of many places in similar circumstances, the Jackson area, or Jackson Hole—a nineteenth-century term for valley—came to rely on tourism because locals ignored or passed over other economic strategies. A western economic regime, as tenuous as it was typical, characterized the region (Wishart 1979; Stone 1956; Merk 1978; James 1936). The limitations that impeded commercial and production-oriented economic endeavor allowed the development of dude ranching, a new kind of tourism. The 76-mile ride from Victor, Idaho, the rocking of the wagon, the difficulty of travel, granted the dude ranch substantial cachet (Burt 1983). Other ranchers hired hands, castrated animals, and conveyed their cattle to the railhead as an essential part of their livelihood, but dude ranchers offered the context of such activities and pursued the same practices as much for the edification of their visitors as for any market value.

By 1915, tourism in Jackson Hole had become one of the most important local industries. A seasonal upper class that mimicked the behaviors of natives of the place but was not subject to its environmental and economic constraints became a fixture on the local scene. For locals in Jackson Hole, their neighbors who ran the dude ranches remained perplexing. These neonatives dressed as did local people and engaged in versions of many of the same activities. But they were different; they wrote books and articles, talked about the issues of the nation rather than those of the region, and did not depend on Jackson Hole for their income. The neonatives skimmed the cream off the top of life at the base of the Tetons; they could afford to appreciate its aesthetic magnificence. To maintain their place astride a wide and widening culture gulf, the hybrid dude ranchers needed the glorious scenery and wild nature of the Tetons and its surroundings. In time, a national park became the answer to their problems.

This solution ran counter to the economic interests and social objectives of many natives of Jackson Hole. A series of conflicts emerged, pitting westerner

against transplant. These disputes began first over two dams along the Gros Ven-
tre River, Buffalo Fork and Spread Creek, constructed by a company that
planned to irrigate poor Wyoming land and expected to sell its water to Idaho
farmers in the aftermath. The fate of the elk herds that migrated to the lower
elevations of Jackson Hole during the winter also juxtaposed locals and the
neonatives attracted by the beauty of the place. State officials established a
570,000-acre state elk preserve north of Moran. Between 1912 and 1913, the
federal government set aside the first National Elk Refuge, almost 3,000 acres in
size. Many locals would have responded to the issue in a different way (James
1936; Saylor 1970; Righter 1982).

After the elk refuge, the preservation of the special nature of Jackson Hole, of
the attributes that drew Struthers Burt and his kind there, became as important
as local livelihood. Struthers Burt freely admitted that this situation stemmed
"partly from clear-sighted selfishness," the desire to preserve the seclusion he so
fervently sought (Burt 1924:4). Others regarded the physical beauty of the
region in more instrumental terms.

By the time the struggle for Grand Teton NP began in earnest after the creation of the NPS in 1916, neonatives such as Burt acquired the status of natives
in the eyes of the law; they had become landowners, enjoying all the influence
that status conferred. Landowners with longer tenure apart from dude ranching
had to share their status with neonatives whose rituals they did not understand
and whose living came independent of their land. For longtime locals, the situation became a conundrum that made expressing their perspective difficult. The
affluent and powerful who spent summers in Jackson Hole were among the
most ardent supporters of a national park and they found a few among the community who joined them. An alliance between the dude wranglers and the NPS
formed, a typical relationship during the Mather years. To outsiders it seemed
that the community of Jackson was split on the issue of a national park; closer
scrutiny revealed that the choice of sides correlated closely with the place of ori-
gin of the individuals involved (Righter 1982).

Grand Teton NP was established in 1929, in no small part to protect the
Tetons from the range of ticky-tack structures, including a dance hall, second-
rate tourist cabins, a rodeo field, and hot dog stands along the highway, that
intruded on the vistas from the valley. John D. Rockefeller Jr. spent more than
$2 million to purchase land for the park. The preservation movement came
largely from the outside, and its triumphs occurred at the expense of conventional local economic endeavor (Righter 1982; Rothman 1989). To many in the
region, the benefits of the park initially did not seem to outweigh the ways it
curtailed their privileges.

Over time, the national park became popular with even the most recalcitrant
locals. The cattle industry had always been shaky and the national park seemed
to obviate the worst features of the dude ranches. The regional experience with

Yellowstone NP to the north helped soften the transition, and the NPS picked local people to represent it in the area. The new park brought resources the region previously lacked. Roads were the most obvious benefit. Built to accommodate tourist travel, they crossed the 8,429-foot-high Teton Pass, the 7,921-foot Rim Pass, and Togwotee Pass, at 9,658 feet, and continued north into Yellowstone NP. Stockmen used them to track their cattle, cutting the losses inevitable in the stock business. At the end of the season, ranchers used the railroads to move cattle to market. National park development facilitated an infrastructure that made local life easier (James 1936).

The cost of the roads did not cut into local pocketbooks. Much of the money came from private or federal sources, not Teton County or the state of Wyoming. Rockefeller invested $50,000 in Yellowstone's roads during the 1920s, and in the 1930s paving began, stimulated by the increasing number of automobile tourists who left the Tetons for Yellowstone. Even all-year mobility became possible. During the winter of 1935–1936, the Hoback and Teton Pass roads were kept open for the first time—the latter with federal money—offering area residents a genuine benefit that they had not anticipated (James 1936; Righter 1982). Locals were able to piggyback on the facilities built to accommodate tourists.

The park also curtailed a growing problem in the region, the cluster of poorly constructed buildings and idiosyncratic service along the road to the mountains that capitalized on the view in the most exploitive of ways. The arrival of the NPS upgraded the quality of service and facilities in the area, forcing the most poorly prepared operators to improve the services they offered or risk being forced out of business. Mather established the policy of selecting one operator for each park and relegating the rest to outside the park in an effort to maintain standards. In 1916 he had thrown a number of concessionaires out of Yellowstone, and at Grand Teton, his legacy held. The combination of the national park and Rockefeller's purchase of adjacent land allowed a pristine view of the Tetons (Shankland 1970; Righter 1982; Winks 1997).

The park also mitigated between the dude ranchers and the locals. The infusion of capital that came with it muted conflict between the two constituencies as the economic benefits of tourism spread beyond the dude ranchers to the locals. The park served as a secondary source of income for locals; they sold some animals to the park and its hotels for food, provided labor and other services, and in some cases contracted for a range of work—from road and building construction to laundry and other services. The result was a healthier regional economy, a growing primacy for tourism, and a backbone that guaranteed that the general economic condition would not fall below a certain point because development in the park would assure a constant flow of dollars—both from the park and from visitors—into the region in even the worst economic circumstances. Although resentment of the federal presence and an acrimonious rivalry between the NPS and the U.S. Forest Service continued until the 1950s, federal dollars and the enormous number of visitors became the mainstay of the regional economy. Grand Teton NP created a more prosperous, more cohesive community than previously existed.

On Indian reservations, national parks played similar roles, supporting economic development and helping communities maintain social and cultural patterns and relationships as circumstances around them changed. The situation on reservations provided a particular challenge. Such communities were the most in need of the infusion of capital that national park areas bring. They were also the most vulnerable to social disruption as a result of rapid, unchecked change. Navajo NM, three noncontiguous archaeological areas in northeastern Arizona on the road between Kayenta and Tuba City, offered a prime example.

Founded in 1909, Navajo NM fit the pattern of many remote national monuments during the first five decades of its existence. Little development occurred and most of the visitors were archaeologists or buffs who braved the more than 100 miles of dirt roads from the end of the pavement. As a result, levels of cooperation far greater than the norm became typical of the relationship between the park and its Navajo neighbors (Rothman 1993). A symbiotic relationship developed, in which Navajos gained economically from the park, which in turn received the benefits of Navajo labor as well as the ability to offer visitors a picture of Navajo life. Local Navajos developed a proprietary interest, truly becoming partners in the park.

Even before the construction of a visitor center and the paved approach road from the main highway in the mid-1960s, park staff and their neighbors enjoyed an interdependent relationship. The park was the long arm of an industrial society, receiving its goods and services from across the nation, but in the remote backcountry of Arizona it also relied on its neighbors. Area Navajos also benefitted materially from their relationship with the park. Besides employment, the park offered communications, transportation, support, and medical facilities unavailable to most of the people in the region. In addition, both the NPS and the Navajo had to battle the often inclement climate of the area. Neighbors and often friends, park staff and area Navajos looked out for one another. Gestures of personal concern reflected the feeling of community that transcended cultural and institutional lines at the monument (Binnewies 1991).

The web of relationships created genuine economic, cultural, and personal interdependence, spawning close friendships among people of different cultural backgrounds. Park officials offered area Navajos the institutional and cultural benefits of modern facilities. In the winter, the park's snowplow could be found plowing the way to various hogans—Navajo dwellings—in the region. The park also allowed Navajos to fill their 55-gallon water barrels at the park, loaned tools, and generally worked to promote harmonious relations. A young Navajo woman who worked as a seasonal ranger at the park received encouragement to return to school to earn a teaching certificate. She became the first Navajo with credentials to teach in the Shonto district. The park also fed people in times of heavy snow, took in local Navajos in need of temporary care, and served as a communications center for the people of the region. In reality, Navajo NM was an island among the Navajo people. In a harsh land, cooperation and adaptation to circumstances assured the survival of all (Black 1991; Hastings 1991; Binnewies 1991; White 1990).

For Navajos, the park brought employment opportunities. By the late 1940s, Navajos in the vicinity of the monument had become avid workers in a range of programs. Many had typical day labor positions, but after World War II Navajos engaged in other work as well. In 1948, Seth Bigman, one of the many Navajo who fought in the war, became the first Navajo seasonal ranger at the monument. He served two years. Bigman was followed by Hubert Laughter, another Navajo war veteran. Laughter also served as an interpretive ranger at the monument during his three-year stay (Brewer 1947; Laughter 1991; Black 1991).

The most important aspect of this dimension was that it kept Navajos at home. After the stock reductions of the 1930s, Navajo men were compelled to seek outside employment. Typical were Hubert Laughter and Delbert Smallcanyon. A veteran of World War II, Hubert Laughter returned to the reservation with a Purple Heart and the desire to make a life. He found a job in Winslow, Arizona, as an airplane mechanic, but because his wife was from a very traditional Navajo family that did not want the couple to move away, he stayed in the Shonto area. There were few economic opportunities on the western reservation, and the park was a solution. It offered him economic opportunity at home—although his wife's family long debated whether he should take the job at the park. For Laughter, his park experience became a springboard. He later served as a Navajo tribal policeman and a member of the tribal council (Laughter 1991).

Delbert Smallcanyon's experiences revealed a different set of goals the park could support. Born around 1920 in the Navajo Mountain area, he tended sheep for his family into adulthood. He first left the reservation to work for the railroad during World War II and later followed it from place to place, working in Montana, Salt Lake City, Chicago, and elsewhere in the West. This pattern of seasonal movement typified the experience of many Navajos of his generation. Smallcanyon left home only because his family needed the income from his labor. He did not enjoy the work, its pressures, or the places he went. It was his duty. His paychecks sustained his family after the local subsistence economy plummeted. A permanent job close to home allowed Smallcanyon to maintain a traditional lifestyle. He first came to the monument in 1968 as a stonemason. Each day he drove the 50 miles from his home on Navajo Mountain, returning after a full day's work. This allowed him to remain in his homeland, maintain his traditional lifestyle, and support his family—all as a result of his job at the park (Smallcanyon 1991).

After the signing of a memorandum of agreement between the park and the Navajo Nation in 1962, opportunity for Navajos who sought work at the park increased. Paving of the highway and later of the approach road to the monument headquarters brought many more travelers and increased the demand for services at the park. Navajos soon recognized that career NPS employees generally filled the desirable permanent ranger positions, prompting some younger Navajos to enter the NPS. Maintenance positions were available for local people, as was seasonal employment. By the 1960s, the maintenance staff was exclusively Navajo except for the supervisor. During the 1980s, a Navajo was appointed supervisor of maintenance, the first in a permanent supervisory capacity at the monument. This helped cement the Navajo character of the maintenance staff.

Yet until the middle of the 1980s, structural problems with the distribution of employment at Navajo NM remained. In 1982, five of the nine permanent employees at the monument were Navajo. Three Anglos worked at the park, along with one Hispano. All had higher General Schedule (GS) ranks than did the five Navajos, leaving a skewed structure that reflected the slow process of the changing patterns of leadership in the American and federal work forces. After the appointment of the Navajo maintenance supervisor and the subsequent appointment in 1986 of a Navajo, Clarence N. Gorman, as superintendent, the historic limitations ended. Gorman's appointment reflected the importance of close relations with local people. Many of the Navajo employees experienced a stronger feeling of belonging after Gorman's appointment, knowing that they would return to work each day with other Navajos, speak their language, and enjoy a certain feeling of accomplishment. There was a stronger pride in working for the park for Navajos working for a Navajo superintendent. "It's good to see your own people working here," Delbert Smallcanyon said in the Navajo language (Smallcanyon 1991; Black 1991). By 1990, the monument had eleven full- and part-time employees. Eight, including the superintendent, the head of maintenance, and the entire maintenance department, were Navajo. The park more accurately reflected the demography of the area around it (Switzer and Carlin 1982; Gorman 1991; Laughter 1991).

Gorman's presence widened the role of Navajos at the park. Because of its unique geographic position in relation to the location of labor, the park could hire area Navajos without going through standard federal employment procedures. Support programs that included Navajos grew, and Navajo history and culture played an expanding role in interpretation to visitors. Efforts to include high school students from the area in summer activities at the park followed. In the summer of 1988, five young Navajos from the Shonto Chapter, one of the internal divisions within the Navajo Nation, worked at the monument. The park had become integral in regional life.

By the 1990s, Navajo NM served a function typical of national parks in remote areas and on Indian reservations. It was an economic backbone in a place with few other options, providing employment, expertise, and facilities. On the reservation it created an intermediary space for Navajo people, allowing them to stay home and maintain community in an area largely devoid of other employment opportunities. Even more, it did not require that they give up the cultural patterns of being Navajo, a trade-off so common for Indian people in other kinds of employment. In Shonto, Navajo NM both supported the people of the region and stood between them and the onslaught of the outside world.

By the 1980s, national parks were integral parts of the economies in the places that surrounded them. In the Carlsbad area, oil and gas, the park, and its companion to the south, Guadalupe Mountains NP, served as the mainstays of the regional economy. In 1991, the park employed the equivalent of ninety-five full-time employees. The concessionaires employed thirty-five people full-time throughout the year and another fifty-five during the peak travel season. The payroll injected more than $3.3 million into the area, coupled with the more than $50 million directly generated by tourism and an additional $5 million in secondary benefits (Sellars 1997). Oil and gas only generated slightly more gross revenue. Carlsbad Caverns was significant in the regional economy, on par with almost every other industry in the region. In Jackson, increasingly overrun by the superrich, Grand Teton NP served an important function in maintaining the social fabric and mitigating the impact of growth in addition to its long-standing enormous economic contribution. At Shonto, the national monument offered social and economic advantages to local people. It permitted Navajos to stay close to home and maintain cultural traditions as it provided an economic backbone in a remote area.

Often overlooked as an economic engine, national parks provided enormous economic and social benefits, especially in rural areas. As these examples show, they create infrastructure, provide employment opportunities, and maintain the social fabric, mitigating the kind of dislocating change found in unregulated tourist communities. In many places having a national park area, for local people, means the difference between making a living at home and being forced to leave in search of work elsewhere.

To date, the role of national parks as a tool of development has been overlooked, often even by the sponsoring agency. As the national and global economy becomes more service oriented, national parks can play an enormous and significant role as a replacement for declining industries such as mining, agriculture, and ranching. Existing parks have the ability to put people to work, creating an economic backbone in declining regions. These may be as diverse as southern Utah or rural South Carolina, but in each there is a similarity of needs and one way to answer them: by using national park areas as tools of economic development. The greatest local value of national parks may be the ways in which they create opportunity that cushions communities and individuals against the impact of wholesale change.

References

Binnewies, W. G. 1991. Interview with Hal Rothman, April 4.

Black, B. 1991. Interview with Hal Rothman, translated by Mary Lou Smith and Clarence N. Gorman, January 5.

Brewer, J. L. 1947. *Memorandum for the Regional Director.* December 25, Navajo Wage Board Matters. Denver: Denver Federal Records Center.

Bryant, R. 1985. Cashing in on the caves. *New Mexico Business Journal* 11: 53–55.

Burt, N. 1983. *Jackson Hole Journal.* Norman: University of Oklahoma Press.

Burt, S. 1924. *Diary of a Dude Wrangler.* New York: Scribner's.

Catton, T. 1996. *Wonderland: An Administrative History of Mt. Rainier National Park.* Seattle: National Park Service.

Demaray, A. E., to Thomas Boles, May 27, 1927. NA, RG 79: 7. Carlsbad Caverns.

Gorman, C. 1991. Interview with Hal Rothman, January 5. Navajo National Monument.

Hastings, F., to Hal Rothman, February 25, 1991.

Ise, J. 1961. *Our National Park Policy: A Critical History.* Baltimore: Johns Hopkins University Press.

James, P. L. 1936. Regional planning in the Jackson Hole country. *The Geographical Review* 26: 442.

Jones, B. M. 1967. *Health-Seekers of the Southwest, 1817–1900.* Norman: University of Oklahoma Press.

Laughter, H. 1991. Interview with Hal Rothman, translated by Clarence N. Gorman, January 5.

Merk, F. 1978. *History of the Westward Movement.* New York: Alfred A. Knopf.

Righter, R. W. 1982. *Crucible for Conservation: The Creation of Grand Teton National Park.* Boulder, CO: Colorado Associated University Press.

Ripp, B. 1984. Greetings from White's City. *Albuquerque Living.* March: 70–71.

Rothman, H. 1989. *Preserving Different Pasts: The American National Monuments.* Urbana: University of Illinois Press.

———. 1993. Partners in the park: Navajo people and Navajo National Monument. *Nevada Historical Society Quarterly* Summer: 106–25.

———. 1998. *Promise Beheld and the Limits of Place: A Historic Resource Study of Carlsbad Caverns and Guadalupe Mountains National Parks and the Surrounding Area.* Santa Fe, NM: National Park Service.

Saylor, D. J. 1970. *Jackson Hole Wyoming: In the Shadow of the Tetons.* Norman: University of Oklahoma Press.

Scrattish, N. 1985. *Historic Resource Study: Bryce Canyon National Park.* Denver: National Park Service.

Sellars, R. W. 1997. *Preserving Nature in the National Parks.* New Haven: Yale University Press.

Shankland, R. 1970. *Steve Mather of the National Parks* (2d ed.). New York: Alfred A. Knopf.

Smallcanyon, D. 1991. Interview with Hal Rothman, translated by Clarence N. Gorman, January 5.

Sproul, D. 1998. Interview with Hal Rothman, February 11.

Stone, I. 1956. *Men to Match My Mountains: The Opening of the Far West, 1840–1900.* Garden City, NY: Doubleday.

Switzer, R. R., and Edward D. Carlin. 1982. *Management Evaluation, Navajo National Monument, August 24–26.* Navajo National Monument, A5427. Denver: National Park Service.

Truman, K. 1996. Interview with Hal Rothman, September 11.

White, A. 1990. Interview with Richard B. McCaslin, June 11.

Winks, R. W. 1997. *Laurence S. Rockefeller.* Washington, DC: Island Press.

Wishart, D. 1979. *The Fur Trade of the American West, 1807–1840.* Lincoln: University of Nebraska Press.

Chapter 4

The Transboundary Relationship between National Parks and Adjacent Communities

Francis T. Achana and Joseph T. O'Leary

National parks have existed in North America for nearly 130 years, during which time the principal objectives for their creation have evolved greatly. The motivations of the early park movement were dominated by a desire to protect watersheds, scenic beauty, tourism, and recreational values (Zube 1989; Stankey 1989; Runte 1987, as cited in Stankey 1989). Park planning and management objectives were often oriented toward satisfying the needs of outsiders to the park area, while the interests of local populations were not seriously considered.

The values associated with parks broadened with time. The importance of some park areas as "nature banks" that protect unique examples of ecosystems became prominent. By the 1930s, the shift of focus toward nature conservation was very apparent (Zube 1989), as national parks were seen predominantly as nature conservation preserves (Stankey 1989). For this reason, it was often thought desirable to separate people from parks, or to severely control and restrict human activities in and around them, as people were seen as intrusions in a natural world (Agrawal and Gibson 1999).

Human communities are almost always located close to national parks. Because of this close alignment, the Yellowstone model of national parks that views parks essentially as instruments of conservation with minimal human involvement has not been enthusiastically embraced by adjacent local communities. Tensions that originate from the adoption of some exclusionary natural science-based park management policies are translated in local communities as a failure to address their transboundary concerns (concerns beyond park boundaries).

Dryzek (1997:8) states that "environmental problems by definition are found at the intersection of ecosystems and human social systems." The natural and social sciences thus complement each other in attempting to deal with park management issues, where environmental and social problems intersect. Managers of national parks are expected to understand not only the environmental aspects of national parks, but also the social and cultural contexts within which policies and programs are implemented. The shift in park management strategy required to achieve this implies that local residents need to be brought into the decision-making process of parks, and that the current technical, rational, and systematic top-down management approach of park professionals needs to be modified (Solecki 1994; Pedlar 1996).

Attempts to ensure that park planning takes the concerns of local communities into consideration, at least after a park has already been established, are not new within the NPS. O'Leary (1974) showed that the NPS's administrative policies were already making such efforts in the early 1970s. More recently, the NPS has become more amenable to supporting the social aspects of parks or cultural landscapes (such as historical sites shaped by humans), as it does unique natural landscapes (Roberts 1994; La Pierre 1997).

But in spite of outreach efforts by the NPS to harmonize the interests of local communities and parks, the natural sciences still contribute the most input in the planning stages of park creation. Social science factors such as the concerns of local residents are given much less credence (La Pierre 1997).

This chapter examines the various social science perspectives from which the functions of national parks can be viewed as affecting the residents of neighboring communities, and vice versa, in the North American context. The influences of social, cultural, political, economic, and other social science domains on the success or failure of the cohabitation between national parks and neighboring human communities are the principal themes examined.

Conceptual Framework

The study of community has a long tradition in social sciences, particularly in the areas of sociology, political science, and anthropology. Machlis (1999) provides an excellent summary of the social sciences and notes that a wide range of research techniques—observation, social surveys, and experiments—are used throughout. Observation and social surveys that look at relationships between various social units (e.g., individuals, groups, and institutions) have dominated community research both within and across community boundaries.

The impact of local circumstances has always been important in shaping the destinies of national parks (O'Leary 1974; Dustin and McAvoy 1982; Lemons and Stout 1984; Lemons 1987; Stankey 1989; Vining et al. 1990; Searle 1990; Fiske 1992; Lee 1993; Dawson et al. 1993; Donnelly 1993; Driver et al. 1996). Although there are many facets associated with such shaping, a review of the research literature associated with U.S. national parks suggests the following major themes: (a) quality of life, (b) economic contribution, (c) environmental quality, (d) social/psychological benefits, (e) equitable access, (f) heritage preservation, and (g) tourism. The following sections will explore each of these.

Social Science, Communities, and National Park Impacts

Recently, the social science literature has shown strong research thrust toward examining the sociocultural impacts of parks on adjacent communities in developing countries. However, this cannot be said about the examination of impacts in industrialized countries such as the United States. Social science research regarding national parks located in industrial countries tends to concentrate on issues related to on-site recreational uses such as the analysis of activity preference and participation levels, carrying capacity, and user conflicts. There is a relative neglect of the transboundary impacts of national parks, which could generate conflicts or offer opportunities for cooperation between park management and local communities.

The contribution of natural science knowledge in the feasibility studies that precede the designation of areas for conservation as national parks sometimes takes priority over the contribution of the social sciences, as technical feasibility in terms of biological, ecological, and technological variables is emphasized (Meis 1990). Research involving social science analysis of the economic, cultural, political, managerial, and social feasibility of planned national parks tends to be underestimated. The designation of natural resource sites for protection is, however, not just a function of natural science attributes (Meis 1990). The selection of the resources to be protected is a social decision-making process, which is strongly influenced by the social paradigms of the day (see, for example, Light and Katz 1996).

Dearden (1995) summarized the social and natural science functions of national parks in the United States by dividing them into social and ecological roles. His list of the functions of national parks includes:

Social roles of national parks:

- "Museum" role: This casts park functions in the light of institutions that preserve the vestiges of natural monuments of the American wilderness. In this museum role, parks also preserve cultural monuments such as historical landmarks.
- Role as art galleries: National parks preserve some of the most scenic examples of the aesthetic appeal of the landscape.
- Role as recreational centers: National parks serve as playgrounds and places of relaxation that allow people to escape from the everyday realities of urbanized environments.
- Role as spiritual centers: The parks provide opportunities for close contact with nature, which nourishes the spirit.
- Economic role: National parks offer opportunities for some people to make a living by supplying goods and services to visitors.

Ecological roles of national parks:

- Nature bank role: National parks serve as stores of genetic capital, which preserve genetic diversity by providing the right habitat for their perpetuation.
- Natural laboratories for research: The protection of biodiversity in national parks makes it possible for scientific studies to be conducted on rare species that would otherwise be difficult to locate.
- Open-air classrooms: National parks provide opportunities for educational hands-on immersion in the natural world by all sorts of people.

This list shows that both the social and the natural sciences have a role to play in examining the impacts of national parks on their surroundings. In addition, virtually all include some type of transboundary effect. Let us explore some of these impacts in detail.

Enhancement of Quality of Life in a Community

Little (1993) states that outdoor recreation is intended to improve people's quality of life through their participation in outdoor activities. He argues that this process is multifaceted. Parks provide opportunities for many outdoor recreation experiences that help develop physical, mental, and emotional wellness. Because they are also convenient meeting places for social and cultural interaction, they can expand people's leisure and stress-reducing opportunities. Parks can, therefore, add to the quality of life of neighboring communities.

Some parks develop special programs for the elderly, at-risk youth, women, and marginal groups aimed at building self-esteem, developing collaboration skills, and generally feeling appreciated (Hultsman and Little 1995). This is another characteristic of national parks that has the potential to improve the quality of life of various sectors of the community.

Donnelly (1993) and Kelly (1996) argue that communities could get some peacetime dividends from the ending of the Cold War if some of the closed military bases were turned into parks to serve community needs. Military base closures could thus be an opportunity to offer more communities enhanced quality-of-life services such as recreation and open space.

The argument supporting the role of national parks in enhancing the standard of living of local communities cuts both ways. Some communities fight attempts to designate sites for national parks in their areas, fearing that the resultant external involvement in land-use decisions will erode their standard of living (Fiske 1992; Jobes 1993). Reading et al. (1994) found that, while a large majority of people living in the Greater Yellowstone area accepted the need for coordinated management of Yellowstone NP to check threats to the integrity of its ecosystem, they were worried that integrated management would lead to a local loss of political and economic control. They perceived negative impacts on the lifestyles and natural resource–based industries of the region resulting from large-scale external intervention in the management of the park (Solecki 1994).

For forty years, the communities of Baker and Ely, in the neighborhood of what was to become Great Basin NP in Nevada in 1986, strongly opposed conversion of the multiple-use Lehman Caves NM, the Wheeler Peak Scenic Area, and Humboldt National Forest into a national park. It was feared that park designation would lead to a loss of grazing, mining, and even recreational opportunities. However, in spite of the doubling of levels of visitation since the park was designated, there has been little disruption of local lifestyles, and the demands on local infrastructure were not excessive (Dawson et al. 1993; Lambert 1991). Some concessions were made to local residents when the park was designated whereby grazing and mining were permitted.

The lessons could be that if there is local involvement in the park designation process, the basic misunderstandings that may arise could be clarified up front, and national parks could achieve their goals while contributing to the enhancement of the standard of living of adjacent communities.

Economic Contributions of Parks to Local Economies

Economic impact analyses (EIAs) often reveal that parks and park-related tourism generate millions of dollars of income, sizeable multiplier effects, and new jobs in neighboring regions (Bergstrom et al. 1990; Cordell et al. 1992). Merrifield and Gerking (1982), in their study at Grand Teton NP in Wyoming, found that the park significantly affected the economy of Teton County by providing 27 percent of the county's income and employment. However, the best available data used in the economic model came from a variety of sources, and some were several years old, making the findings less reliable. Wallace et al. (1990) also found large positive economic impacts associated with Theodore Roosevelt NP. The input-output model used in the study estimated that, over a two-year period, visitation to the park generated more than $100 million of economic activity in North Dakota, and created more than 2,000 new jobs. However, a 50 percent response rate and respondents' problems in recalling and estimating amounts spent within the target region make it difficult to ascertain the accuracy of these findings (Dawson et al. 1993). Dawson et al. (1993) also found some modest positive impacts of visitor expenditure on the total gross output, value added, and employment levels in a three-county area around Great Basin NP in Nevada and Utah.

Generally, methodological obstacles such as incomplete or outdated secondary data, small, unrepresentative survey samples, and problems in computing the multiplier effects of a multifaceted industry like tourism result in huge variation in estimates of local and regional economic impacts of national parks and the tourism they generate (Dawson et al. 1993). This variation in estimates is common in economic impact analyses. One of the often-cited external benefits of parks, enhancement of real estate values of properties adjacent to parks, provides an example of the level of variation of these estimates.

An increase in the economic value of property due to proximity to parklands is termed "location rent." Corrill et al. (1978) found that in Boulder, Colorado, the prices of housing declined an average of $4.20 for each foot that a house was situated away from a greenbelt. On the other hand, Schroeder (1982) found no monetary value for property in Du Page County, Illinois, as a consequence of proximity to recreation and park facilities. At the other extreme, Gartner et al. (1996) actually found that the location of private property adjacent to public land was significantly and negatively correlated with property value.

The results of research on location rent are therefore complex and indeterminate. In some of the places where high location rent has been reported, the values of the properties that were directly adjacent to the park were depressed. It is likely that any negative impacts caused by park users on neighboring properties will be felt most in the properties that are directly adjacent to the park.

Other studies reported that properties facing open-space parks had location rent while those facing parks developed for intensive recreation use did not (Weicher and Zerbst 1973). A likely implication is that the effect of parks on the value of adjacent properties varies according to the attributes of the parks and the social context. Apparently, intensive-use parks, which are more likely to produce negative impacts such as noise and vandalism on their surroundings, produce fewer external benefits. This may suggest that there is some degree of incompatibility between on-site benefits of parks and their external benefits. Maximization of on-site recreation benefits may diminish some off-site benefits.

Communities in the neighborhood of a national park are likely to have their own unique relationships with the park, as has been seen with urban parks. Unique community-park relationships are more likely to determine the impacts of a national park on the local community than a general theory of location rent (Rudzitis 1996).

Other economic benefits of national parks to gateway communities are derived from the twin objectives of parks: efficiency and equity (Driver and Peterson 1996). Equity refers to fairness in the distribution of economic and nonmonetary benefits generated by a park, through equitable access to all publics. Efficiency is concerned with the cost-effective production of those benefits. It measures the relative extent to which park investments add or subtract from economic well-being. By helping to index the monetary worth of goods and services, efficiency analyses may make it possible to quantify benefits such as the spiritual value of a park, which would otherwise be difficult to measure. This helps prevent wasteful allocation of scarce resources.

In trying to generate economic gain, some parks allow concessionaires to operate within their borders, or immediately beyond them. Local entrepreneurs are some of the most likely people to benefit from concessions such as motels, transportation services, stores, and small businesses. When activities such as hunting or fishing are permitted in a park, as they are in Mojave NPres, local people will be able to continue these practices as they did before the creation of the park (Soden 1995). Other economic activities of an extractive nature, on the other hand, are more likely to be seen as less compatible with the objectives of most parks (Dawson et al. 1993). While the economic impacts of some of these activities may be felt in the local area, they are more likely to be undertaken by larger external industries. Generally, when the economic activities permitted in parks are more service oriented, local entrepreneurs such as restaurant owners, tour guides, and whitewater or mountain-climbing guides are more likely to take advantage of the park's presence to make a living. The biosphere reserve model, which creates core preservation zones surrounded by buffer and transition zones in which local communities can engage in sustainable economic activities, appears to be more inclusive of the land-use concerns of local residents, and may be more politically acceptable for establishing new conservation areas in the future (Solecki 1994).

Alward (1986) establishes that the geographical distribution of expenditures related to parks and recreation activities ensures that most of the direct economic impacts occur in the "support area" immediately adjacent to the park or recreational site. Expenditures on labor, equipment, food, lodging, supplies, and materials thus tend to occur in the communities near the park. The implication of this is that national parks can still have a significant economic impact on the local community, if the "leakage" (loss of expenditure from the local area) is not excessive.

Apart from the direct employment-generating capability of parks for local and regional communities, Crompton et al. (1997) found that parks, recreation opportunities, and open spaces were some of the essential elements of quality-of-life considerations in company location and relocation decisions. This was particularly true of "footloose" knowledge-based service companies such as those involved in research, insurance, finance, and high technology. Generally, the financial performance of these companies is less dependent on location than on highly qualified personnel, who may prefer remote locations with desirable quality of life. The employees of such companies tend to be well paid, and could be welcome additions to the local community in economic terms. The presence of a national park could, therefore, serve as a catalyst for location of top-quality businesses in the neighborhood, producing several economic and social benefits. At the same time, some of these changes could also create significant disruption. For example, some new residents attracted to a national park area are accused of attempting to "Californicate" or "Coloradicate" the area, making it more like an area they experienced before (Jobes 1993). On the other hand, other new residents are said to want to "lock it up" to "save" it from exploiters.

Positive examples of the economic impact of amenity-seeking migrants are the rural counties that include the towns of Boulder, Colorado, and Escalante and Kanab in the canyon lands of Utah. Amenity resources tend to give these rural counties an advantage over other rural areas by enabling them to diversify their economies through relocation of amenity-seeking migrant companies looking for access to rural recreation opportunities for their employees (The Wilderness Society 1999). Retirees are another important sector of amenity-based migration, and their nonlabor income (e.g., Social Security benefits, pensions) generates additional jobs in the local economy. In 1996, 39 percent of total personal income in Garfield and Kane Counties in Utah came from nonlabor income, reflecting the amenity-based migrant retiree communities in those counties. Some of the fastest-growing counties in the United States are said to be located next to federally designated wilderness areas (Rudzitis and Johansen 1989; Geisler 1993).

Environmental Quality and the Impact of Parks on Local Communities

Since the 1930s, one of the principal objectives of parks in the United States has been to conserve natural ecosystems (Stankey 1989). This environmental conservation function of parks often has a beneficial impact on the lives of local residents because it helps protect the natural resources vital to their lives, such as watersheds and clean air. Parks also help educate people about natural processes by preserving unique wilderness areas and bringing people into contact with nature (Dearden 1995).

Of the 95 million acres of the National Wilderness Preservation System that existed in the United States at the end of 1992, about 39.1 million acres were in national parks (Petersen and Harmon 1993). From a natural science perspective, even though the protection that parks give to unique fauna and flora (within the relatively pristine habitats they offer) does not necessarily guarantee the survival of all threatened species, it is sometimes the only way of avoiding the extinction of certain species. Parks thus contribute to maintaining genetic diversity and allow scientists to learn more about nature under natural conditions.

The existence of national parks and wilderness areas in proximity to human communities has other beneficial consequences of a social nature. Parks and wilderness areas tend to be cited by some residents of adjacent communities as important attributes that define their communities and make them appealing to outsiders and to themselves.

In examining the attitudes of the general public in 100 counties of the northern Intermountain West of the United States, Rudzitis et al. (1995) found that 92 percent of respondents were concerned with how federal lands in their counties were being managed. Fifty-five percent of the respondents had moved to that area in the last fifteen years, and the attributes that featured prominently in the decisions of many to move there included outdoor recreation opportunities, the landscape and scenery, and the general quality of the physical environment. National parks and wilderness areas were major factors in creating this image.

The majority of the respondents surveyed by Rudzitis et al. (1995) preferred federal lands in their counties to be managed principally for protection of watersheds and habitat for fish and wildlife, for recreational use, and for preservation of ecosystems and wilderness values. Timber harvesting was also considered important. In another study, Rudzitis and Johansen (1991) surveyed 2,670 residents of wilderness counties nationwide and found that the presence of wilderness was an important reason 53 percent of the people moved to or lived in those areas.

Other studies also suggest that environmental resource amenities such as national parks are considered very important to community stability and growth in communities close to preserved natural resources. Shindler et al. (1993), citing Whitelaw (1992), state that the quality of life in Oregon is what spurs its economic growth, and that if the state can maintain its environmental assets, businesses seeking favorable living conditions for their employees will continue to be attracted. This suggests that local communities, incoming businesses, and prospective migrants are keenly interested in the environmental attributes and land-use policies of preserved public lands in a target region, and the attributes of national parks are an integral part of this appeal.

Besides the utilitarian benefits that protected natural resources bestow on adjacent communities, the residents of those communities may also be interested in the natural resource–related beauty of their immediate environments simply for aesthetic reasons. The existence of wildlife and scenic and cultural landscapes in proximity to a community can enhance the uniqueness of the place. In Britain, various natural resource–based community initiatives, such as "Common Ground" and "Jigso," encourage this kind of aesthetic environmental awareness in combination with a celebration of the cultural landscape and a place identity (Roberts 1994). This shows how the social sciences can bridge the gap between different domains of endeavor by combining environmental concerns, cultural heritage interests, and place attachment into one uniting concept of "meaningful space," thereby contributing to better management of natural resources.

The Social-Psychological Issues of Parks and Local Communities

One possible way of viewing transboundary national park impacts is to consider local communities around a national park part of the park (Alward 1986). In this case, the boundary becomes transparent. Active users of national parks, such as hikers and campers, are not the only beneficiaries of the opportunities offered by the parks. Ulrich and Addams (1981) argue that park research puts an excessive emphasis on active park users and the space they occupy, ignoring the psychological benefits of parks to passive users and nonusers. National parks may allow passive users in nearby communities to have a place of private refuge away from their usual daily chores, and offer a serene atmosphere for social interaction both in and around the park. For some nonusers in adjacent communities, the mere presence of a park may also be a source of psychological satisfaction. They may simply enjoy knowing that they have an option to use the park when they want to, or that it is likely to be there in the future for their children.

A national park may bring fame and aesthetic variety to a local area and serve as an identifying symbol of the locality. This could be of interest to all local residents, as it allows even those who do not use the park to feel a common bond to it. When local residents are made to feel proud of the park as an asset to their community, they may be encouraged to contribute their time and effort, through volunteer work, for example, toward maintenance of the park. The uniting influence of a common psychological investment in the park may create the solidarity and sense of common purpose among residents that help to promote the community concept (Huang and Stewart 1996).

Soden (1995) found that, among middle- and senior-level managers of various organizations surveyed in places within an hour's drive of a national park, 70.2 percent rated the quality of the relationship between the national park and local communities (in terms of mutual benefits and costs) as being positive. It appears, therefore, that sections of the public view the relationships between national parks and local communities to be quite healthy.

O'Leary (1974), however, draws attention to some of the negative social and psychological impacts that the establishment of a park may have on a local community. In a study of the response of a small natural resource–dependent community adjacent to North Cascades NP in Washington state when the park was first created, he documents the impacts of the park on the local community. Some of the problems created within the community were related to the congestion resulting from the sudden increase in the number of visitors to the area. Residents felt a loss of control of events in their community, as tourist businesses from outside the community came in and gave little consideration to the concerns of local people and businesses. The increased external interest in the area also led to higher prices and taxes, and local residents were crowded out of some leisure and recreation activities. As a result, local residents felt the rural character of the area and the quality of life of its people had deteriorated.

Some historical antagonisms already existing within the community were compounded by the novelty of having to confront these externally generated problems. The result was a breakdown in the traditional rural decision-making process in the community. O'Leary (1974) speaks of the inevitability of change when nonlocal intervention occurs in rural communities. Such communities become divided between those who embrace the new ideas that outsiders bring, and the traditionalists who attempt to cling to the old ways of doing things. It would appear that, in this case, at the planning stages of park creation, the NPS did not consider the possible impacts of the creation of the park on adjacent communities to be a priority issue. When local communities are marginalized in the process of creation of a park, they may be unprepared for the increased volume of visitors to the community, and the centrifugal forces that the new crowds may unleash in the social and cultural domains.

Equal Opportunity Mechanism

Burdge (1996) argues that land management agencies are increasingly confronted with a diverse clientele and the changing values and demographics of America. This requires abandonment of the assumption that national park users are all seeking the unidimensional, mainstream middle-class cultural experience. While appropriate for some, an emphasis on solitude in the outdoor experience of a national park may not be in tune with the values of all cultural or ethnic groups. Burdge (1996) advocates development of new management strategies, programs, and facilities to meet current needs of the changing users of natural resource sites. These changing needs have led to calls in the literature for creation of nontraditional national parks, especially in socially and culturally diverse urban areas (Burdge 1996). Foley (1990) advocates a "human service–oriented park administrative system" that builds coalitions with local communities and uses the educative and self-esteem-enhancing aspects of national park and recreation experiences to integrate social problem solving into the park experience. Cooperation between residents of the local community and national park authorities also helps control park-related social problems such as noncompliant visitor behavior. Local residents can bring such visitor behaviors as vandalism and failure to follow park rules to the attention of park management (Johnson and Kamp 1996).

Equitable access to on-site recreational use of parks, as well as provision of quality facilities, staff, and programs to cater to clients of different ages, genders, economic and cultural backgrounds, and levels of ability, will help ensure social equity in the distribution of benefits of parks in the local community. Kraus (1987) states that studies in Northampton, Massachusetts, show that 87 percent of park users were under age forty. Older people appear to be using the parks at lower levels. Ethnic minorities are also often reported to underutilize parks. Participation in community recreation in parks has been shown to help the disabled develop friendships and build self-esteem, and yet there are often barriers to their participation in these activities (Green 1992; Heyne and Schleien 1992). More deliberate efforts aimed at equitable access for all in parks could help alleviate some of these problems.

Heritage Preservation

Many national parks are centered around preservation of cultural landscapes, such as historic or prehistoric landmarks, or some other feature of the landscape that is associated with human culture and history. Examples of these in the United States include the Longfellow's Wayside Inn NHS in Massachusetts; the Wick Farm, part of the Morristown National Historical Park (NHP) in New Jersey; the Frederick Law Olmsted NHS in Massachusetts; and the Marsh-Billings-RockeFeller NHP in Vermont. Issues concerning these attractions are often dear to the hearts of local residents, whose ancestors may have been involved in their creation, or who grew up around the features and therefore may consider them essential parts of the meaning of the place.

Traditionally, when the NPS acquires land to preserve historical features, it tends to phase out existing uses of the land that are considered incompatible with this historical perspective. The NPS may also try to restore the landscape to its appearance in the historical period of interest, although for local people, the same landscape may be associated with various historical events over the centuries. Therefore, there is often a challenge, in the historical preservation of a landscape, to determine the precise point of history to which to restore or maintain the landscape (La Pierre 1997). Landscapes are dynamic and assume changing roles over time. People may associate them with various important past events simultaneously. A predilection for specific past events associated with a place, and the role of those events as reference points for the continuity of our cultural heritage, should not make us simply crave for some cliché ideal of the past in relation to the selected events, and ignore all the other historic occurrences that are also a part of that heritage. These circumstances make it even more crucial for local residents to be consulted before such decisions are made in national parks. Consultations with local residents allow discussions to occur about the values attached to the place, and this may help avoid strong opposition by residents to the policies of the NPS, or the policies of a particular national park.

Additionally, choosing to restore historic views may involve certain modifications such as the clearing of trees, vegetation, and buildings, which can change the character of a place completely. Besides the resultant feelings of nostalgia by local residents for the place as they have always known it, some natural resource issues could also be at stake. An example of this is Wick Farm in the Jockey Hollow Unit of Morristown NHP. It served as an encampment for the Continental Army from 1779 to 1780 during the Revolutionary War. The historical view of the farm from that period extended across orchards, fields, and open space that are today covered by forest. This forest currently serves as habitat for wildlife. Any reconstruction of the landscape to reflect the historical character of the farm would involve clearing the forest and thus would negatively affect wildlife and recreational opportunities for local residents in the area (La Pierre 1997). Therefore, it becomes necessary to seek a balance in the pursuit of preservation of natural and cultural resources in national parks.

La Pierre (1997) cites the collaboration between the NPS and the local community of Middlesboro, Kentucky, in plans to restore a historic trail in Cumberland Gap NHP. The gap was used as an access route by Indians, American pioneers, Civil War soldiers, and settlers. Now the main access route for the city of Middlesboro also runs through it. The local community is receptive to the possibility of restoring the trail and removing the paved road, after the building of a tunnel through the mountain. This demonstrates that an informed local community may be willing to undergo some inconveniences to preserve its historical heritage in a national park. Cultural landscapes in national parks are some of the park assets that require the most support from neighboring communities. However, that support may only be forthcoming if the public is well informed about planned policies, and has opportunities to participate in the decision-making process.

Agrawal and Gibson (1999) have stressed the utility of adopting a political approach to community when seeking a partnership to further conservation goals. This implies an emphasis on collaboration with institutions within the community rather than on some amorphous concept of community based simply on the geographic and residential proximity of local people, without reference to their social cohesion and shared purpose. Therefore, national park managers may find avenues for cooperation that enhance the prospects of achieving their heritage preservation goals by establishing partnerships with professional groups and private organizations in the local community that are interested in heritage preservation. Diminishing park budgets mean that the NPS could do a better job if it shared some of the restoration and maintenance costs of cultural landscapes with such partners. This could take the form of permitting some compatible economic or cultural activities in some parks by local residents (Dawson et al. 1993; Roberts 1994).

The traditional view that all human economic activities in parks are bad may have to evolve to accommodate some of these partnerships. Agriculturalists have often become partners to park managers in this way (La Pierre 1997). An example of an agricultural partnership is Fort Hill, which was historically used to cultivate hay before it was incorporated into Cape Cod National Seashore (NS) in Massachusetts in 1963. The NPS maintained its historic open appearance by mowing. The Olmsted Center, however, recommended that, as a cost-cutting measure, the area be leased out for the historic use of hay cultivation (La Pierre 1997). This could lower maintenance costs while achieving the same result of preventing an invasion by permanent vegetation. The challenge is to protect historically significant landscapes in ways that do not clash with local residents' ideals of heritage preservation.

Tourism, Parks, and Local Communities

Tourism was one of the early objectives for establishing national parks. Attributes such as spectacular scenery, readily visible wildlife, rare geological features, wonderful outdoor recreation opportunities, and unique historical monuments attract millions of visitors to national parks each year. Tourist expenditure in local communities can be a very important part of the economy in some places (Huang and Stewart 1996). The shrinking budgets of national parks, and the attempts by adjacent rural areas to develop their communities economically, create an opportunity for partnerships to promote park-related tourism to increase employment opportunities and improve the availability of economic, social, and recreational infrastructure and amenities for local residents. Roads, health services, and leisure opportunities are some of the amenities that can be improved in this context.

Park-driven tourism brings local communities other benefits besides economic development. These include support for cultural and natural area preservation, enhancement of cross-cultural understanding, and encouragement of community pride and identification with a community attractive enough to be of interest to outsiders (Schroeder 1982).

Communities may then have to deal with some of the negative consequences of tourism that affect the quality of life of local residents, such as seasonal population fluctuations; external corporate control of decision making in community issues; and increased social nuisances such as crime, noise, litter, traffic congestion, pollution, inflation, land speculation, and infrastructures inadequate to support high volumes of visitors (O'Leary 1976; Rothman 1978; Thomason et al. 1979; Mathieson and Wall 1982; Milman and Pizam 1988; Solecki 1994).

Tourist actions can also damage the fragile environments of national parks (Glick 1991; Holland and Crotts 1992; Dearden and Rollins 1993). Even when attempts are made to manage tourism development in natural areas with conservation as a guiding principle, as has been the case in Banff National Park in Canada, cumulative environmental impacts become substantial in the long run (Nelson 1994).

Additionally, unless the benefits of tourism are sustainable over the long term, they may not be worth the social, cultural, and environmental disruptions to rural communities that tourism brings in its wake. Tourism development that is overtly committed to a policy of "no net loss" of environmental, cultural, and social value, as well as to economic gains, could produce enough positive and durable effects on a local community to distinguish itself from conventional development in terms of its sustainability (Geisler 1993). Often, however, many gains to local communities resulting from tourism fail to meet that test. Outside owners of tour companies and hotels reap most of the economic benefits while local residents take on low-paying jobs in hotels and restaurants, and are sucked into "addictive" and perpetual social and cultural changes (Freudenburg 1992; Geisler 1993).

Involvement of the local community in the operation of a national park is, however, more likely to motivate residents to help stem some of these park-related tourism problems than if park management had no local cooperation. Allen (1991) concluded from a study of ten rural communities in Colorado that the local residents most likely to view tourism development favorably are either those at tourist destinations with low economic activity and low current tourism development, or those at destinations with high economic activity and high tourism development. The former have high expectations about tourism development, while the latter have an economy that can capture all the ripples of tourist expenditure and may already have attained some of the economic benefits of tourism. The study found that communities with mixed levels of economic activity and tourism development (high economic activity and low tourism development or the reverse) have less favorable attitudes toward tourism development. Either the need for tourism development is not manifest where there is high economic activity and low tourism development; or expectations about the economic benefits of tourism have not been realized where high tourism activity has not produced high economic development.

The situation of communities surrounding Great Basin NP tends to support this model of destination attitudes to tourism. The three counties in the vicinity of the park have low economic activity and tourism development. Residents have been shown to have a positive attitude toward tourism development. The proportion of residents in the area who thought that the national park had a positive effect on economic development opportunities was 58.2 percent, and 83.4 percent felt that the park improved the potential for tourism development in the region (Dawson et al. 1993). The attractiveness of a national park may serve as a magnet for a large number of visitors. However, many national parks are situated in rural areas whose economies may not be adequately developed to provide the additional inputs that will capture all the direct, indirect, and induced economic impacts of the expenditures of such large numbers of people (Dawson et al. 1993). Some of the inputs may have to be brought in from outside the region, and this leakage of economic activity from the local area will reduce the economic impact of the park on the local and regional economy. Under those circumstances, an increase in visitation and expenditure may not produce a proportional increase in economic activity in the local or regional economy. This can cause the unsatisfactory mixture of high tourism activity producing low economic impact at the local and regional levels.

Conclusion

The literature reviewed shows that there are both benefits and costs in relationships between national parks and nearby communities. A national park can have profound economic, social, and environmental impacts on the local community and the region. The literature reviewed for this paper noted seven impact areas: (a) quality of life, (b) economics, (c) environmental quality, (d) social-psychological benefits, (e) equity in access, (f) heritage preservation, and (g) tourism.

Earlier it was noted that environmental problems are often found at the intersection of ecosystems and human social systems. If this is true, then the literature review identifies several shortcomings in our knowledge of relationships between national parks and nearby communities. First, it points toward no consistent research program that systematically explores one individual park and local community relationship over time. Second, there is no research that uses the same method and looks at several parks in the same way. Third, there is no research that develops an experimental design (e.g., big park versus small park; urban versus rural; east versus west) and then uses the same methodology to explore impacts within the design framework. A potential model for this could be the National Science Foundation's Long-term Ecological Studies project, except that it is applied to human communities and national parks.

A number of studies dealing either with the broad concept of community in general or with communities and natural resource issues (e.g., reservoirs, community stability, agriculture, rural communities) could be used as stepping stones for developing both applied and basic research frameworks in this area. But no tradition to study national parks and their impacts on nearby communities in this way appears to exist in the United States.

In the introduction to the book *Nature and the Human Spirit: Toward an Expanded Land Management Ethic* (Driver et al. 1996:1), the editors cite a speech by President Bill Clinton in 1993:

> Clearly, we are moving toward a new era in the stewardship of public lands. This new era is one in which we must blend environmental values with the needs of people in such a way that the [public lands] represent diverse, healthy, productive, and sustainable ecosystems.

If we are to achieve this goal, then usable social science knowledge that explores the park/community relationship will be required to produce successful public land management policies in the next century.

References

Agrawal, A., and Gibson, C. C. 1999. Enchantment and disenchantment: The role of community in natural resource conservation. *World Development* April, 27(4): 629–49.

Allen, L. R. 1991. Benefits of leisure services to community satisfaction. In *Benefits of Leisure*, ed. B. L. Driver, P. J. Brown, and G. L. Peterson, 331–50. State College, PA: Venture.

Alward, Gregory S. 1986. Local and regional economic impact of outdoor recreation development. *A Literature Review, The President's Commission on Americans Outdoors—Values*, 47–55. Washington, DC: U.S. Government Printing Office.

Bergstrom, J. C., H. K. Cordell, G. A. Ashley, and A. E. Watson. 1990. Economic impacts of recreational spending on rural areas: A case study. *Economic Development Quarterly* 4(1): 29–39.

Burdge, Rabel, J. 1996. Introduction: Cultural diversity in natural resource use. *Society and Natural Resources* 9(1): 1–2.

Cordell, H. K., J. C. Bergstrom, and A. E. Watson. 1992. Economic growth and interdependence effects of state park visitation in local and state economies. *Journal of Leisure Research* 24: 253–68.

Corrill, M., J. Lillydahl, and L. Single. 1978. The effects of greenbelts on residential property values: Some findings on the political economy of open space. *Land Economics* 54: 207–17.

Crompton, John L., Lisa L. Love, and Thomas A. More. 1997. An empirical study of the role of recreation, parks and open space in companies' (re) location decisions. *Journal of Park and Recreation Administration* 15(1): 37–58.

Dawson, Scott A., J. Dale Blahna, and John E. Keith. 1993. Expected and actual regional economic impacts of Great Basin National Park. *Journal of Park and Recreation Administration* 11(4): 45–59.

Dearden, Phillip. 1995. Park literacy and conservation. *Conservation Biology* 9(6): 1654–56.

Dearden, P., and R. Rollins. 1993. *Parks and Protected Areas in Canada: Planning and Management.* Toronto, Ontario: Oxford University Press.

Donnelly, Peter. 1993. The right to wander: Issues in the leisure use of countryside and wilderness areas. *International Review of the Sociology of Sport* 28(2–3): 187–202.

Driver, B. L., and George L. Peterson. 1996. The values and benefits of outdoor recreation: An integrating overview. In *A Literature Review, The President's Commission on Americans Outdoors—Values,* 2–9. Washington, DC: U.S. Government Printing Office.

Driver, B. L., Daniel Dustin, Tony Baltic, Gary Elsner, and George Peterson, eds. 1996. *Nature and the Human Spirit: Toward an Expanded Land Management Ethic.* State College, PA: Venture.

Dryzek, John S. 1997. *The Politics of the Earth: Environmental Discourses.* New York: Oxford University Press.

Dustin, D. L., and L. H. McAvoy. 1982. The decline and fall of quality recreation opportunities and environments? *Environmental Ethics* 4: 49–58.

Fiske, Shirley J. 1992. Sociocultural aspects of establishing marine protected areas. *Ocean and Coastal Management* 18: 25–46.

Foley, Jack. 1990. Taking back the parks. *Recreation Canada* 48(3): 11–19.

Freudenburg, W. 1992. Addictive economies: Extractive industries and vulnerable localities in a changing world economy. *Rural Sociology* 57(3): 305–32.

Gartner, William C., Daniel E. Chappelle, and T. C. Girard. 1996. The influence of natural resource characteristics on property value: A case study. *Journal of Travel Research* 351: 64–71.

Geisler, Charles C. 1993. Rethinking SIA: Why ex-ante research isn't enough. *Society and Natural Resources* 6(4): 327–38.

Glick, D. 1991. Tourism in Greater Yellowstone: Maximizing the good, minimizing the bad, eliminating the ugly. In *Nature-tourism: Managing for the Environment,* ed. T. Whelan, 58–74. Washington, DC: Island Press.

Green, F. P. 1992. The impact of community recreation on friendship between adults with mental retardation and their nondisabled peers. In *Abstracts of the Proceedings of the 1991 National Recreation and Park Association Leisure Research Symposium (October), Baltimore, Maryland,* 26. Alexandria, VA: National Recreation and Park Association.

Hammer, L. F., T. Adams, F. W. Loede, C. J. Storey, and F. B. Williams. 1974. Public recreation: A study of parks, playgrounds and other outdoor recreation facilities. In *Metropolitan America; Regional Plan of New York and its Environs,* 256. *Regional Survey of New York and its Environs,* 5. (Rev. ed.). New York: Anro Press.

Heyne, L., and S. J. Schleien. 1992. Friendship development between children with and without disabilities through participation in school and neighborhood recreational activities. In *Abstracts of the Proceedings of the 1991 National Recreation and Park Asso-*

ciation Leisure Research Symposium (October), Baltimore, Maryland, 26. Alexandria, VA: National Recreation and Park Association.

Holland, S. M., and J. C. Crotts. 1992. A strategic planning approach to tourism development in rural communities. *Visions in Leisure and Business* 11(1): 14–23.

Huang, Yueh-Huang, and William P. Stewart. 1996. Rural tourism development: Shifting basis of community solidarity. *Journal of Travel Research* 34(4): 26–31.

Hultsman, W., and B. Little. 1995. Recommendations for a Youth-at-Risk Initiative: Comments from the Academy. *Journal of Park and Recreation Administration* 13(1): 10–25.

Jobes, Patrick C. 1993. Population and social characteristics in the Greater Yellowstone Ecosystem. *Society and Natural Resources* 6(2): 149–63.

Johnson, D. R., and M.E.V. Kamp. 1996. Extent and control of resource damage due to noncompliant visitor behavior: A case study from the U.S. national parks. *Natural Areas Journal* 16(2): 134–41.

Kelly, J. T. 1996. Military base closures can change lands to parks. *Parks and Recreation* 31(1): 70–76.

Kraus, Richard. 1987. Serving ethnic minorities: A submerged issue? *Parks and Recreation* 22(12): 46–50.

Lambert, D. 1991. *Great Basin Drama.* Niwot, CO: Robert Rhinehart.

La Pierre, Yvette. 1997. The taming of the view. *National Parks* 71(9–10): 30–33.

Lee, Kai N. 1993. *Compass and Gyroscope: Integrating Science and Politics for the Environment.* Washington, DC: Island Press.

Lemons, John. 1987. Title 16 United States Code §55 and its implications for management of concession facilities in Yosemite National Park. *Environmental Management* 11(4): 461–72.

Lemons, J., and D. Stout. 1984. A reinterpretation of national parks. *Ecology Law Quarterly* 8: 1–54.

Light, Andrew, and Eric Katz. 1996. *Environmental Pragmatism.* London: Routledge.

Little, Alton. 1993. Outdoor recreation revisited. *Parks and Recreation* 28(8): 42–44.

Machlis, G. E. 1999. New forestry, neopolitics, and voodoo economies: Research needs for biodiversity management. *In Ecosystem Management: Adaptive Strategies for Natural Resource Organizations in the Twenty-First Century,* ed. J. Aley, W. Burch, B. Conover, and D. Field, 5–16. Philadelphia: Taylor and Francis.

Mathieson, A., and G. Wall. 1982. *Tourism: Economic, Physical, and Social Impacts.* Harlow, Great Britain: Longmans.

Meis, Scott M. 1990. The socio-economic function of the Canadian parks service as a model for the U.S. National Park Service and other agencies: An organizational framework for managing natural resource recreation research. In *Social Science and Natural Resource Recreation Management,* ed. Joanne Vining, 33–46. Boulder, CO: Westview Press.

Merrifield, J., and S. Gerking. 1982. *Analysis of the Long-term Impacts and Benefits of Grand Teton National Park on the Economy of Teton County, Wyoming.* Laramie: University of Wyoming, Institute for Policy Research.

Milman, A., and A. Pizam. 1988. Social impacts of tourism on central Florida. *Annals of Tourism Research* 15: 191–204.

Nelson, J. G. 1994. The spread of ecotourism—Some planning implications. *Environmental Conservation* 21(3): 248–55.

O'Leary, Joseph T. 1974. "Community Conflict and Adaptation: An Examination of

Community Response to Change in Natural Resource Management and Policy Strategies." Ph.D. diss., University of Washington.

———. 1976. Land use redefinition and the rural community: Disruption of community leisure space. *Journal of Leisure Research* 8(4): 263–74.

Pedlar, Alison. 1996. Community development: What does it mean for recreation and leisure? *Journal of Applied Recreation Research* 21(1): 5–23.

Petersen, Margaret, and Dave Harmon. 1993. Wilderness management: The effect of new expectations and technologies. *Journal of Forestry* 9(2): 10–14.

Reading, Richard P., Tim W. Clark, and Stephen R. Kellert. 1994. Attitudes and knowledge of people living in the Greater Yellowstone Ecosystem. *Society and Natural Resources* 7: 349–65.

Roberts, G. 1994. The cultural landscape. *Landscape Research* 19:(3) 133–36.

Rothman, R. A. 1978. Residents and transients: Community reaction to seasonal visitors. *Journal of Travel Research* 16: 8–13.

Rudzitis, Gundars. 1996. *Wilderness and the American West.* New York: John Wiley.

Rudzitis, Gundars, Christy Watrous, and Harley Johansen. 1995. *Public Views on Public Lands: A Survey of Interior Columbia River Basin Residents.* Moscow, ID: The Migration, Regional Development, and Changing American West Project. University of Idaho, Department of Geography.

Rudzitis, Gundars, and Harley E. Johansen. 1989. *Amenities, migration, and nonmetropolitan development.* Final report written and produced by the University of Idaho to the National Science Foundation. Washington, DC.

———. 1991. How important is wilderness? Results from a United States survey. *Environmental Management* 15(2): 227–33.

Runte, A. 1987. *National Parks: The American Experience.* Lincoln: University of Nebraska Press.

Schroeder, T. D. 1982. The relationship of local public park and recreation services to residential property values. *Journal of Leisure Research* 14(3): 223–34.

Searle, Mark S. 1990. Empowering the citizen: Advocacy for recreation and parks. *Recreation Canada* 48(2): 36–38.

Shindler, Bruce, Peter List, and Brent S. Steel. 1993. Managing federal forests: Public attitudes in Oregon and nationwide. *Journal of Forestry* 91(7): 36–42.

Soden, Dennis L. 1995. Community perceptions of national parks as economic partners. *Journal of Park and Recreation Administration* 13(2): 11–28.

Solecki, W. D. 1994. Putting the Biosphere Reserve concept into practice—Some evidence of impacts in rural communities in the United States. *Environmental Conservation* 21(3): 242–47.

Stankey, George H. 1989. Linking parks to people: The key to effective management. *Society and Natural Resources* 2(3): 245–50.

Thomason, P., J. Crompton, and R. Kamp. 1979. A study of the attitudes of impacted groups within a host community toward prolonged stay of tourist visitors. *Journal of Travel Research* 13: 179–90.

Ulrich, R. S., and D. L. Addams. 1981. Psychological and recreation benefits of a residential park. *Journal of Leisure Research* 13(1): 43–65.

Vining, J., R. Graham, and R. J. Payne. 1990. Customary and traditional knowledge in Canadian national park planning and management: A process view. In *Social Science and Natural Resource Recreation Management,* ed. J. Vining, 125–50. Boulder, CO: Westview Press.

Wallace, G., P. Reed, and J. McKean. 1990. *The Impact of External Development on the Economic and Aesthetic Values of Theodore Roosevelt National Park.* Final report to the National Park Service. Fort Collins: Colorado State University.

Weicher, J., and R. Zerbst. 1973. The externalities of neighborhood parks: An empirical investigation. *Land Economics* 49: 99–105.

Whitelaw, E. 1992. Oregon's real economy. *Old Oregon* 72(2): 31–33.

Wilderness Society, The. 1999. *Stand by Your Lands: Crown of the Canyons.* http://www.wilderness.org/standby/uta/atlas/economic.htm

Zube, Ervin H. 1989. National parks in a changing world. *Society and Natural Resources* 2(3): 241–43.

Discussion

The chapters in Part One converge around several key themes. The first is that economic development is central to the trajectory of rural development. This argument is essential to understanding the tension between national park management and rural development strategies, particularly in the western United States. As Rothman notes, revered icons of nature such as Yellowstone NP were also engines of growth for gateway communities. And not all was tourist based: construction of infrastructure (by the CCC and others) was also economically important.

A second theme, emphasized by Summers and Field as well as Marcouiller and Green, is that local economies are affected by regional, national, and international forces. Combined with the common rural pattern of dependency on single industries, a general policy prescription emerges: development strategies must be multisectoral and diverse. This directly leads to a third theme emphasized by several authors. Tourism should be considered an element of rural development strategies near parks: overreliance on tourism has its strategic dangers.

The authors diverge on several key points. While overreliance on tourism is generally agreed to be unattractive and unwise, the authors do not wholly agree on the level to which parks actually contribute to local economies. Achana and O'Leary, in particular, note that the economic influence of parks is highly variable. And while Rothman provides several examples of parks established with at least modest local participation (Navajo NM and Carlsbad Caverns NP), Achana and O'Leary provide examples (such as North Cascades NP) where local involvement or federal concern for local interest was relatively lacking. They remind us that the interests of federal agencies and national conservation groups may not always correspond to the interests of rural regions and local communities.

Part Two

CASE STUDIES

The following five case studies examine the role of national parks in rural development. Each reflects a unique relationship between parks and their surrounding communities. While the social, economic, historical, and environmental processes described in Part One are regularities experienced by most parks and surrounding regions, there is a distinctiveness to these case studies. The distinction is driven, in part, by the unique historical period of park establishment and development, the unique mix of cultures involved, and specific environmental and economic conditions. Hence, these chapters reflect a "sense of place" critical to understanding the relationship between national parks and rural development.

In the first case study, John Miles discusses three parks in the Pacific Northwest. He describes park establishment in a rugged terrain and harsh climate, which inhibited tourism development in adjacent rural towns. Communities were supported primarily by extractive economies that developed parallel to the parks. Mt. Rainier NP (established in 1899), Olympic NP (1930), and North Cascades NP (the late 1960s) were each surrounded by public lands and somewhat isolated from pressures of private enterprise. In the author's analysis, all three parks were seasonal parks, with visitors mainly coming for day trips from nearby cities that already had established tourism economies. These "founding conditions" directed the relationship between these national parks and their surrounding regions.

The Grand Canyon NP case study addresses a current and critical issue related to land use and development around national parks. Julie Leones and George Frisvold describe in detail the complex problem and extensive negotiations surrounding the location of visitor services and visitor and staff lodging. The case study is especially relevant because of the importance of Grand Canyon NP in American culture, and for its application to other relatively isolated parks with high rates of visitation.

In Alaska, though there are also large tracts of federal lands surrounding the Alaska parks, the pattern was different. Federal legislation mandated the inclusion of residents in managing the parks. Hence, the case of Alaska is distinct from other regions of the United States in its history, scale, and important issues affecting both park management and rural development. Darryll Johnson provides a description of the historical and current subsistence use of Alaska's wildlands, and the balance between parks, native communities, and contemporary natural resource management.

An urban counterpart to Alaska is Bill Kornblum's case study of Cape Cod NS. In the Northeast, urban settlements and stable manufacturing-based economies were well established before the creation of national parks, seashores, and historic sites. Hence, these urban communities are not dependent on the park to build or boost their economies. Rather, residents are concerned about how the park is and will be used. In this case, the communities and the NPS have had to work together, often through significant conflict, to arrive at compromises and agreements regarding park management.

The final case is Yellowstone NP. Established in 1872, Yellowstone was the nation's first and the world's first national park. Since its founding, Yellowstone NP has been viewed as both a refuge for wildlife and a catalyst for economic development. Dennis Glick and Ben Alexander describe historical and recent events in the Greater Yellowstone Ecosystem (GYE). They illustrate both the positive and negative impacts of development affecting Yellowstone NP and Grand Teton NP, as well as the parks' surrounding communities. Yellowstone NP is both a cultural icon and a potential environmental model for protection and rural development. Many of the issues regarding rural development in the Rocky Mountain region are common and critical to many other places in the western United States.

Chapter 5

Three National Parks of the Pacific Northwest

John C. Miles

The Pacific Northwest is variously defined, but for this review of the impact of national parks on rural development in the region it will include the states of Oregon, Washington, and Idaho. The region, so defined, contains twenty units of the National Park System, including four national parks. The earliest unit in the region was designated in 1899 as Mount Rainier NP, while the most recently established unit, City of Rocks National Reserve (NRes), was authorized in 1988. The size of the units ranges from Olympic NP, at nearly a million acres, to the small visitor center that comprises the Klondike Gold Rush NHP in Seattle. National Park System units are diverse in the Pacific Northwest as they are in most geographic regions.

The effort to describe the impact of the National Park System on rural development in this region is complicated by this diversity. At Mount Rainier NP, for instance, the story of this impact is a long one affected by many historical forces. The earliest visitors arrived by train and horse-drawn conveyances; then the advent of the automobile changed everything. The North Cascades National Park Service Complex, which includes Ross Lake NRA and Lake Chelan NRA along with the park, has a brief history only stretching back to 1968 and has been less affected by the forces of general social and technological change than its older counterpart. Also, different types of units involve greater or lesser degrees of development, with less in wilderness parks than in national recreation areas. The great range of unit size is another complicating factor, as are geographic factors associated with the dramatic climatic differences between the eastern and western sides of the Cascade mountain range. All of this suggests that some narrowing of focus is necessary for any meaningful examination of the impacts of national parks on rural development in the region. Consequently this case study, which can only be a brief summary of the situation, will focus on the three national parks in the state of Washington, all of which are relatively large, primarily managed for natural values and wilderness, and located on the moist western side of the Cascade range. Their common qualities make study of them feasible in a short report, yet their diverse histories provide a range of experience for analysis. This approach excludes one Oregon national park and diverse smaller park system units in the region. Any insights drawn from this exploration will thus be limited to the large North Cascades and Olympic Mountains NPs. Though Crater Lake NP will not be examined, its many similarities with the three parks studied allow some extension of insights from them to it.

The aim of this chapter is to present a case study of the impact of these parks on rural development, so definitions of "rural," "development," and the region are necessary. Rogers and Burdge (1988) define "rural" as characterized by people living in small communities of fewer than 2,500 in open country and on farms. This accurately describes the human community surrounding the three parks examined here, although the parks also affect larger communities on access routes to them. An example is Port Angeles, Washington, a small city very close to Olympic NP and the site of the park headquarters. As for "development," Rogers and Burdge define it as social change resulting in higher incomes and levels of living that come from modern production methods and improved social organization. [*Editors' Note:* For additional discussion, see chapters 1 and 10.] Assessment of the presence or absence and level of development associated with a national park in this region involves looking for jobs added to or subtracted from the economy directly or indirectly as a consequence of the park. It involves assessment of park-induced changes in the nature of these jobs, in income levels, and in the composition and organization of the people living in the rural region surrounding the parks.

The Region

The Pacific Northwest encompasses three states, as noted, and is geographically diverse. It is bounded on the north by the international boundary with Canada's province of British Columbia. This boundary sweeps through the Strait of Juan de Fuca, which reaches eastward from the Pacific Ocean between Canada's Vancouver Island and the Olympic Peninsula of Washington state. It turns north through the San Juan Archipelago to the forty-ninth parallel, then runs along this parallel through Washington's North Cascades, Okanogan highlands, and Kettle Range to the Selkirk Mountains of northern Idaho. The region's eastern edge drops south through the Cabinet, Bitterroot, and Beaverhead Mountains to the hot, dry Snake River Plain of southern Idaho. Turning back west, it follows the boundaries of Idaho and Oregon across the northern Great Basin, mostly high desert, to the Siskiyou Mountains of the coast range and back to the Pacific Coast.

The geology, climate, and ecology of the region are diverse. Storms track off the North Pacific, dropping copious precipitation west of the Cascade mountain divide. East of this divide is a dry rain shadow, and plateaus rise to western subranges of the Rocky Mountains. Coastal maritime climatic conditions, wet and mild, characterize the western part of the region, yielding to semidesert in the interior basins and to continental mountain conditions marked by greater temperature fluctuations and less precipitation than in the maritime mountains.

Temperate rain forests, famous for their large trees, dominate the maritime region, while the semidesert areas grow few trees and feature a range of drought-adapted communities. Much wheat is grown in parts of this semidesert area. The continental mountains yield timber and offer range to cattle and sheep.

The human population of the region is concentrated west of the Cascades along the north-south interstate corridor stretching from Vancouver, British Columbia, through Seattle and Portland to Eugene, Oregon. Culturally and politically a "Cascade curtain" separates the "Inland Empire" of the geographic majority of the region from the population majority in the coastal cities.

The three parks examined in this case study are located in the maritime mountains of the western part of the region (see map 5.1). They are mountain parks and lie close to large population centers. No claim is made here that these large parks (as measured in budgets, staff, visitation, and acreage they are significantly larger than the other units in the region with the exception of Crater Lake NP) are representative of all National Park System units in the region. Their homogeneity makes a meaningful case study possible by confining the scope of the examples examined. Another reason to focus on these parks is that, while information on their impact on rural development is sparse, it is greater than that found for other units in the region.

Economic Impact Studies

There is a dearth of literature on the impact of national parks on rural development in this region, and what little there is focuses primarily on economic impact. Byers (1970) studied the economic impacts in 1968 of Mount Rainier NP and Olympic NP. He found that visitor spending and NPS operations expenditures pumped large sums into the economies of the communities in the vicinity of these two parks. Yet he concluded that "a minority of generated income accrued to Washington residents" (Byers 1970:8) and that visitor expenditures were highly seasonal, resulting in seasonal fluctuations in generated employment and income. This descriptive study examined a single year; and while it suggests positive economic impacts of the parks on local economies, which in turn might affect development in a positive way, it can only suggest such development impact.

Another economic impact study of Mount Rainier NP was done by Aldwell (1986), who attempted to assess whether there had been any significant change in economic patterns since the Byers study. He found that change was negligible and reaffirmed Byers's conclusion that the park was a significant source of income to the locality of the park and of seasonal employment for the local economy. These studies focused narrowly on economic impacts and drew no conclusions about consequences for development of the economic impact described.

Other studies have attempted to analyze the tourism markets of the regions around Olympic NP and North Cascades NP and offer insight into their impact on development. The Dean Runyan Associates (1995) analysis of the north Olympic Peninsula described the visitors to the region and noted that 70 to 80 percent of visitors came for the attractions of the national park and the scenic wonders of the area. The report notes that annual visitation to the park was uniform between 1983 and 1993 and that the travel industry in the region, as measured by taxable lodging sales, has grown modestly. No effort was made to correlate these rates of growth (1.8 to 6.2 percent per year) specifically to the

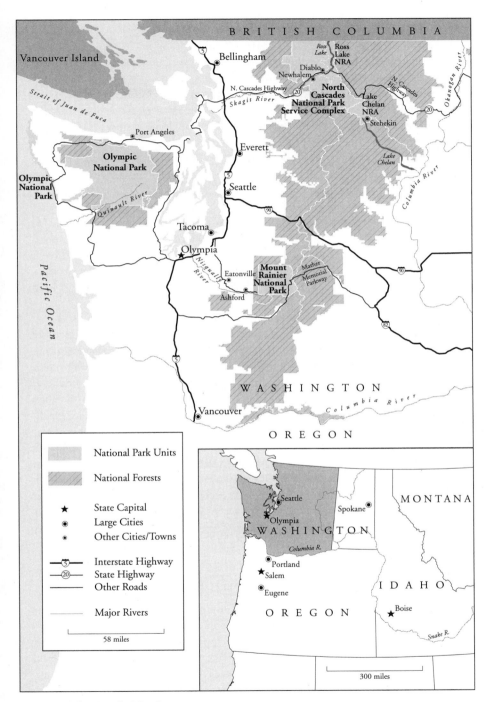

Map 5.1. The Pacific Northwest

presence of Olympic NP. Allaway (1997) studied tourism in the upper Skagit River Valley, which is the primary access to the North Cascades National Park Service Complex. He found data on visitation and highway use unreliable and the picture of visitation and use trends consequently cloudy. Nonetheless, he concluded that a significant number of tourists pass over the North Cascades Highway (Washington State Highway 20) and have done so since its opening in 1972, yet there is a "low capture of revenue" by the local economy from these tourists that he attributes to "factors such as marketing, lack of match between products or services offered and those desired, or other business management considerations, rather than too few tourists" (Allaway 1997:28). Allaway suggests that while there is a "large pool of prospective customers passing by their doorsteps daily in the summer," (1997:29) this pool remains untapped. His analysis of why this may be concludes that the seasonality of tourism is a special problem in the Skagit Valley because the highway is closed by snow for three to four months annually. Allaway concludes that tourism is significant in his study area but has not greatly enhanced development in the form of restaurants, lodgings, gas stations, or other businesses.

These are the only studies of economic impacts of parks in the region that an exhaustive search of the literature could unearth, and what can be concluded from them? Clearly the parks result in the addition of revenue to the economies of communities close to them, but exactly how this translates into development has simply not been examined. One feature of the economic picture noted in all studies is an extreme seasonality of visitation. The tourist season in the three Washington parks is brief. The pattern in the North Cascades is typical with significant visitation confined to the period of June through September. Dean Runyan Associates (1995) describe a similar situation for the north Olympic Peninsula, and Byers (1970) and Aldwell (1986) for Mount Rainier NP. All three are mountain parks that receive extreme amounts of precipitation in the winter months. They become inaccessible except in minor ways from November to April. This near total five-month hiatus in visitation and associated economic activity has been a major factor in depressing park-related development in rural areas around the parks.

Historical Perspectives from Mount Rainier NP

Mount Rainier has the longest history of any national park in the region, and its experience may yield insights into what appears to be a situation of relatively low impact of national parks on rural development in the Pacific Northwest. The park was established in 1899 during the period in the expansion of the National Park System when many of the "crown jewel" parks in the West were served by railroads that supplied a large portion of the visitors. [*Editors' Note:* For additional discussion, see chapters 3 and 9.] The early stages of Mount

Rainier NP's history were not as tied to railroads transporting tourists from distant cities as was the case for other western parks. The cities of Seattle and Tacoma provided the driving force for park development and a concentrated population of park users (Catton 1996). Thus, from an early stage, park visitation to Mount Rainier was dominated by in-state tourists who made relatively brief visits.

With the advent of the automobile, the road system in the region surrounding the park grew gradually. Most of these roads were constructed for reasons other than access to the park, and over the years, park development was affected by road development outside its boundaries. Modest accommodations were built in the park, and visitation, concentrated on weekends in July, August, and September, increased steadily through the 1930s. A concessionaire, the Rainier National Park Company, held a transportation monopoly from the Seattle-Tacoma area in the 1920s, but as autos became more common, the visitation pattern changed. Railroads and concessionaire-provided transport brought tourists who stayed in hotels, while autos brought tourists who stayed in campgrounds or visited for the day. As roads and autos improved, the proportion of day users among the visitors increased.

Tourist-related businesses on the routes approaching the park appeared during the period of growing automobile tourism, but they seem to have been few. The principal difficulty again was the shortness of the tourist season. To offset this, pressure grew in the 1930s for winter recreation development in the park, with proposals for aerial trams to serve skiers in two locations. Skiing increased at Paradise, but overnight visitor facilities were limited and weather often made access difficult. For a decade after World War II, the pressure grew on the NPS to develop for winter use. Lobbyists, such as a group from the community of Eatonville on the principal access route to Paradise, calling themselves "Operation Bootstrap," clamored for all-year, overnight accommodations at Paradise and for a chairlift. After a decade of debate about such proposals, during which the NPS opposed ski development on various grounds, the issue declined as other ski areas were developed in the region. Park visitation remained highly seasonal and businesses needing a steadier flow of tourists throughout the year remained marginal.

The campaign for overnight facilities in the park was not over, however. By 1956, day use accounted for 92 percent of park visitors, while overnight campers comprised 5 percent and hotel visitors only 3 percent. Promoters and politicians pushed for more hotel development in the park, but conservationists and NPS consultants pointed out that such development would require a large government subsidy and be inconsistent with primary park values. Ultimately a new visitor center was built at Paradise, but Mount Rainier would continue to be a park for day users and campers. In 1988, Congress passed a Washington Park Wilderness Act (1988), which designated approximately 95 percent of the park's total land base as the Mount Rainier Wilderness. This precluded much additional development within the park.

This history of pressure to build year-round overnight accommodations in the park and to develop winter recreation is instructive. Those who wished to capitalize economically on the park, including the park concessionaire, recognized that unless there was more year-round activity in the park their businesses would struggle. Studies of potential development within the park by consultants to the NPS indicated that considerable public subsidy of such development would be necessary to make hotels and related enterprises feasible. Business was simply not steady or extensive enough to make private investment in such development worthwhile. No major development of such facilities was privately undertaken in the park region, presumably for the same reason. Ski areas were eventually constructed on national forest land in the Mount Rainier area, which reduced pressure for such development on the park. Such developments could occur on national forests and be compatible with their multiple-use management. The extensive modification of the mountain landscape required for an economically viable winter recreation area was not consistent with the scenic and natural value emphasis of national park management. At Mount Rainier NP, preservation of scenic integrity won out over winter recreation development, although not without a long struggle (Catton 1996).

Mount Rainier, like the other Pacific Northwest national parks, is surrounded by public land, and this is another factor that has retarded development. A private tree farm reaches close to the western boundary, but the park's neighbors to the north, east, and south are national forests. One explanation for the relative lack of tourist development on private lands outside the park boundaries is that those lands are quite limited. Furthermore, the principal use of much of this private land has historically been timber production. Most of the national forest and private land near Mount Rainier NP has been logged, and a so-called working forest where clear-cut logging is extensive is not prime for development because of the aesthetic impact of such operations. Also, the presence of national forests has depressed development opportunity. For instance, the Mather Memorial Parkway, which approaches the park from the east, has been managed by the U.S. Forest Service as a scenic highway since 1931, precluding development along the 50-mile scenic drive outside the park boundary.

The Mount Rainier region has also been relatively free from the so-called gateway community pattern of development, though this may be changing. Some tourist development has occurred outside the Nisqually entrance, but the approach roads have been relatively free of it. The decade of the 1990s, a period of economic boom in the Pacific Northwest, has brought signs that gateway communities may be a prospect for the Mount Rainier region. Studies have shown that people move to gateway communities for the scenic beauty and high quality of life to be found in them (Howe et al. 1997). Factors that may account for the lack of gateway development near Mount Rainier NP to this point may be the weather, which is wet and dreary for much of the year, and the industrial forestry practiced on the landscape in accessible areas outside the park boundaries.

These obstacles to development near the park may be lessening. The Park Junction Resort has been proposed at Ashford, 11 miles from the Nisqually entrance. This resort is to include a 270-room hotel, a conference center, a golf course, 200 homes, 225 time-share condominiums, and a 40,000-square-foot shopping plaza, all on a 400-acre site. The NPS has expressed several concerns about the project in its response to the draft Environmental Impact Statement (EIS). The gist of its response is that the scale of the proposed development may be inappropriate for the location. The current level of park visitation is high and if the resort does not provide adequate recreation for its guests on its site, this may increase visitation to already heavily used (and affected) park areas during the summer period of peak visitation. Park Junction proposes to operate its conference season during the park's off season, thus bringing more visitors to the park during its shoulder seasons when it can accommodate them. Skeptics doubt whether such an approach will minimize great pressure on the park during the peak season when, after all, the weather is the best, the mountain is visible (which it rarely is at other times of the year), the flowers are in bloom, and a visit to the park is the most pleasant.

Should Park Junction Resort be constructed (which seems likely at this point) and be successful, it might change the historic problem of extreme seasonality that has retarded development around the park. It will change the character of one approach to the park, and might lead to more development and the growth of a true gateway community. The NPS is currently participating in planning efforts with communities in the Nisqually River Valley to define business centers and promote growth around these points. The agency is also part of a long-range planning effort being undertaken by Pierce County with the goal of long-term and appropriate development.

The outcome of the resort proposal and planning efforts by government in the region is uncertain. Nonetheless, the Park Junction proposal indicates renewed development pressures are at work in the area, which may lead to a gateway community and other development-related changes.

What insights into the rural development situation may be derived from this Mount Rainer experience? From its founding the park drew most of its visitors from nearby urban areas. This was possible, of course, because such urban concentrations were present. The growth of communities in the region paralleled that of the national park idea and of Mount Rainier NP itself. From its earliest days the park drew on a significant regional visitor base and this was both a cause and an effect of limited resort development in and around the park. Another serious retardant of resort development was the short visitor season—investment in hotels and related facilities was unwise in such a short season. In addition, as the automobile became more ubiquitous, tourists could visit the park in a day from Seattle or Tacoma, and they did just that. Mount Rainier NP became another attraction of the Pacific Northwest, a stop on the tour, but people lodged and dined and spent their tourist dollars in host cities such as Seattle and Tacoma rather than in resorts around or in the park. The historic pattern of national park development in the Mount Rainier case seems to have resulted, at least until recently, in relatively little impact on rural development of the region around the park itself.

The Olympic National Park Experience

The next national park established in the Pacific Northwest was Olympic NP, in 1938. This park is much larger than Mount Rainer NP—922,654 acres as opposed to Mount Rainier's 235,613 acres. It entered the system well into the automobile age and in very different circumstances than had its older counterpart. The economy of the Olympic Peninsula was quite developed by the time the park appeared on the scene, and from its beginnings it had been almost entirely centered on harvest of the exceptional timber resource found there. For this reason, peninsula communities vigorously opposed any designation of public land that would result in less access to this pivotal timber resource. After decades of debate, direct intervention by President Franklin Roosevelt was necessary for establishment of an approximately 634,000-acre park in 1938. Roosevelt enlarged the park in 1940 to include the northern and eastern forks of the Quinault River and the north shore of Lake Crescent, while the coastal strip was added by President Truman in 1953. While Mount Rainier NP had been carved out of nearly unsettled public land, portions of what became Olympic NP had been long settled and inhabited. A 1956 NPS report noted that inholdings in the park, mostly in the 1940 additions, amounted to 7,354 acres in 800 tracts held by more than 600 landowners (NPS 1990).

Like Mount Rainier NP (and the North Cascades National Park Service Complex), Olympic NP was, from its beginning, close to a large population of visitors who came for day trips or to camp, backpack, or climb mountains. Its core was a vast, roadless wilderness, and most of the lands around its boundaries were public. Little tourist development had occurred on the peninsula, since nearly all of its inhabitants were engaged in timber-related work and expected to be so in the future. Access to the park by road was limited, and the visitation season was also constrained by weather—snow in the mountains, heavy winter rains in the lowland valleys, and winter storms that pounded the west coast of the peninsula.

Throughout its history Olympic National Park has been primarily a wilderness park. In 1938 a NPS management study team recommended that the wilderness features of the park be preserved at the expense of visitor access (NPS 1990). During the 1950s there was support by Superintendent Fred Overly and other interests for a more "parks are for people" approach. Overly's 1952 Master Plan called for more overnight accommodations, trail-building, skiing, and other winter use, but a NPS study of this initiative indicated that demand for winter use was relatively light. Campgrounds were built and expanded during Mission 66, a ten-year effort conceived by National Park Service Director Conrad Wirth in 1955, to catch up on maintenance and new facility development that had fallen behind during and after World War II. (The goal was to achieve the upgrade of park facilities by the 50th anniversary of the National Park Service Act, thus its name "Mission 66.") However, in the 1960s the emphasis on the wilderness resource was reasserted and little development of visitor facilities was undertaken. The 1988 Washington Park Wilderness Act designated 876,669 of the park's 922,654 acres as part of the National Wilderness Preservation System.

In the debate over establishment of Olympic NP, opponents argued that the "locking up" of valuable timber resources would be at best damaging and at worst disastrous to the economic health of the timber-dependent communities on the Olympic Peninsula. The Washington State Planning Council concluded in 1936 that anything but a minimalist park (they could accept a 360,000-acre park) would "cripple financially any local government unit" (WSPC 1936:7). Such dire predictions did not come to pass. Olympic Peninsula communities continued to grow. Manufacturing became the leading source of personal income, with forest product industries dominating. Timber production of national forest and state and private lands increased until both Clallam and Jefferson Counties, the two counties with the most land base in the park, reached record timber output peaks in 1964 (WDCED 1968). Statistical evidence of economic development impact in either positive or negative directions from the park is scarce as noted earlier, but the general pattern during the sixty-year life of the park seems to be one of minimal effect. No doubt there has been impact. A portion of the Olympic Peninsula timber base was removed when the park was created, and this is timber that sooner or later was not available to feed mills and provide timber jobs. This negative impact may have been felt only recently, when timber supplies in national forests, and on state and private lands, have been reduced by extensive harvest. Rates of harvest for remaining timber have also been reduced on federal lands by implementation of the National Forest Management Act and the Endangered Species Act. It may be argued that the presence or absence of Olympic NP or any other national park containing timber would not have changed the eventual effect of the interplay of rates of timber harvest, depletion of timber supply, and impact of measures to protect biological diversity on the timber economy of the region. The additional available timber might have bought only a little time for the timber economy.

Has Olympic NP stimulated development in the region? It probably has, but precisely how and to what extent has not been determined. As noted earlier, Byers (1970) concluded that park-related tourism brought significant economic benefits to communities near the park. No bursts of development can, however, be attributed directly to the influence of the park. Tourists came to Olympic NP, as to Mount Rainier NP, in a strongly seasonal pattern. The majority came during summer from the Pacific Northwest and stayed one or two nights (Dean Runyan Associates 1995). The park built more campgrounds in the 1950s to accommodate growing numbers of visitors; and hotels, motels, and restaurants in Port Townsend, Port Angeles, and other peninsula communities met tourists' needs. Despite this, the economy remained largely timber oriented.

In the 1960s, the Washington Department of Commerce and Economic Development (WDCED) predicted that growth of the timber industry would be slowed and that future economic growth in the region would lie in other directions. A department report said of Jefferson County, "The future of economic growth . . . may be in a different direction. The combination of proximity to salt water beaches and Olympic NP represent a potential for recreation of a very high order. It would appear that recreation may become one of the basic, if not the basic, functions of the Jefferson County economy in future years" (WDCED 1968:49). Counties on the peninsula did not, however, heed this view, arguing that their future would lie in timber. They thought constraints on the tourist industry were that it was too seasonal, that the community was opposed to developing privately owned recreational facilities (presumably because of direct impacts on them), that public resources to support tourist development were too scarce, and that promotion of the county's attributes as a recreational, historical, and cultural center were and would continue to be inadequate (Jefferson County Board of Commissioners 1978). The Washington State Research Council reported in 1982 that efforts to develop a tourist industry on the peninsula had largely failed and that the history of Washington state travel and tourism is "largely a tale of missed opportunities" (WSRC 1982:2). In 1990, an Olympic Peninsula Regional Diversification Strategy Plan called for development of a tourism industry because of projected loss of jobs stemming from timber harvest restrictions. "There is untapped potential to capture visitor expenditures on routes to major destinations, to develop more destination lodging facilities, and to increase off-season tourism" (WDTED 1990:25).

When examining the history of economic development on the peninsula, it is difficult to say that the locking up of resources by the national park had a significant negative impact on the communities there. The restrictions on timber harvest of the 1990s, which came after decades of record high harvests, have had much greater impact. What can be said is that there are potential positive economic impacts from the park that have not yet been fully realized. Tourism has begun to grow in recent years, yet even the 1994 county profiles of Jefferson and

Clallam Counties list it as an underdeveloped resource (WSESD 1995; WSESD 1992). This may be due to constraints originally listed in the 1978 Jefferson County Office of Economic Development and Planning report that are difficult to overcome and continue to constrain tourism development. Access to the Olympic Peninsula has greatly improved since the establishment of the park, but the location of the park surrounded by national forest limits access. The number of campgrounds and hotel/motel facilities has increased in both counties, but promotion of the park has not improved. The peninsula communities still need to provide incentives for tourists to stop and stay in their facilities instead of simply driving through to the next access point (WDTED 1990). The major impact of Olympic NP on rural development is still a potential.

North Cascades National Park Service Complex

The last park to be examined is North Cascades, and in this case the park is part of an NPS-administered complex that includes the Ross Lake NRA and Lake Chelan NRA. This complex was added to the National Park System in 1968 and has both similarities and differences with the other two parks. The North Cascades National Park Service Complex is bisected by the North Cascades Highway, opened in 1972. Two developed areas are included in the complex. One is the Skagit Hydroelectric Power Project of Seattle City Light, which includes three dams on the Skagit River and the associated company communities of Newhalem and Diablo in the Ross Lake NRA. The other is the community of Stehekin at the head of Lake Chelan in the Lake Chelan NRA. Such extensive developments were not a feature of the other two parks when they were established, though significant inholdings were present in Olympic NP, as noted earlier.

Despite this development, access to the North Cascades complex is limited. The principal approach from east and west is Washington State Highway 20, while a southern entry may be made to Stehekin via boat on Lake Chelan. All units in the complex total 684,614 acres of which 634,614 are in the Stephen Mather Wilderness, so designated in the Washington Park Wilderness Act of 1988. The park and recreation areas are surrounded on the west, south, and east by 6 million acres of national forest lands, of which 1.4 million acres are designated wilderness. To the north, across the international boundary with Canada, are parks and forest lands administered by the province of British Columbia (NPS 1987).

As with Mount Rainier NP and Olympic NP, North Cascades NPS Complex features mountains, and many of the same forces that have constrained visitation, and thus development in and around these parks. Seasonality of visitation is again the principal constraint, as noted earlier in review of the Allaway tourism planning study. There has been no discernible burst of tourism-related development on the approaches to the complex since 1968 although visitor use of the North Cascades Highway has increased steadily since its 1972 opening. The scenic nature of the highway, like the Mather Memorial Parkway at Mount Rainier NP, has been an additional constraint on development. Like the Parkway, the North Cascades Highway traverses national forest on each side of the park; and the U.S. Forest Service, in cooperation with the NPS, has managed significant stretches of the road for scenic values. The Washington State Wilderness Act of 1984, recognizing the "remarkable scenic values, representing a unique aesthetic travelway through the Cascade Mountains," directed that management plans for the Mount Baker-Snoqualmie and Okanogan National Forests "preserve the scenic value of this highway corridor" (S837, Sect. 8). Thus, in addition to land within the park service complex adjacent to the highway managed for such value, approximately 88,000 acres of national forest along the highway are also precluded from development that might adversely affect the scenery. More than 60 miles of the highway are so managed.

On the southern edge of the national park complex, the community of Stehekin and its experience since the Lake Chelan NRA was established also constitute case study. Creation of the North Cascades complex had several consequences for this small, isolated community. Just before congressional approval of the NRA, the rate of building in the Stehekin Valley increased as residents feared the NPS would curtail building and development (Georgette and Harvey 1980). The NPS proceeded to acquire privately owned land in Stehekin, which reduced the possible extent of development of private holdings, but property values rose and development of remaining private land increased, resulting in population growth and rising demand for valley resources such as firewood. This in turn resulted in conflict over regulation of these resources by the NPS.

The community and the NPS have struggled for thirty years with the core issue of how to perpetuate a small, independent community inside the North Cascades NP Complex while protecting the resource values of the Stehekin River Valley, the very values that led to the valley's inclusion in the complex by Congress. When the Lake Chelan NRA was established, approximately 1,700 acres in the valley were privately owned, with the rest managed by the U.S. Forest Service. Stehekin's economy was based almost entirely on tourism, and it functioned as a self-contained and self-sufficient economic unit. The U.S. Forest Service's presence and level of control were low.

The legislation creating the park complex stipulated that the eighty-year-old community should continue to exist, and that it should be allowed to continue to use certain public resources for community purposes, but that its future would be quite strictly controlled. Congress limited future use by authorizing

> such management, utilization, and disposal of renewable natural
> resources and the continuation of such existing uses and develop-

ments as will promote or are compatible with, or do not significantly impair, public recreation and conservation of the scenic, scientific, historic, or other values contributing to the public enjoyment (S1321: Sect. 402a, 1968).

Interpretation of this language by the community and the NPS has at times differed, resulting in continual tension between the two parties.

The NPS has purchased 1,200 of the 1,700 acres of private land in the valley from willing sellers as authorized by Congress. Visitation of tourists to Stehekin has increased significantly because of the greater visibility provided by
inclusion in a unit of the National Park System. Where one U.S. Forest Service
employee lived all year in the valley, there is now a considerable year-round NPS
presence. Summer employment and vacation residential use have grown, and
private businesses at the landing used by the daily boat up Lake Chelan have
become NPS concessions. Private businesses elsewhere in the valley have
increased modestly and demand for homesites and for natural resources has also
increased.

The NPS management goal has been to carefully and stringently control
development in the valley. While some development has occurred and more is
proposed, the NPS has attempted to maintain the character of the community
as it was when the park was established while minimizing impacts on resources.
In this Stehekin case, the impact of the North Cascades National Park Service
Complex on rural development has been a complex combination of stimulus
and constraint. There is a higher level of economic activity as a direct result of
the park, yet development and growth have been strictly controlled, to the con-
sternation of some residents who believe that national park regulations unduly
interfere with their lifestyles and economic opportunities. The NPS has zoned
the valley very carefully for various uses, strictly limiting the development zone,
and this has and will unquestionably restrain development in this rural community.

Conclusions

This attempt to examine the impact of national parks on rural development in
the Pacific Northwest is based on review of literature about park-related economic development, historical studies of three Washington national parks, and
exploration of statistical and planning information on the communities and
counties around these parks. One conclusion from this review is that there is
much work to be done to truly understand the impact of national parks on rural
development in the region. With the exception of the Stehekin situation, no
studies have scientifically affirmed that a decision to create a park or implement
a management policy has resulted in a specific impact on development. One can

infer that a decision not to develop a park for winter recreation at any and all of these parks resulted in seasonality of visitation and marginality of businesses seeking to reap tourist revenues from park visitors. No studies have, however, correlated that decision with that effect. The scant literature on which to draw in this regional case study is anecdotal and speculative. Queries to economic development and planning agencies in the regions of all three parks elicited a consistent response—no, we don't have information on that, but we sure wish that we did.

With these limitations of information clearly in mind, several speculative conclusions can be drawn. First, the overall impression that comes from investigations involved in this study is that the national parks in the Pacific Northwest region have not stimulated rural development to the extent that national parks have in other places. Gateway communities have not sprung up. The roads leading to these parks are not lined with tourist shops and restaurants, motels, hotels, gift shops, and other tourist-oriented businesses. The overriding question is why this has been so.

Common to the three parks studied are their climatic and topographic features, related, of course, to geographical location of all three in an area subject to storms yielding heavy precipitation off the North Pacific Ocean. This precipitation, which is dropped on the mountains where the parks are located, imposes a severe seasonality on visitation. Economic development on approach routes seems to have been limited by this confinement of heavy visitation to four months each year. Winter recreation has not proved feasible because it requires development within parks that is not compatible with the parks' principal resource values: scenery, naturalness, and wildness. Winter recreation development would also require significant public subsidy, if the Mount Rainier NP experience is any indicator, and this has not been forthcoming. Increases in general popularity of winter backcountry recreation in the past two decades have not resulted in a significant change in winter use patterns in the three Pacific Northwest parks because of unpredictable weather, inaccessibility, and periodic severe avalanche potential. Thus, the geographic locations of the parks in this region and associated climatic conditions have depressed development in surrounding rural areas.

Another geographical factor at work to depress development in and around these parks is simply the rugged topography. The dream of building a road through the North Cascades, for instance, took nearly a century to come to fruition. Development of any sort, for mining, recreation, or any other enterprise, has proved extremely difficult in the mountains of the Pacific Northwest. Building roads, railroads, and other projects is one thing; maintaining them in the face of immense snowpack, avalanche, and flood is entirely another. Development of the most basic sort within the parks, such as hotels and roads, which would attract and concentrate visitors and thus be a catalyst for development around the parks, has simply proven to be very difficult and expensive, park resource value issues aside.

All of these parks are surrounded by predominantly public land administered for multiple uses by the U.S. Forest Service. Washington state lands and private holdings close to these parks have, like the national forests, been managed primarily for timber production, and industrial forestry operations do not make good neighbors to recreational development. Access to park boundaries through these working forests has been very limited, and in many cases timber operations have reached right to park boundaries. In other cases, national forest wilderness areas abut the park boundaries, virtually prohibiting access for all but the hardiest visitors from these directions. No one made a decision to surround these parks with working forests. They were carved out of federal forest reserves, with the areas of national-park quality being designated as such. But the effect of this history has been to reduce opportunity for development immediately adjacent to the parks.

Another factor common to all three parks is their wilderness quality and the decision made to manage them as such. Mount Rainier was wild when designated a park, largely because the timber industry in the Pacific Northwest was still relatively young and had not yet reached the rugged region surrounding the mountain. The lands included in the other two parks were still wild at the relatively late dates of their establishment because of the rugged topography mentioned earlier. Timber, the principal resource of these areas, was expensive to extract, so it was left while more accessible timber was harvested. Whatever the reason, these parks were wild, and the NPS over the years chose, with considerable encouragement from the conservation community, to keep them that way. One reason winter recreation and other development were not pursued was that they would adversely affect the wilderness quality of these parks. Schemes for chairlifts, gondolas, hotels, backcountry shelter systems, and other visitor facilities have been proposed, debated, and rejected. The Washington Park Wilderness Act of 1988 was the ultimate expression of a public desire to keep the parks wild. Multitudes of tourists have visited them, but most have used the automobile to briefly touch the edges of these wild places and moved on. Those who stay for any extended period tend to be in the backcountry. Thus the pattern of visitation, linked to the decision to manage the parks for wilderness values, has not provided as much opportunity for tourism development in the surrounding country as would a park that provided other developed amenities such as hotels, lodges, and roaded development on the pattern of the Yosemite or Yellowstone model. The backcountry user neither needs nor wishes to spend money, and the auto-bound visitor is not around long enough to spend much.

One other factor may be responsible for tourism development as a potential rather than an actuality in rural regions surrounding these parks, and that is the timber culture of the region. Timber jobs have been lucrative and a set of values associated with working in the woods has provided coherence to rural communities in the timber-rich regions of the Pacific Northwest. This is perhaps most manifest on the Olympic Peninsula where, as pointed out earlier, there has been reluctance to heed the predictions, indeed the warnings, that the timber economy cannot and will not last forever and that tourism is one field of future opportunity. Unquestionably the service jobs associated with tourism do not pay as well as those that have evolved in the timber industry, and the outdoor setting and excitement of timber work would be absent. The lifestyle associated with tourism work is very different, and people have been understandably reluctant to embrace this change. It is impossible to say how much or even whether this sociocultural dimension has added to the slowness of rural communities around the parks to embrace tourism development, but it may have been a factor.

A question that is unanswerable but which brings a useful perspective to this inquiry is what might have been the rural development history of the regions around these parks had they never been designated. What might the rural development histories of these places have been, and how different would they have been from what they are? The three parks discussed contain heavily timbered areas that would have undoubtedly been logged had they not been included in national parks. Strong opposition to the designation of the Olympic and North Cascades parks was led by timber interests. Had these interests prevailed, roads would have been extended into currently wild areas and timber harvest there would have, for a time, added to the local economies. Designation of the parks reduced opportunity for timber industry growth. Perhaps, on the other hand, the growing wilderness preservation movements of the 1930s and 1960s, when the Olympic and North Cascades parks were established, would have preserved portions of the current parks as wilderness. One can speculate that in either scenario there would have been more timber harvest than has been the case with designation of the parks. In summary, the decisions made to allocate portions of the resources of Mount Rainier, the Olympic Mountains, and the North Cascades have resulted in constraint of rural development in these parts of the Pacific Northwest.

References

Aldwell, Patrick. 1986. *Economic Impacts of Mount Rainier National Park in Washington State*. Seattle: University of Washington, Cooperative Park Studies Unit, College of Forest Resources.

Allaway, Jim. 1997. *Tourism Planning and Environmental Education in the Upper Skagit River Valley*. Unpublished report to the Skagit Environmental Endowment Commission.

Byers, William B. 1970. *An Economic Impact Study of Mount Rainier and Olympic National Parks*. Seattle: University of Washington, Department of Geography.

Catton, Theodore. 1996. *Wonderland: An Administrative History of Mt. Rainier National Park.* Seattle: National Park Service, Cultural Resources Program.

Dean Runyan Associates. 1995. *Tourism Market Analysis: North Olympic Peninsula.* Portland, OR: Dean Runyan Associates.

Georgette, Susan E., and Ann H. Harvey. 1980. *Local Influence and the National Interest: Ten Years of NPS Administration in the Stehekin Valley, Washington—A Case Study.* Publication No. 4. Santa Cruz: University of California, Environmental Field Program.

Howe, Jim, Ed McMahon, and Luther Propst. 1997. *Balancing Nature and Commerce in Gateway Communities.* Washington, DC: Island Press.

Jefferson County Board of Commissioners. 1978. *Jefferson County Overall Economic Development Plan.* Olympia, WA: Department of Commerce and Economic Development.

National Park Service (NPS). 1990. *Olympic National Park: An Administrative History.* Seattle: National Park Service, Pacific Northwest Region.

———. 1987. *North Cascades Draft General Management Plan and Environmental Assessment.* Washington, DC: U.S. Department of the Interior, National Park Service.

Rogers, Everett M., and Rabel J. Burdge. 1988. *Social Change in Rural Societies.* 3rd ed. Englewood Cliffs, NJ: Prentice-Hall.

United States Congress. 100th Congress, second session, November 16, 1988. S2165: Washington Park Wilderness Act.

United States Congress. 98th Congress, first session, July 3, 1984. S837: Washington State Wilderness Act of 1984.

United States Congress. 90th Congress, second session, October 2, 1968. S1321: North Cascades Complex.

Washington Department of Commerce and Economic Development (WDCED). 1968. *Economic Regions in Washington State.* Olympia, WA: WDCED.

Washington Department of Trade and Economic Development (WDTED). 1990. *Olympic Peninsula Region Diversification Strategy.* Olympia, WA: WDTED.

Washington State Employment Security Department (WSESD). 1995. *Jefferson County Profile.* Olympia, WA: WSESD.

———. 1992. *Clallam County Profile.* Olympia, WA: WSESD.

Washington State Planning Council (WSPC). 1936. *The Proposed Mount Olympus National Park.* Olympia, WA: WSPC.

Washington State Research Council (WSRC). 1982. *The Washington State Visitor Industry, Economic Impacts, and Database Development.* Olympia, WA: WSRC.

Chapter 6

Park Planning beyond Park Boundaries: A Grand Canyon Case Study

Julie Leones and George B. Frisvold

Grand Canyon NP's unique beauty has made it a truly international attraction. The park has been designated a World Heritage Site, and two of five visitors come from other countries. It is second only to Great Smoky Mountains NP in number of annual visitors. Park visitation fluctuates from year to year affected by such factors as gasoline prices and the Asian economic crisis. Fluctuations aside, park visits have increased dramatically, from an average of 3 million people per year in the 1980s to more than 4.5 million in the 1990s. The NPS projects the average number of visitors to reach 6.8 million by 2010 (GCNP 1995).

The popularity of the park has led to growing congestion and has placed stress on its infrastructure. The average number of vehicles entering the South Rim of the park (where 90 percent of the visitation occurs) has risen from 0.76 million in the 1980s to 1.28 million in the 1990s. On summer peak visit days, 6,500 cars compete for 2,400 parking spaces (Chilson 1998). During summer, visitors often face traffic congestion, crowding at park educational exhibits, and long lines at concessions. Public funds and private incentives to supply housing and community services to park and local concession employees have been lacking (USFS 1997a, 1999g, 1999h; Chilson 1998).

In 1995, the NPS released its General Management Plan (GMP) for the park. The GMP sought solutions to congestion and infrastructure problems that reached beyond park boundaries. The plan called for construction of a mass transit staging area, park employee housing, lodging, food service, community facilities, and educational exhibits in and around the community of Tusayan— a 144-acre enclave of private land within the Kaibab National Forest, located 1 mile from the park's south entrance. The GMP also called for the elimination of most automobile traffic in the park by 2010 by expanding mass transit within the park. The NPS has subsequently decided that this will be a light rail system (GCNP 1997).

In 1997, the Kaibab National Forest released its *Draft Environmental Impact Statement for Tusayan Growth* (DEIS). The DEIS considered several development alternatives to provide lodging and other services near the park's south entrance. Most controversial has been the proposal to construct Canyon Forest Village (CFV), a gateway community to the park. Besides providing land for community services and housing for park service employees, CFV would include 1,270 lodging units and 270,000 square feet of retail space. The project is contingent on a land exchange where the CFV developer would receive U.S. Forest Service lands near Tusayan in exchange for 2,200 acres of scattered private in-holdings within the Kaibab National Forest. Construction of CFV would mean significant commercial development at the boundary of the park. Moreover, the land exchange would reconfigure the spatial pattern of public and private land ownership adjacent to the park. By doing so, it would alter the distribution of proximity rents captured by existing hotels, restaurants, and other establishments serving park tourists in Tusayan and outlying communities.

Using the debate over gateway development near Grand Canyon NP, this chapter draws policy lessons concerning park management and its relationship to surrounding communities. The NPS and U.S. Forest Service, by looking beyond park boundaries to solve visitation growth problems, were forced to confront more far-ranging economic consequences of their actions. Efforts to evaluate development alternatives were hampered by the lack of a comprehensive perspective or approach to evaluating the role of the park in the regional economy. The chapter also raises questions about the use of land exchanges as a policy tool. In particular, land exchanges place federal agencies managing public lands at the center of local development, investment, and private land-use issues beyond their administrative borders.

Regional Setting

Grand Canyon NP lies wholly within the boundaries of Coconino and Mohave Counties, Arizona, but is part of the broader Colorado Plateau region that includes Apache and Navajo Counties in Arizona; Kane, San Juan, and Washington Counties in Utah; and Clark County, Nevada (see map 6.1). The region claims Bryce NP, Canyonlands NP, and Zion NP; Lake Mead NRA and Glen Canyon NRA; and several national monuments (such as Canyon de Chelly NM, Wupatki NM, Sunset Crater Volcano NM, and Grand Staircase-Escalante NM). The Las Vegas metro area is the largest in the region, with a population of over 750,000. In this western portion of the Colorado Plateau, jurisdiction over land and natural resources is fragmented among three states, eight counties, five sovereign Indian nations, the NPS, the Bureau of Land Management, the U.S. Forest Service, and several city governments.

The primary access points to the North and South Rims of the park lie within Coconino County. Like many western, nonmetro counties, Coconino has experienced high rates of population and economic growth on a limited private land base. Only 5 percent of the land in the county is privately owned. Between 1990 and 1997, population grew 17.4 percent compared to 7.6 percent for all nonmetro counties. Employment growth has also exceeded the nonmetro county average of 1.3 percent annually. In addition, the county has high housing cost burdens. More than 25 percent of households have housing costs exceeding 30 percent of household income.

Like many southwestern counties, Coconino County has persistently high rates of unemployment and poverty, despite high economic growth rates. Unemployment rates exceed 1.5 times the U.S. average. One in four residents lives below the poverty level and the county is characterized by the U.S. Department of Agriculture as a "persistent poverty county" (one with 20 percent or more of the population in poverty in each of the census years 1960, 1970, 1980, and 1990). The high poverty and unemployment rates are attributable, to

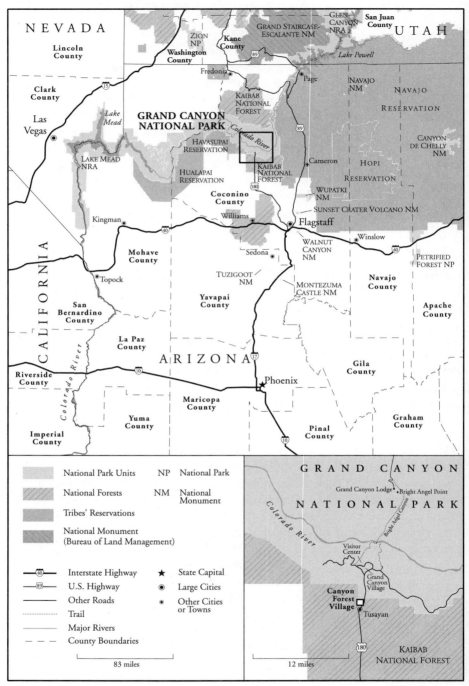

Map 6.1. Grand Canyon and the Colorado Plateau

a large extent, to the large Native American population in the county (29 percent) and the dire economic conditions on the Hualapai, Havasupai, and Navajo reservations, with poverty rates of 55 percent, 30 percent, and 49 percent, respectively (Grand Canyon Trust 1997). Native Americans account for 60 percent of the county's households in poverty, and reservation unemployment rates range from 20 to 50 percent.

Role of the Park in the Regional Economy

Grand Canyon NP may be classified as a destination park. Destination parks often provide the primary motivation for tourists to come to a region. These parks can be distinguished from others by the sheer number of visitors and by the large share of visitors from foreign countries and distant parts of the United States. Examples would include Grand Canyon NP, Yosemite NP, and Yellowstone NP. Grand Canyon also indirectly draws visitors to surrounding national parks and national monuments. Visitors often include these side-trip parks in their itineraries when en route to and from Grand Canyon. The side-trip sites enrich the travelers' experience but do not usually motivate travel to the region. Examples include Montezuma Castle NM, Walnut Canyon NM, and Tuzigoot NM.

Because of the large number of distant visitors, most spending associated with Grand Canyon NP visits occurs outside the local area. For example, visitors to Williams, who come primarily to visit the park, spent $37 million in Williams itself, but spent $159 million on airfare and $99 million on car rentals outside the area (Leones and Ralph 1997). A 1994–1995 Grand Canyon visitor survey asked where visitors stayed the night before and the night after visiting the park (USFS 1997a). According to the survey, 58 percent of the visitor nights were spent outside northern Arizona (mostly in Las Vegas or Phoenix). Lodging and other expenditures associated with overnight stays generally account for the bulk of local tourism expenditures (Leones et al. 1997).

Although Coconino County captures a small share of the total expenditures from park visitation, tourism-related services are still relatively important to the local economy. While economic accounts do not include a tourism sector per se, one can approximate the economic role of tourism by examining sectors that are heavily used by visitors. These include transportation by air, eating and drinking establishments, lodging establishments, and amusement and recreation services. These sectors account for 12 percent of total income in Coconino County, compared to 7 percent in Arizona, and 3 percent in the United States as a whole (Grand Canyon Trust 1997).

Because lodging and other services within the park itself are quite limited, several communities in Coconino County capture economic rents from proximity to the park. These communities include Tusayan, Williams, Flagstaff,

Valle, Cameron, Fredonia, and Page. In general, the relative importance of park tourism to the local economy increases with proximity to park entrances and decreases with the population size. For example, the relative importance of park tourism to Tusayan (1 mile south of the park, population less than 600) is greater than in Flagstaff (80 miles south of the park, population greater than 52,000). One indicator (albeit an imperfect one) of the importance of tourism to a locality is the ratio of hotel rooms relative to the local, permanent population. Table 6.1 shows that this ratio can be quite large in some northern Arizona communities.

Particular communities are highly dependent on park tourism. For example, input-output analysis of the impacts of tourism on Williams found that visitor expenditures in Williams alone created 1,033 jobs and $20 million in income through direct effects. Including indirect and induced effects, Williams visits contributed 1,339 jobs and $30 million in income to Coconino County (Leones and Ralph 1997). Most of the direct effects would be felt in Williams itself, a town of less than 2,700. In surveys, 82 percent of visitor parties indicated that visiting the Grand Canyon was the major reason for staying in Williams. This figure was close to 100 percent for parties with international travelers. These parties accounted for about a quarter of visitors, but spent relatively more money per day (Leones and Ralph 1997).

In Tusayan and Grand Canyon Village (located within the park itself), the local economies are based almost entirely on the park. Grand Canyon Village exists to provide housing and services to NPS and concession employees. Its population was 1,500 in the 1990 census, but rises to 2,100 with summer peak employment. Tusayan's population was 555 in 1990 and its population is estimated to double during the summer with the influx of seasonal workers (USFS 1997a).

Table 6.1. Number of Hotel Rooms in 1996 Compared to Permanent Local Populations

Location	Miles from Grand Canyon NP	Hotel/Motel Rooms	1990 Population	Rooms as a Percentage of Local Population
Grand Canyon Village	0	1,033	1,499	68.9
Tusayan	1	931	555	167.7
Valle	30	73	123	59.3
Cameron	30	493	45	9.1
Williams	60	1,350	2,532	53.3
Flagstaff	80	4,500	45,857	9.8

Source: U.S. Forest Service 1997b

Though tourism is important to certain localities, it is instructive to consider park tourism in the broader perspective of the regional economy. In Coconino County, 10 percent of the jobs are in high-skilled service sectors—health, engineering, and legal services (Grand Canyon Trust 1997). Regional amenities such as climate, environmental amenities, and educational opportunities (Northern Arizona University is located in Flagstaff) appear to be main attractions for these more highly skilled workers (Grand Canyon Trust 1997). High-skilled services account for a comparable number of jobs to tourism-related jobs. They also pay substantially more. In Coconino County, wages in hotel and lodging and retail trade are roughly half those of high-skilled service-sector jobs. From 1969 to 1994, retail trade accounted for 26 percent of job growth, but only 6 percent of labor income growth (Grand Canyon Trust 1997). So, although tourism growth appears to be contributing to job growth, these jobs are often low paying, seasonal, or both.

The relationship between park management, tourism, and the livelihoods of Native Americans in the Grand Canyon area has often been contentious. In 1882, the Havasupai people, who previously roamed over the entire South Rim area, were confined to a 518-acre reservation around Havasu Canyon and were excluded from the area that was to become Grand Canyon NP. When the park was established in 1919, the Havasupai were allotted 150,000 additional acres for grazing, although grazing permits for the most valuable traditional Havasupai grazing areas were issued to white settlers (Hough 1991).

In 1975, Congress passed the Grand Canyon National Park Enlargement Act. The Act incorporated Grand Canyon NM and Marble Canyon NM into Grand Canyon NP and returned 185,000 acres of land to the Havasupai. This included the NPS campground in Havasu Canyon. The Havasupai, who had continued to fight for expansion of their 518-acre reservation, had previously opposed park enlargement. The Act was passed over the objections of the NPS and the Sierra Club, in part because they highly prized lands in the reservation enlargement area for inclusion in the park (Sierra Club 1974; White 1994; Morehouse 1996). This land was not returned unconditionally. The Act prohibited logging and mining and required the preparation of formal land-use plans for other activities. The Act also designated 93,500 acres within the park as "Havasupai Use Lands" that could be used for grazing and other traditional activities, again subject to federal agency approval. Although the Act removed several historical sources of antagonism between the NPS and the Havasupai, continued federal oversight over land use by the Havasupai in the park and on the reservation continues to be a source of contention (Hough 1991; Morehouse 1996).

Tourism has become an important source of income for some of the Indian nations in the Grand Canyon area. About 12,000 people visit Havasu Canyon per year and the Havasupai economy depends primarily on tourist spending and federal programs (Hough 1991; USFS 1997a). The Hualapai tribe is also becoming increasingly dependent on tourism (Grand Canyon Trust 1997; USFS 1997a). The Hualapai tribe is planning the expansion of Grand Canyon West, a tourist facility that currently serves 3,000 visitors a month. Tourist development also includes plans for lodging, food service, and a craft center. In addition, the tribe operates the only American Indian–owned rafting company on the Colorado River. Park tourism presents the Indian nations with a dilemma, however. Tourist expenditures are an important source of income, yet tribal members often view the seasonal influx of tourists as intrusive (Hough 1991; White 1994).

Although tourism has grown in importance, the Indian nations capture a small percentage of northern Arizona's share of the economic rents from proximity to the park. Four factors account for this. First, reservations have limited lodging facilities, reducing the potential to capture expenditures from overnight stays. Second, attractions on reservation lands are often far less accessible to tourists than areas within the park itself. For example, Havasu Canyon is 8 miles from the road and 60 miles from the nearest town and through road (Hough 1991). Attractions often involve more "rugged" experiences that do not necessarily involve large consumer purchases. Third, the nations have no presence in Tusayan, the major node of tourist activity. More than 99 percent of the visitors to the South Rim pass through Tusayan (USFS 1997a). Finally, the remoteness of the reservations can make it more difficult for tribal members to take advantage of employment opportunities in major tourist nodes.

In sum, while park tourism is important in particular communities and sectors in Coconino County, there are also important, core areas of income and poverty linked less closely to the park. About 16 percent of jobs are in manufacturing and high-skilled service jobs not tied directly to tourism. These jobs pay substantially more than tourism-related jobs. Retiree benefits account for another 14 percent of county income (Grand Canyon Trust 1997). There is also a significant core population living in persistent poverty, many on Indian reservations. While tourism revenues do provide some earning opportunities for Native Americans, high unemployment and poverty remain significant problems.

Park Management Plan: Seeking Solutions outside Park Boundaries

The NPS initiated studies and consultations to develop a GMP for Grand Canyon NP in 1990. The GMP sought to address congestion problems, infrastructure needs, and visitor services in light of growing visitation. As noted at the outset, visitation growth has led to peak-season traffic congestion, parking problems, and congestion at concessions and interpretive exhibits (USFS 1997a,

1999e). Within the park there is hotel lodging for 1,067 people, but during the summer, demand exceeds supply at current prices. Visitors unable to find lodging within the park must then turn to Tusayan or outlying areas.

The population of Grand Canyon Village and Tusayan rises from 2,300 to 3,200 during the summer months because of seasonal employment (USFS 1997a, 1999e). Housing for NPS and concession employees is, by the NPS's own admission, often "substandard" (GCNP 1995). Some NPS employee housing includes old trailers left over from construction of Glen Canyon Dam in the 1960s. About 940 employees live in Tusayan during the peak season, with most living in employer-provided housing. A third of the housing units in Tusayan are dormitories, while 44 percent are apartments or trailers. Although land is zoned for residential development in Tusayan, landowners have an economic incentive to devote as much of the limited space as possible to tourist services.

Virtually all the local community services for Grand Canyon Village and Tusayan are located in the park itself. These include the school, medical clinic, recreation facilities, and day care facilities (USFS 1997b). The local school is currently operating at capacity and any increase in the number of students might require that they be bused to other school districts. Communities usually allocate space for such services and fund them to varying degrees through local property taxes. Tusayan landowners, however, have benefited from the fact that these services have been provided by the federal government.

To address visitor growth, the NPS faced three choices to head off future congestion problems. First, it could limit visitation to the park. The GMP considered doing this through a reservation system. Second, it could expand housing, community services, and visitor facilities within park boundaries. More construction of roads and buildings would leave a larger imprint on the land and contribute to fragmentation of habitat in sensitive areas (GCNP 1995; Grand Canyon Trust 1997). The third option, and the one ultimately chosen, was to expand development of facilities outside the park boundaries. This option would require greater coordination and consultation with outside parties and agencies, at the federal, state, and local levels.

The NPS released its GMP in 1995 proposing several significant changes. First, it called for the eventual elimination of almost all automobile traffic along the South Rim by expanding mass transit in the park and developing a staging area outside the park (GCNP 1995). The NPS has subsequently decided to construct a light rail system (GCNP 1997). Second, it would cap residential growth and community facilities in the park, proposing that these needs be met outside the park. Third, there would be only minor increases in visitor services within the park. These too would be expanded outside the park. Fourth, the GMP proposed the area north of Tusayan as the future site of gateway information and orientation centers, parking facilities, and community services. Implementing this plan would involve changing land uses on U.S. Forest Service land in the

Kaibab National Forest. The costs of implementing the GMP for the entire park were more than $300 million. The costs of constructing proposed facilities in Tusayan alone would be substantial, $20–$30 million compared to the park's annual revenues of $19.4 million (GCNP 1995; U.S. Department of the Interior and U.S. Department of Agriculture 1998).

Tusayan Land Exchange—The Proposals

Because the NPS's GMP proposed land near Tusayan in the Kaibab National Forest as the site of future gateway development, the U.S. Forest Service, not the NPS, became the lead agency in presenting and evaluating development alternatives. During this period, the Kaibab National Forest received numerous requests to use or acquire lands adjacent to Tusayan (USFS 1999d, 1999e). The U.S. Forest Service initiated work on a *Draft Environmental Impact Statement for Tusayan Growth* (DEIS) to evaluate competing proposals in a comprehensive fashion in light of the objectives set out in the NPS's GMP.

When the DEIS was released in 1997, two competing proposals emerged as the front-runners for gateway development. The first was put forward by the Grand Canyon Improvement Association (GCIA), a group of Tusayan land and business owners. The GCIA proposal (also referred to as Alternative D) would expand tourist-related services and businesses through redevelopment of Tusayan. Alternative D called for construction on 117 acres of U.S. Forest Service land, including a parking capacity of 4,500 vehicles, 710 lodging units, 220,200 square feet of retail space, and a park orientation and interpretive center. A local government entity would purchase U.S. Forest Service land for employee housing and community services. Under the Townsite Act of 1906, federal land can be purchased for public purposes (e.g., public housing, schools) but not commercial development. The U.S. Forest Service would also have to issue a Special Use Permit to allow construction of a mass transit staging area.

The second proposal was to construct CFV, a gateway community to the park. The developer proposing CFV had purchased twelve private in-holdings totaling 2,200 acres within the Kaibab National Forest and offered to trade these for U.S. Forest Service land between Tusayan and the park boundary. The U.S. Forest Service has authority to exchange land with private landowners under the General Exchange Act of 1922 and the Federal Land Policy and Management Act of 1976 (USFS 1997a, 1999f). By law, federal and private lands exchanged must be of equal market value. Further, the agency implementing the exchange must demonstrate that the exchange is "in the public interest" (USFS 1999f).

The DEIS considered two land exchange alternatives that would allow construction of CFV, representing different scales of commercial development. Alternative B called for construction on 672 acres of U.S. Forest Service land, a parking capacity of 8,000 to 10,000 vehicles, 3,650 lodging units, and 250,000 square feet of retail space. Alternative C called for construction on 380 acres of U.S. Forest Service land, a parking capacity of 6,000 to 8,000 vehicles, 2,000 lodging units, and 180,000 square feet of retail space (USFS 1997a). Under both land exchange alternatives a mass transit staging area would be constructed on acquired land. CFV would design, finance, and build a community center, library, fire station, sheriff's office, post office, and day care center. It would also donate improved land to the school district for a school site, and construct infrastructure and make sites available for primary health care and church facilities.

Both the GCIA and CFV proposals called for constructing 270 single-family units for local employees. The CFV proposal (Alternatives B and C in the DEIS) however, called for construction of 1,800 to 2,265 apartment/dormitory units, while the GCIA proposal called for 566 mobile home/apartment/dormitory units. Both proposals would institute local associations to control or subsidize rents for NPS and concession employees.

In her study of the enlargement of Grand Canyon NP in 1975, Morehouse (1996) examined how particular geographical configurations of land-use authority emerged from political and jurisdictional competition for space and resources. She argued further that "these configurations establish important preconditions for subsequent contests" (Morehouse 1996:46). The history of the consolidation of federal holdings in Kaibab National Forest did indeed establish important preconditions affecting the debate over gateway development options.

The Kaibab National Forest was originally a checkerboard of federal lands mixed with private and railroad indemnity lands (Morehouse 1996). In 1922, the U.S. Forest Service began consolidating its holdings through land exchanges, aligning its boundaries more closely with actual forested lands. Since 1922, Kaibab National Forest acquired nearly 100,000 acres of private in-holdings through exchanges (USFS 1999f). When "blocking up" federal lands in Kaibab, the area of Tusayan was left in private hands, along with twenty-one scattered holdings that were part of federal grazing allotments. Tusayan, then, became a 144-acre island of private land adjacent to the national park and to major roadways. This pattern of federal land acquisition positioned Tusayan landowners to capture economic rents from proximity to the park. Because private land adjacent to the park was limited, and because the Kaibab National Forest provided a buffer zone, proximity rents could also be captured by outlying areas such as Williams and Flagstaff. Subsequently, the CFV developer acquired the twelve inholdings closest to the park, indicating that he would develop some of these if the land exchange were not implemented (Chilson 1998; USFS 1997a). More dispersed development would involve more road building and habitat fragmentation in the national forest. The threat of more dispersed development gave the CFV developer additional leverage in bargaining with the U.S. Forest Service over terms of an exchange.

At first glance, the CFV proposals had several attractive features. First, they provided the U.S. Forest Service and NPS with more certainty about the nature of development near the park. In contrast, the GCIA proposal left many of the details of future gateway development in the hands of Tusayan landowners. More lodging could be constructed, but the type, placement, and timing remained unspecified. The GCIA proposal would form a County Improvement District that would make land acquired from the U.S. Forest Service "available to other governmental entities to build community services and facilities" (USFS 1997a:87). How school or fire districts would fund these purchases was not discussed, however. In contrast, CFV precommitted to financing and building specific community facilities up front. The land exchange would allow the U.S. Forest Service (and NPS) to negotiate with one developer beforehand about a wide range of issues and have more of a direct say in the structure of the gateway development. Second, a land exchange would also have certain budgetary and administrative advantages. Through a land exchange, the U.S. Forest Service can secure construction of certain facilities as part of the terms of the exchange rather than requiring congressional appropriations. So, construction that might be incurred by the federal government can be implemented "off budget" through administrative (rather than legislative) measures. Finally, through an exchange, the U.S. Forest Service could acquire the twelve closest in-holdings to the park, precluding future development and establishing contiguous federal authority of a much broader area south of the park.

Tusayan Growth—The Controversy

Despite certain advantages, the CFV proposals proved highly controversial. There were three main areas of controversy: (a) the sheer size of the proposed development so close to the park, (b) impacts on groundwater resources, and (c) impacts on existing tourism-based establishments in Tusayan and outlying communities.

The largest development proposal (Alternative B) would quadruple the private land area adjacent to the park and triple the number of lodging units in Tusayan. These features, combined with the large area of retail space, drew fire from a number of sources questioning the appropriateness of scale of the project (Hoffman 1998; *Tucson Citizen* 1998; Palmeri 1997; No on Canyon Forest Coalition 1997; Chilson 1998). These included American Indian tribes, officials in outlying communities, Tusayan landowners, and environmental groups.

The two CFV proposals would require 140–147 million gallons of water a day, and consequently additional well construction and groundwater use. Groundwater would come from the Redwall-Muav Aquifer, which lies 2,500 feet below the surface. Discharges from the aquifer feed Havasu Springs on the Havasupai reservation and Blue Springs on the Navajo reservation. Smaller discharges occur within the park at Indian Garden Springs and Hermit Springs and throughout the South Rim area in smaller seeps and springs (USFS 1999i). Although seeps and springs account for a small share of the water and land resources, they support a disproportionately high share of its biodiversity. Springs support 610 species per square km compared to 220 species/km^2 for riparian areas and 15 species/km^2 for uplands (Grand Canyon Trust 1997). The seeps and springs around the canyon are also considered sacred by many of the local Indian tribes, who have formally expressed concern over the potential impact of development (USFS 1999i).

The most persistent and vocal opponents of CFV have been local government officials and hospitality industry businesses in Tusayan and outlying northern Arizona communities. Opponents formed the No on Canyon Forest Village Coalition. The coalition includes a Flagstaff city councilman as its chair and a committee that includes the mayors of Kingman, Williams, Winslow, Fredonia, Sedona, and Page as well as members of local chambers of commerce. A major concern of CFV opponents is the amount of hotel, restaurant, and other business, the number of jobs, and the volume of sales taxes CFV will displace from their own businesses and communities.

CFV opponents criticized the analysis of these displacement impacts presented in the DEIS on several grounds (BBC Research and Consulting 1997; Chilson 1998; Foster and Eastwood 1997; Hoffman 1998; No on Canyon Forest Village Coalition 1997). First, they argued that the DEIS overstated future visitation growth and thus the growth in northern Arizona lodging demand and the ability of the market to support CFV and existing establishments. Second, by doing so, the DEIS understated the negative impact of CFV operation on existing tourism-related establishments in Tusayan and outlying communities. Third, the DEIS failed to include multiplier effects from the displacement of tourist-related business in northern Arizona. Fourth, opponents of CFV argued that the lands to be exchanged between the CFV developer and the U.S. Forest Service were not of equal value. Fifth, the DEIS relied on analysis of the economic impacts of CFV from the same consultants employed by CFV. Sixth, the DEIS did not adequately address potential impacts on groundwater resources. In all, the U.S. Forest Service received more than 900 comments on the DEIS, many of which were critical of the hydrological and socioeconomic analysis (USFS 1998).

Forest Service Considers New Alternatives

After the close of the comment period for the DEIS, three environmental groups—the Grand Canyon Trust, the Environmental Defense Fund, and the Natural Resources Defense Council—approached the CFV developer to work on a revised land exchange proposal (De Paolo 1998; NRDC 1998). The new proposal that emerged from these negotiations differed in several important respects from the earlier land exchange proposals. First, the scale of development was greatly reduced. Development would occur on 272 acres instead of 380–672 acres. The number of lodging units was also scaled back from 2,000–3,650 units to 1,220 units. Second, rather than relying on pumping groundwater, the project would rely on purchased surface water from the Colorado River. Water would be shipped by rail from Topock, Arizona (near Lake Mead), to Williams and piped to CFV. Third, a 1 percent charge would be placed on gross sales and applied to an environmental trust fund. The charge is estimated to raise $1.2 million per year and be devoted to purchase of environmentally sensitive lands, habitat restoration, groundwater monitoring, environmental education, and other conservation activities (NRDC 1998; USFS 1998). Fourth, 20,000 square feet of retail space would be devoted to a Native American Marketplace to sell traditional arts and crafts. CFV would build and donate the space to a Native American business organization that would run the facility. Fifth, the buildings would include several "sustainable design" features, emphasizing water and energy conservation, and recycling.

This new proposal has been dubbed the "environmental proposal" by environmental group supporters, which now include the Grand Canyon Trust, Environmental Defense Fund, Natural Resources Defense Council, National Parks and Conservation Association, The Wilderness Society, American Rivers, Global Environmental Options, Scenic America, and The National Trust for Historic Preservation. It has also received support from former Interior Secretary Stewart Udall of Arizona (Udall 1997) and Paul Babbitt, chairman of the Coconino Board of Supervisors and brother of Interior Secretary Bruce Babbitt (Chilson 1998). This new proposal actually calls for more retail space than earlier CFV proposals. The CFV developer claims that the larger retail space is needed to defray the added costs of environmental mitigation features. For example, the estimated cost of surface water is 23 cents per gallon, compared to a 3-cent-per-gallon cost of well water (NRDC 1998).

In July 1998, the U.S. Forest Service released a supplement to the DEIS that attempted to address some of the earlier criticisms of the DEIS (USFS 1998). It revised its visitation and lodging demand projects downward and provided more discussion of the development potential of the 2,200 acres of in-holdings owned by the CFV developer to be offered in the exchange. CFV opponents had argued that these in-holdings were grazing lands with no development potential. The supplement pointed out that although development potential on the tracks was uneven, it was high on some tracks. In particular, one 160-acre parcel is one-eighth of a mile from the private property boundary of Tusayan. Another 320-acre parcel fronts Highway 64, one of the main arteries into the park.

The supplement also included three new gateway development alternatives.

Alternative F, combining elements of earlier proposals, was a revised plan to meet park objectives through Tusayan redevelopment. Alternative H was the new land exchange proposal negotiated between CFV and environmental groups. The U.S. Forest Service's preferred Alternative G called for an even smaller version of CFV (900 lodging units) that relied on groundwater and excluded most of the other environmental mitigation features included in Alternative H. The U.S. Forest Service's apparent attempt at a compromise between a larger CFV and no CFV pleased no one, however (Yozwiak 1998). Alternative G still allowed construction of CFV, which was opposed by interests in outlying cities. Even though it called for less development than Alternative H, it also took away many of the key elements that environmental groups had helped to craft in Alternative H. The environmental groups cited above are arguing for the larger level of development implied by Alternative H. By spring 1999, the U.S. Forest Service had eliminated Alternative G from consideration "because it received little public support" (USFS 1999e:2). Although the U.S. Forest Service has narrowed its choices down to Alternatives F and H, it missed its June 1999 deadline for release of the final EIS and its final decision.

Policy Lessons

This case study illustrates some of the dilemmas that federal agencies face when park management involves changing land uses beyond park boundaries and raises questions about land exchanges as a policy tool. The land exchange options allowed for more direct influence by the U.S. Forest Service and the NPS over the design of gateway development at the Grand Canyon. Many of the details could be negotiated in advance with a single developer. However, as solutions to immediate park management problems move beyond park boundaries, the socioeconomic impacts of park management take on broader regional implications. By changing the configuration of public and private land ownership, land exchanges place the NPS, U.S. Forest Service, Bureau of Land Management, and other federal land management agencies at the center of local land-use planning, growth, and development issues. Land exchanges imply that federal agencies accustomed to managing uses of public lands will get drawn increasingly into county-level development and investment issues on private lands.

Some of the controversy over development options might have been averted if more attention were paid to developing generally agreed-upon baseline assumptions and projections. Future visitation demand, and its linkage to demand for particular lodging sites, was the major source of debate (USFS 1999j). Yet no independent econometric study of the supply and demand for lodging in northern Arizona was conducted to inform this debate. In draft EISs for federal land exchanges, it is common for federal agencies to rely on economic analyses conducted by or for private exchange proponents. This can lead to questions about the objectivity of such analyses, as it did in the Tusayan Growth DEIS. For the most part, analyses of development options were commissioned either by opponents or proponents of the exchange. As a result, these analyses were incomplete and difficult to compare. One problem was the wide discrepancy in baseline economic assumptions between studies. In particular, studies differed widely in their assumptions about what would happen if CFV were *not* built (BBC Research and Consulting 1997; Foster and Eastwood 1997; Pollack and Company 1998; USFS 1997a, 1997b, 1998). Another problem was the failure to maintain internal consistency of assumptions, even within studies.

Efforts to evaluate development alternatives have also been hampered by the lack of a comprehensive perspective or approach to evaluating the role of the park in the regional economy. Before the CFV controversy, the supply of new lodging units had been increasing rapidly in northern Arizona (USFS 1997a). CFV brought issues of intercity competition for limited visitors out into the open sooner than might otherwise have been the case. Yet a broader consideration of how many tourism-related establishments northern Arizona can support is still missing. Nor has an internally consistent and comprehensive answer to the question of how alternative gateway development options will affect the employment and income distribution throughout Coconino County been attempted. Rather, the debate has centered on narrow rent seeking by individual communities.

The jury is still out about whether CFV will be a model for future gateway development. Yet the evolution of proposals for CFV has explicitly raised the issue of public capture of proximity rents from gateway development. For the opportunity to capture these proximity rents, the CFV developer has had to make up-front commitments concerning provision of community services, mitigation of environmental impacts, and sharing of proximity rents with Native Americans. It remains to be seen, however, if such precommitments ultimately satisfy local interest groups.

The EIS process also dramatically reduced the scale of initial development proposals. Although this downsizing will mitigate some of the negative impacts on outlying business and communities relying on Grand Canyon tourism, certain tourist-dependent communities will still be affected. A lesson here is that the configuration of public and private land ownership in the West is dynamic. This is made more so by the federal government's increased use of land exchanges. Gateway communities to national parks currently capturing proximity rents cannot take these rents for granted. One potential lesson from CFV for current gateway communities is the importance of forming alliances and opening dialogue with the Native Americans and environmental groups in planning long-run sharing of proximity rents.

Post Script

On August 6, 1999, Eleanor Towns, regional forester, U.S. Forest Service, Southwestern Region, announced the selection of Alternative H, Canyon Forest Village (USFS 1999b) along with the release of the *Record of Decision, Final Environmental Impact Statement for Tusayan Growth* (USFS 1999c). The decision was appealed by the cities of Williams and Flagstaff, the Northern Arizona Council of Governments, and the Grand Canyon chapter of the Sierra Club, among others (USFS 1999a). On November 10, 1999, Chief of the Forest Service Mike Dombeck upheld the selection of Alternative H (USFS 1999a). CFV development will be regulated through the county zoning and through two covenants offered by CFV governing water use and sustainable development (USFS 1999k). The goal of the covenants is to make the commitments in the EIS binding conditions and to provide for external oversight of CFV development (USFS 1999k). In March 1999, Julie Leones died after a long and brave battle with breast cancer. Any errors or omissions in this final text are my responsibility————GF.

References

BBC Research and Consulting. 1997. *Review of Tusayan Growth Draft EIS Economic Analysis.* Denver: BBC Research and Consulting.

Chilson, P. 1998. The Grand Canyon struggles with reality. *High Country News* 30: 1–4.

De Paolo, T. 1998. "Forest Village Meets Everyone's Needs." *Tucson Citizen,* June 22, 1998, p. 7A.

Foster, D., and J. Eastwood. 1997. *A Comment on the Draft Environmental Impact Statement for Tusayan Growth.* Bureau of Business and Economic Research, College of Business Administration. Flagstaff: Northern Arizona University.

Grand Canyon National Park (GCNP). 1995. *Final General Management Plan and Environmental Impact Statement.* Grand Canyon National Park, AZ: National Park Service.

————. 1997. *Final Environmental Assessment, Mather Point Orientation/Transit Center and Transit System.* Grand Canyon National Park, AZ: National Park Service.

Grand Canyon Trust. 1997. *Beyond the Boundaries: The Human and Natural Communities of the Greater Grand Canyon.* Flagstaff, AZ: Grand Canyon Trust.

Hoffman, J. 1998. "Federal Report Backing Project Lacks Facts." *Tucson Citizen,* June 22, 1998, p. 7A.

Hough, J. 1991. The Grand Canyon National Park and the Havasupai People: Cooperation and Conflict. In *Resident Peoples and National Parks: Social Dilemmas and Strategies in International Conservation,* ed. P. C. West and S. R. Brechin, 215–30. Tucson: University of Arizona Press.

Leones, J., D. Dunn, and V. Ralph. 1997. *Travel and Tourism in the Globe-Miami Region 1995–1996.* Tucson: University of Arizona Cooperative Extension.

Leones, J., and V. Ralph. 1997. *The Williams 1995–96 Visitor Study.* Department of Agricultural and Resource Economics. Tucson: University of Arizona Cooperative Extension.

Morehouse, B. J. 1996. Conflict, space, and resource management at Grand Canyon. *Professional Geographer* 48: 46–57.

Natural Resources Defense Council (NRDC). 1998. *Canyon Forest Village "Alternative H": Creating a Sustainable Future for the Grand Canyon.* Washington, DC: Natural Resources Defense Council.

No on Canyon Forest Village Coalition. 1997. *A Summary of the No CFV Situation: "Environmental Disneyland."* Grand Canyon, AZ: No on Canyon Forest Village Coalition.

Palmeri, C. 1997. "Shopping, Anyone?" *Forbes,* July 7, 1997, http://www.forbes.com/forbes/97/0707/6001045a.htm

Pollack, E. D., and Company. 1998. *The Economic and Fiscal Impact of Alternative H of Canyon Forest Village.* Scottsdale, AZ: E.D. Pollack.

Sierra Club. 1974. Statement of Position of the National Native American Issues Committee—Havasupai and the Grand Canyon National Park Bill (§1296, H.R. 5900), March 30, 1974. Legislative Assistant Files, Box 25, 93rd Congress, Morris Udall Archives, University of Arizona Library, Special Collections, Tucson, AZ.

Tucson Citizen. 1998. "Grand Canyon: New Plans Kept Under Wraps." *Tucson Citizen,* June 22, 1988, p. 6A.

Udall, S. 1997. "Canyon Forest Village Best Hope for Grand Canyon's Future." *Arizona Republic,* October 21, 1997, p. B6.

U.S. Department of the Interior and U.S. Department of Agriculture. 1998. *Recreation Fee Demonstration Program: Progress Report to Congress.*

U.S. Forest Service (USFS). 1997a. *Draft Environmental Impact Statement for Tusayan Growth.* Williams, AZ: Kaibab National Forest.

———. 1997b. *Executive Summary of the Draft Environmental Impact Statement for Tusayan Growth.* Williams, AZ: Kaibab National Forest.

———. 1998. *Supplement to the Draft Environmental Impact Statement for Tusayan Growth.* Williams, AZ: Kaibab National Forest.

———. 1999a. *And the Decision Is?* Williams, AZ: Kaibab National Forest.

———. 1999b. *Rationale for the Decision on the Tusayan Growth Environmental Impact Statement.* Williams, AZ: Kaibab National Forest.

———. 1999c. *Record of Decision, Final Environmental Impact Statement for Tusayan Growth.* Williams, AZ: Kaibab National Forest.

———. 1999d. *Tusayan Growth Environmental Impact Statement Briefing Paper.* Williams, AZ: Kaibab National Forest.

———. 1999e. *Tusayan Growth Environmental Impact Statement: Bulletin Number 11.* Williams, AZ: Kaibab National Forest.

———. 1999f. *Tusayan Growth Environmental Impact Statement: Bulletin Number 12.* Williams, AZ: Kaibab National Forest.

———. 1999g. *Tusayan Growth Environmental Impact Statement: Bulletin Number 13.* Williams, AZ: Kaibab National Forest.

———. 1999h. *Tusayan Growth Environmental Impact Statement: Bulletin Number 14.* Williams, AZ: Kaibab National Forest.

———. 1999i. *Tusayan Growth Environmental Impact Statement: Bulletin Number 15.* Williams, AZ: Kaibab National Forest.

———. 1999j. *Tusayan Growth Environmental Impact Statement: Bulletin Number 16.* Williams, AZ: Kaibab National Forest.

————. 1999k. *Tusayan Growth Environmental Impact Statement: Bulletin Number 19.* Williams, AZ: Kaibab National Forest.

White, D. 1994. Tourism as economic development for Native people living in the shadow of a protected area: A North American case study. *Society and Natural Resources* 6: 339–45.

Yozwiak, S. 1998. "Canyon Village Plan Is Chosen: No One Pleased." *Arizona Republic,* July 3, 1998, p. A22.

Chapter 7

National Parks and Rural Development in Alaska

Darryll R. Johnson

Managers of Alaska national parks created by the Alaska National Interest Lands Conservation Act (ANILCA: Public Law 96–487) face several different issues than their counterparts in the rest of the United States. In the lower forty-eight states, issues associated with gateway communities, tourism, and the social and economic impacts of parks from large numbers of recreational visits are dominant aspects of rural development and national park discussions. In Alaska national park units established by ANILCA, visitation is sparse, and in a few cases is almost nonexistent. With few exceptions, consequences to rural development from recreational visits, although present, have been and continue to be limited. Subjects such as integration of humans as natural predators in models of national park wilderness management, and the impact of park management policy on the continuation of customary and traditional Alaska rural lifeways, are often as important locally as discussions pertaining to the role of conventional tourism in rural economic development.

My goals in this writing are first to explain the unique ecological, cultural, economic, and legal circumstances surrounding Alaska's national parks and rural communities, and second, to discuss the distinct challenges and opportunities these conditions bring to their mutual evolving relationships. My focus is entirely on the approximate 45 million acres of land added to the National Park System by ANILCA in 1980 that, in terms of acreage, constitute more than half of the total acreage managed by the NPS in the United States (see map 7.1). Throughout this discussion my conceptualization of "rural development" includes, and indeed emphasizes, the impact of national parks on evolving rural culture, social structure, and human resources, as opposed to a more narrow orientation directed exclusively toward economic development and enhanced personal income.

Alaska's Geography and Population

Alaskan ecological conditions range from the dry arctic tundra of the North Slope to the heavily timbered rain forests of the southeast (Cornwall 1982). Although largest in area,[1] it is the second least populated (607,800) of the states after Wyoming. About 30 percent of Alaskans lived in communities of 2,500 or fewer or in dispersed dwellings in 1997.[2] Alaska rural communities, to varying degrees, are isolated and many lack services taken for granted in urban areas of Alaska and throughout the lower forty-eight states (e.g., running water, year-long road access, a wide selection of retail outlets). This is especially true of communities near units of the National Park System, many of which are inaccessible by road. For example, one of Alaska's most isolated traditional Native American villages, Lime Village near Lake Clark NP and Pres, first began to provide electricity to residences in 1998. Its first school was built in 1974.

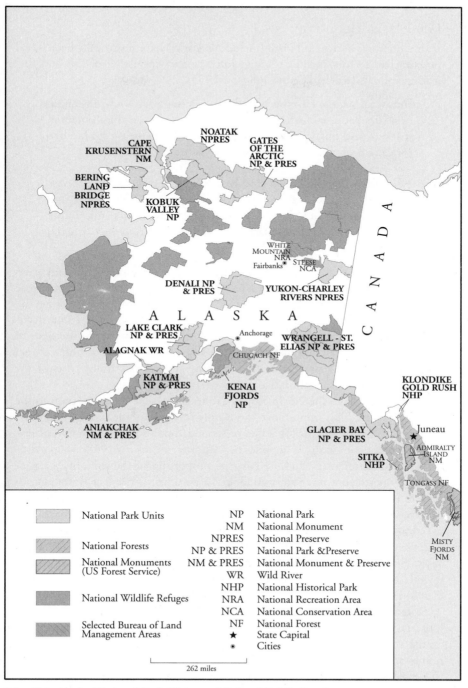

NOATAK
NPRES

CAPE
KRUSENSTERN
NM

GATES
OF THE
ARCTIC
NP & PRES

BERING
LAND
BRIDGE
NPRES

KOBUK
VALLEY
NP

WHITE
MOUNTAIN
NRA
Fairbanks

STEESE
NCA

C A N A D A

DENALI NP
& PRES

YUKON-CHARLEY
RIVERS NPRES

A L A S K A

LAKE CLARK
NP & PRES

Anchorage

WRANGELL - ST.
ELIAS NP & PRES

ALAGNAK WR

CHUGACH NF

KLONDIKE
GOLD RUSH
NHP

KATMAI
NP & PRES

KENAI
FJORDS
NP

ANIAKCHAK
NM & PRES

GLACIER BAY
NP & PRES

Juneau

ADMIRALTY
ISLAND
NM

SITKA
NHP

TONGASS NF

MISTY
FJORDS
NM

National Park Units	NP	National Park
	NM	National Monument
	NPRES	National Preserve
National Forests	NP & PRES	National Park &Preserve
	NM & PRES	National Monument & Preserve
National Monuments (US Forest Service)	WR	Wild River
	NHP	National Historical Park
National Wildlife Refuges	NRA	National Recreation Area
	NCA	National Conservation Area
Selected Bureau of Land Management Areas	NF	National Forest
	★	State Capital
	⊙	Cities

262 miles

Map 7.1. Alaska National Park Units and Related Public Lands

The Alaska Economy

Cash economies in the Far North (including Alaska) have historically been based on extractive sectors such as mining, forestry, and harvesting of fish and fur-bearing animals (Kochemer and Johnson 1995).

> Industrial sectors have been difficult to sustain without substantial subsidies because of small population, long distances from potential markets, and unfavorable climate. Consequently, the North has historically been a net importer of manufactured goods. . . .
>
> Northern economies have repeated "booms and busts" in response to cycles of resource discovery and depletion and supply and demand in world markets. This has occurred with furs and mining and will probably take place with petro-chemicals and fisheries (Kochemer and Johnson 1995:46–47).

Cornwall (1982) stated that although rich in natural resources, in many ways Alaska was still a developing region. This is still true. The Alaska economic base is largely a combination of fish harvesting and processing; timber harvesting; oil, gas, and hard mineral extraction; government services; and tourism. Its harsh climate and isolation add considerably to costs of production and to the costs of imported goods, especially in remote rural areas. Subsistence hunting, fishing, gathering, and to a lesser extent, fur trapping remain important parts of the economy in much of rural Alaska.

Oil revenues from the North Slope have recently been very important to the Alaska economy. This importance is not only reflected in the money that flows directly to Alaska residents for wages or services, but also in the amount of revenue the petroleum industry supplies to state government. In 1968, when petroleum was discovered in Prudhoe Bay, the proportion of the state budget supported by petroleum revenues was about 12 percent; in 1984, it was about 90 percent (Chance and Andrews 1995). In response to a decline in oil revenue, it has declined at present to about 70 percent with the decrease being covered by withdrawals from cash reserves (Goldschmit pers. comm., 2000). Alaska residents pay no personal state income or sales taxes; rather, they receive annual per capita dividends (children included) from the Alaska Permanent Fund (created by oil royalties). These have ranged from $827 to $1,541 in recent years (1988–1998).

State spending is large and in the mid-1990s accounted for 33 percent of the jobs and $3 of every $10 of Alaska personal income (Jackstadt and Lee 1995). In the rural interior, we can intelligently speculate that somewhat more economic activity emanates from state spending, perhaps as much as 40 percent.[3] Oil royalties also flow directly into some borough governments such as the North Slope Borough, which is largely populated by Inupiat Eskimo. This borough taxes oil revenues from Prudhoe Bay, from which it has realized millions of dollars to build a modern infrastructure and a set of services that are very unusual in the Far North.

Alaska's Rural Mixed Subsistence-Market Economies[4]

Many, if not most, Alaska rural communities can be characterized as having "mixed subsistence-market economies." This concept recognizes:

> . . . that there exists a "subsistence sector" to the community's econ-
> omy and social life, and a "market sector," and that the socioeco-
> nomic system [as a whole] is viable because the sectors are comple-
> mentary and mutually supportive (Wolfe 1983:252–53).

Even households that harvest wildlife and other natural resources in quantity for subsistence purposes use modern equipment such as snow machines, boats, traps, motors, and firearms. Equipment requires maintenance, motorized vehicles use fuel and oil, and firearms use ammunition, all of which are purchased. Accordingly, households that harvest substantial amounts of local foods must also generate cash to purchase necessary equipment and supplies. This mix of cash income and locally harvested resources combines to form the economy of most of rural Alaska. An estimated 43.7 million pounds of wild foods are harvested and consumed annually in rural areas, or about a pound a day per person. Harvests of wild foods contain 242 percent of the minimal protein requirements of the rural population and 35 percent of the caloric requirements (Bosworth 1995). Valuing this harvest of local food at $3–$5 per pound results in an estimated replacement value between $131.1 and $218.6 million annually.

In isolated communities, locally harvested food may be more reliable than wage employment. Thus, local food is a safety net that many families, even those that typically import foods, depend on during economic downturns (Sumida and Anderson 1990). Shared subsistence harvests are also a form of security for those who are unable to fish or hunt such as older people or single mothers with small children—especially in Native American communities.

Finally, we note that food is not the only subsistence use of wild resources. Other primary uses of subsistence products include:

Fuel: Wood is a major source of fuel in rural homes for heat and for some cooking. Wood is also used extensively for smoking and preserving fish and meat. In some areas, wood is used extensively to fuel steam baths.[5]

Construction: Spruce, birch, hemlock, willow, and cottonwood are used to build such things as houses, shelters, sleds, and fish racks.

Ceremony: Traditional products are used in funerals, potlatches, marriages, and community gatherings.

Cash sale: Furs are sold for cash to obtain equipment and to otherwise supplement subsistence lifeways. Grass, wood, bark, and skins are also crafted into items for sale and for personal use.

Overall rural Alaskans are more directly dependent on wildlife and other natural resources for food, fuel, and in some instances, construction materials than are rural residents of any other state.

Cultural Importance of Subsistence Activities

Harvesting, sharing, preparation, and consumption of wild resources are also a distinctive part of rural Alaska culture and important in maintaining viable social structures, especially for Native Americans. An Alaska Department of Fish and Game (1992) report validates the cultural as well as economic importance of subsistence:

> Without subsistence, many rural Alaska communities might become wholly dependent upon transfer payments from the government. Such increased dependencies probably would be associated with increased rates of social pathologies such as chronic substance abuse, domestic violence, suicides, homicides, accidents, and destructive anomie.[6]

Rural communities may attempt to diminish these impacts by continuing traditional ways of living, which include subsistence fishing, hunting, trapping, and gathering (Wolfe and Bosworth 1990). Alaskan Native Americans frequently argue that without traditional subsistence activities, they would cease to exist as culturally distinct peoples (Berger 1985). Harvesting preparation, processing, and sharing of traditional local foods define many social roles in native social structure and consequently may be intimately related to personal identity and self-esteem. Many non–Native American rural households also pursue, by choice, a vanishing Euro-American way of life characterized by substantial harvests of wild resources, accompanied by individual values espousing rugged individualism and self-reliance.

In summary, access to natural resources for subsistence purposes is crucial to Alaska rural communities for both economic and cultural reasons. Discussions of rural development and Alaska national parks established by ANILCA implicitly involve consideration of the impacts of NPS policies on the access that local people have to natural resources for personal consumption because this access may have profound consequences for the evolution of rural culture and social structure as well as the viability of local mixed subsistence-cash economies. This is not to say that a conventional perspective toward national parks and rural development emphasizing opportunities for local people to realize income from tourism is not relevant in Alaska rural areas. It is to say that such a perspective is insufficient to describe the full social and economic impact of the establishment of national parks on the evolution of Alaska's rural communities.

Alaska National Park System Units

Of the total acreage of the National Park System (80.6 million acres), about 55 million acres are in Alaska (see table 7.1). Ten National Park System units and most of this acreage were added to the National Park System on December 1, 1978, by proclamation by President Jimmy Carter. Carter's proclamation was

Table 7.1. Listing and Description of Alaska National Park System Units

Alagnak Wild River	The Alagnak River flows from Kukaklek Lake in Katmai NP & Pres. It is noted for outstanding white-water rafting and abundant species of salmon. 69 miles. Acreage: 24,038. *Recreational visits in 1998: not reported.*
Aniakchak NM and Pres	The Aniakchak Caldera (30 square miles) is one of the world's great calderas. Acreage: NM 137,176; NPres 400,257. *Resident-zone communities: Chignik, Chignik Lagoon, Chignik Lake, Meshik, and Port Heiden. Recreational visits in 1998: 209.* Established by ANILCA.
Bering Land Bridge NPRES	The preserve is a remnant of the land bridge that once connected Asia with North America. Noted for paleontological and archaeological resources; large populations of nesting migratory birds. Acreage: 2,784,960. *Recreational visits in 1998: 3,740.* Established by ANILCA.
Cape Krusenstern NM	Noted for archaeological sites illustrating Eskimo communities of every known cultural period in Alaska and dating back 4,000 years. Older sites also present. Acreage: 659,807. *Resident-zone communities: Kivalina, Kotzebue, and Noatak. Recreational visits in 1998: 2,960.* Established by ANILCA.
Denali NP and Pres	The park contains Mt. McKinley—the highest mountain in North America. Also noted for populations of caribou, Dall sheep, moose, grizzly bears, and wolves. Acreage: NP 5,000,000; NPres 1,500,000. *Resident-zone communities for Denali NP: Canwell, Minchumina, Nikolai, and Telida. Recreational visits in 1998: 372,519.* ANILCA added lands to the park and created the preserve.
Gates of the Arctic NP and Pres	Often referred to as the greatest remaining wilderness in North America. Contains portion of the Central Brooks range and the northernmost Rocky Mountains. With adjoining Kobuk Valley NP and Noatak NPres it is one of the world's largest park areas. Acreage: NP 7,523,888; NPres 948,629. *Resident-zone communities for Gates of the Arctic NP: Alatna, Allakaket, Ambler, Anaktuvuk Pass, Bettles/Evansville, Hughes, Kobuk, Nuiqsut, Shungnak, and Wiseman. Recreational visits in 1998: 8,266.* Established by ANILCA.

continues

Table 7.1. *Continued*

Glacier Bay NP and Pres	Noted for tidewater glaciers and a striking range of plant communities from barren terrain recently uncovered by ice to climax rain forests. A large variety of wildlife is found in the park including mountain goats, brown bears, and whales. Acreage: NP 3,225,284; NPres 57,884. *Recreational visits in 1998: 403,912.* ANILCA added lands to the park and created the preserve.
Katmai NP and Pres	Noted for the Valley of Ten Thousand Smokes, created after the eruption of the Nuarupta Volcano in 1912. Containing a varied landscape of lakes, forests, mountains, and marshlands, the park provides excellent habitat for brown bear. Katmai has renowned sportfishing opportunities. Acreage: NP 3,716,000; NPres 374,000. *Recreational visits in 1998: 45,470.* ANILCA added lands to the park and created the preserve.
Kenai Fjords NP	Contains the 300-square-mile Harding Icefield and coastal fjords, one of the four major ice caps in the United States. Noted for breeding birds and marine wildlife such as sea lions, sea otters, and seals. Acreage: 669,591. Subsistence uses are prohibited in Kenai Fjords NP. *Recreational visits in 1998: 263,948.* Established by ANILCA.
Klondike Gold Rush NHP	The park preserves historic buildings in Skagway and remnants of the Chilkoot and White Pass Trails, all associated with the 1898 gold rush. Acreage: 13,195. *Recreational visits in 1998: 679,980.*
Kobuk Valley NP	The Great Kobuk Sand Dunes are within this area. The park exhibits the northernmost extent of the boreal forest and abundant arctic wildlife. Rich archaeological sites indicating more than 12,500 years of human occupation are reputed to be some of the most significant in the Arctic. Acreage: 1,750,421. ***Resident-zone communities: Ambler, Kiana, Kobuk, Kotzebue, Noorvik, Selawik, Shungnak.*** *Recreational visits in 1998: 5,550.* Established by ANILCA.
Lake Clark NP and Pres	Lake Clark, some 40 miles long, is headwaters for red salmon spawning. The park contains jagged peaks, granite spires, and two active volcanoes and contains the Chilikadrotna, Mulchatna, and Tlikakila Wild Rivers. Acreage: NP 2,636,839; NPres 1,407,293. ***Resident-zone communities for Lake Clark NP: Iliamna, Lime Village, Newhalen, Nondalton, Pedro Bay, and Port Alsworth.*** *Recreational visits in 1998: 11,335.* Established by ANILCA.

Noatak NPres	Contains the Noatak River Basin, the largest virtually unaffected mountain-ringed river basin in the United States. The 65-mile Grand Canyon of the Noatak is a transition zone and migration route for plants and animals between the arctic and subarctic environments. *Recreational visits in 1998: 2,100.* Established by ANILCA.
Sitka NHP	Preserves the site of an 1804 fort and battle that marked the last major Tlingit resistance to Russian colonization. The primary tourist attraction is the best collection of totems in the NP System and the Russian Bishop's House. Acreage: 106 acres, of which 57 are on land. *Recreational visits 1998: 159,965.*
Wrangell-St. Elias NP and Pres	This is the largest unit of the National Park System and with adjacent protected areas in Canada is the largest protected area in the world. Contains the continent's largest assemblage of glaciers and greatest collection of peaks above 16,000 feet. Mt. St. Elias is the second-highest peak in the United States. Acreage: NP 8,331,604; NPres 4,856,721. ***Resident-zone communities: Chisana, Chistochina, Chitina, Copper Center, Gakona, Gakona Junction, Glennallen, Gulkana, Kenny Lake, Lower Tonsina, McCarthy, Mentasta Lake, Nabesna, Slana, Tazlina, Tok, Tonsina, and Yakutat.*** *Recreational visits in 1998: 25,859.* Established by ANILCA.
Yukon-Charley Rivers NPres	The preserve protects 115 miles of the 1,800-mile Yukon River and the entire Charley River Basin. The preserve also contains historical sites associated with the gold rush, important archaeological sites, and nesting sites for peregrine falcons. *Recreational visits in 1998: 4,451.* Established by ANILCA.

superseded by the Alaska National Interest Lands Conservation Act (ANILCA: Public Law 96–487), which was signed into law on December 2, 1980.

ANILCA designated about 38.8 million acres to the ten new National Park System units and renamed most as either national parks or preserves. About 5.9 million acres were also added to three existing NPS units (Glacier Bay NM, Katmai NM, and Mt. McKinley NP). ANILCA designated 32.4 million acres of NPS-managed land in Alaska as wilderness. Substantial acreage was also added to the National Wildlife Refuge System. The act also created Steese National Conservation Area and White Mountain NRA managed by the Bureau of Land Management, created Misty Fjords NM and Admiralty Island NM managed by the U.S. Forest Service, and added lands to the Chugach and Tongass National Forests.

With the exception of Kenai National Fjords and land added to Katmai NP, the National Park System units established by ANILCA are fundamentally different from units established in almost all national parks in the lower forty-eight states. In 1980, the ideal goal of national park natural resource management in the lower forty-eight states was often simplistically stated as restoring national parks as vignettes of primitive (i.e., pre-Columbian) America. Realistically, this goal meant vignettes of primitive America that included whatever impacts occurred from "nonconsumptive" public enjoyment and excluded continuation of impacts resultant from perhaps thousands of years of use by Native Americans. Known as the Yellowstone model of park management, this perspective is oriented toward nature protection and "nonconsumptive" recreation as primary goals of national park management.

Wilderness areas are defined as inherently uninhabited in the Yellowstone model—being places that are ideally imagined to evolve apart from human history (Stevens 1997). Outside designated wilderness in adjacent frontcountry areas, tourism and its associated development (e.g., paved roads in limited-access corridors, lodges, restaurants, large visitor centers, parking lots, and trinket shops) are acceptable. Except for in-holdings (typically viewed as temporary aberrations to be eventually acquired by the federal government), permanent human settlement is prohibited. Maintenance of historical structures, however, may continue. By statute, the primary human use is recreational with emphasis on a set of values that in one form or another emphasizes solitude as a primary indicator of the wilderness recreation experience. Recreational fishing is usually allowed; most traditional consumptive uses by local people are banned—especially taking of wildlife by hunting or trapping, no matter how ecologically benign.

As we shall see throughout this chapter, Congress's vision for ANILCA units of the National Park System, and for lands added to existing Alaska national park units by ANILCA, is unlike the Yellowstone model in many respects—despite the fact that most of this acreage also is either designated as wilderness or being managed by the NPS as de facto wilderness. Rather than using the power of the federal government to coercively eliminate consumptive uses by rural residents, including Native Americans[7] who had occupied these lands for thousands of years, Congress assumed that continued "customary and traditional" subsistence use by local rural residents does not represent inherent contradictions with either the "national park" or the "wilderness" concepts within these new units of the National Park System. Further, it was assumed that the subsistence use by local rural residents was not inherently contradictory with the management of "natural and healthy" wildlife populations within national parks and "healthy" populations within the national preserves.[8] Hunting and trapping by nonlocal people is also allowed in preserves. Congress thereby charged the NPS with a complex and challenging management task (i.e., the management of harvests of wildlife and other natural resources by local rural residents in parks and monuments and by nonlocals in preserves) with which it had little history and which was contradictory to central elements of its organizational culture.[9]

Although lands designated as wilderness, or now managed as de facto wilderness, exclude areas permanently inhabited by Alaska residents, these areas may be interspersed with large tracts of private lands including Native American allotments and corporation holdings and other privately owned tracts that serve not only as residences but also as bases for hunting, fishing, trapping, gathering, or guiding within park wilderness. Although some land exchanges may be in order to correct pressing problems, there is no plan for the federal government to acquire these in-holdings in a large-scale fashion.

Rural People, Subsistence Uses, and the Management of ANILCA-Established National Park System Units[10]

Congress first debated subsistence provisions in ANILCA because of concerns for Alaska Natives, which, it was argued, had not been entirely covered by the Alaska Native Claims and Settlement Act of 1971 (ANCSA). The intent was to create a bill that would be legally acceptable to the state of Alaska, politically feasible in the U.S. Congress, and protective of Native American subsistence needs (Johnson et al. 1995). The result avoided socially divisive issues associated with race, ethnicity, and income, yet recognized that rural Native American people were primary beneficiaries of the Act (C. Stanley Sloss (1991) as quoted in Johnson et al. 1995).

Through Title VIII, Sec. 802, of ANILCA, Congress directed that nonwasteful "customary and traditional" subsistence uses of fish and wildlife by rural Alaska residents be given priority over other consumptive uses on federal lands affected by ANILCA, and stated that:

> The continuation of the opportunity for subsistence uses by rural residents of Alaska, including both natives and non-Natives . . . is essential to Native physical, economic, traditional, and cultural existence and to non-Native physical, economic, traditional, and social existence (Sec. 801).

Further, the language of ANILCA and its associated legislative history indicate congressional intent that the administration of federal lands under the Act would have minimal impact on the evolution of subsistence lifeways in rural communities and that local rural residents are to be conceptualized as part of the natural ecosystem:

With respect to the situation of local residents in and near certain new national parks and monuments established by the Act, the House believes that the establishment of these units should protect the opportunity for local rural residents to continue to engage in a subsistence way of life. The House notes that the Alaska Native way of life in rural Alaska may be the last major remnant of the subsistence culture alive today in North America. In addition, there is also a significant non-Native population residing in rural Alaska which in recent times has developed a subsistence lifestyle that is also a cultural value. . . .

. . . *The National Park Service recognizes and the Committee agrees, that subsistence uses by local rural residents have been, and are now, a natural part of the ecosystem serving as a primary consumer in the food chain.* . . .

. . . *it is the intent of this legislation to protect the Alaska Native subsistence way of life, and the Alaska Native culture of which it is a primary and essential element* . . . *to leave for the Alaska Native people themselves, rather than to Federal and State resource managers, the choice as to the direction and pace, if any, of the evolution of the subsistence way of life and of the Alaska Native culture* (Congressional Record—House; 11/12/80; italics added by author).

ANILCA itself states that the policy of Congress is that:

. . . the utilization of the public lands in Alaska is to cause the *least adverse impact possible on rural residents who depend upon subsistence uses of the resources of such lands* . . . [and that] non-wasteful subsistence uses of fish and wildlife and other renewable resources shall be the priority consumptive uses of all such uses on the public lands of Alaska. . . . (3112:2; italics added by author).

The above notwithstanding, we must also recognize that ANILCA does not establish any of the units of the Alaska National Park System expressly for the purpose of providing opportunities for subsistence use by local rural residents. Nonetheless, the law provides for continuation of subsistence ways of life and subsistence uses by rural residents as long as these uses are consistent with the purposes for which the areas were designated. It is abundantly clear that Congress did not intend for ANILCA to provide a sunset for the continuation of subsistence uses on new NPS-managed units of the National Park System or on lands added to existing units, except as noted above.

Rural Residence and Resident Zones

For ANILCA-created national parks and monuments, the NPS administratively established "resident zones" (see map 7.2) within which it has determined there are significant concentrations of local rural people who "without using aircraft as a means of access for purposes of taking fish or wildlife for subsistence uses (except in extraordinary cases where no reasonable alternative existed), have customarily and traditionally engaged in subsistence uses within a national park or monument" (36 CFR 13.43).[11] All permanent residents, including immigrants, within these zones are considered eligible for subsistence uses within a specific park or monument.[12] Currently fifty-five communities are included within the resident zones of seven Alaska national parks or monuments (see table 7.1). People who permanently reside within the boundary of an ANILCA park or monument (including on private land) are considered as living in the park resident zone and are also eligible for subsistence uses.

Any rural resident whose permanent residence is outside a resident-zone community may apply to the superintendent of a given park or monument for what is called a 13:44 permit. The superintendent shall grant this permit, allowing continued subsistence uses, if the applicant demonstrates:

> Without using aircraft as a means of access for purposes of taking fish and wildlife for subsistence uses, the applicant has (or is a member of a family which has) customarily and traditionally engaged in subsistence uses within a national park or monument (36 CFR 13:44).

Any and all wildlife harvest by people who are not designated as local rural residents on federal lands administered under ANILCA law is outside the legal definition of subsistence use and is, where allowed, accorded a lower priority than harvest by designated subsistence users. In national parks and monuments, this distinction is irrelevant because, as a general rule, there are no legal harvests of wildlife by nonlocals except for noncommercial fishing. In national preserves, however, hunting, trapping, and fishing by nonlocals may legally occur. Here, ANILCA establishes a priority for local rural (subsistence) uses, should allocation of wildlife harvest opportunities become necessary.[13] Subsistence users may also be granted more lenient restrictions with regard to issues such as bag and size limits, length of open seasons, and timing of the seasons.

Although ANILCA states that preserves should be managed in the same manner as parks, except for hunting by nonrural people, the NPS has not defined resident zones or other eligibility systems for subsistence uses within Alaska national preserves. A draft internal NPS document, *Review of Subsistence Law and National Park Service Regulations* (NPS 1995), states: "If an eligibility system is established for preserves, eligibility for subsistence uses should be determined by the same criteria as that for parks." If such determinations had

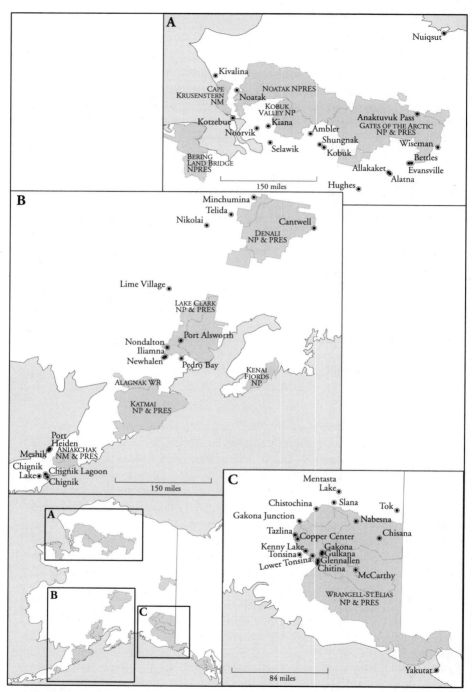

A

Nuiqsut

Kivalina

CAPE KRUSENSTERN NM
Noatak

NOATAK NPRES

KOBUK VALLEY NP

Kotzebue
Noorvik
Kiana

Ambler

Anaktuvuk Pass
GATES OF THE ARCTIC NP & PRES

Wiseman

Shungnak

Selawik

Kobuk

Bettles

BERING LAND BRIDGE NPRES

Allakaket
Evansville

Alatna

Hughes

150 miles

B

Minchumina
Telida

Nikolai

Cantwell

DENALI NP & PRES

Lime Village

LAKE CLARK NP & PRES

Port Alsworth

Nondalton
Iliamna
Newhalen

Pedro Bay

KENAI FJORDS NP

ALAGNAK WR

KATMAI NP & PRES

Port Heiden
ANIAKCHAK NM & PRES

Meshik

Chignik Lake

Chignik Lagoon

Chignik

150 miles

C

Mentasta Lake

Chistochina
Slana
Tok

Gakona Junction
Nabesna

Tazlina
Copper Center
Chisana

Kenny Lake
Gakona
Tonsina
Gulkana

Lower Tonsina
Glennallen

Chitina
McCarthy

WRANGELL-ST. ELIAS NP & PRES

Yakutat

84 miles

Map 7.2. Resident Zone Communities

occurred at the time it was written (e.g., for communities seeking inclusion as resident zones adjacent to ANILCA-affected federal lands), the eight criteria in box 7.1 would have probably been employed to define "customary and traditional." The accompanying exercises likely would have included complex statistical analyses relying on extensive quantitative data from social surveys, secondary data sources, and the like and would have been performed by formally trained social scientists.

At the request of the regional council chairs, in the summer of 1998 a Customary and Traditional (C & T) Committee appointed by the Federal Subsistence Board was in the process of reviewing C & T determinations and recommending changes in the process. The deliberations of that committee indicate the belief that although ANILCA does not require C & T determinations, neither does it preclude them. It was, therefore, concluded that a range of options was possible.

To date, however, NPS has not defined resident zones or other eligibility systems for subsistence uses within Alaska national preserves. An internal NPS document dated August 1997, titled "National Park Service Subsistence Management Program," states:

> There are differences in law between preserves and parks and monuments. If in the future, the NPS determines a need for further eligibility regulations for preserves, it will work closely with subsistence advisory groups to develop those regulations (NPS 1997).

Hence, there appears to be a general move away from rigid top-down formulaic management of subsistence driven by rigid interpretation of regulations and formal analyses like that described above, to more fluid management through negotiation and cooperation between federal agencies (including NPS) and community actors. In this case, the process of defining C & T is now directly associated with institutionalized cooperative management arrangements involving Federal Regional Advisory Councils and Subsistence Resource Commissions (discussed further later in the chapter) and will likely culminate in more active local involvement in processes that potentially limit or constrain local use of natural resources that are associated with the resident-zone designation (although formal analyses still may be done).

Alaska Native and Non-Native Subsistence

Of Alaskans who lived outside the Anchorage, Juneau, and Fairbanks areas in 1997, about 28 percent were Natives.[14] (The word "Native" refers to Eskimos, Indians, and Aleuts.) Physically, many contemporary Native and non-Native rural communities are similar. For example, they are small and relatively isolated, and wildlife and other locally harvested resources are important in their economies. Overall, however, Alaska Native and non-Native communities differ in their use of local wild resources.[15]

Box 7.1. Eight Factors That Exemplify Customary and Traditional Uses of Specific Fish Stocks and Wildlife Populations

According to 50 CFR 0.16 and 36 CFR 242.16, Customary and Traditional Use Determination Process, the Federal Subsistence Board will identify specific community or area uses of specific fish stocks and wildlife populations through application of the following eight factors, which exemplify customary and traditional use:

1. Long-term consistent pattern of use, excluding interruptions beyond the control of the community or area;
2. A pattern of use recurring in specific seasons for many years;
3. A pattern of use consisting of methods and means of harvest which are characterized by efficiency and economy of effort and cost, conditioned by local characteristics;
4. The consistent harvest and use of fish or wildlife as related to past methods and means of taking near, or reasonably accessible from, the community or area;
5. A means of handling, preparing, preserving, and storing fish and wildlife which has been traditionally used by past generations, including consideration of alteration of past practices due to recent technological advances, where appropriate;
6. A pattern of use that includes the handing down of knowledge of fishing and hunting skills, values, and lore from generation to generation;
7. A pattern of use in which the harvest is shared or distributed within a definable community of persons; and
8. A pattern of use that relates to reliance on a wide diversity of fish and wildlife resources of the area and that provides substantial cultural, economic, social, and nutritional elements to the community or area.

On average, rural Alaska Natives harvest more and a greater variety of wildlife than their non-Native counterparts. They also share wild foods throughout the community to a greater extent. This said, however, it would be a mistake to convey the impression that many rural non-Native households do not harvest high amounts of local food and other resources, from a variety of sources, and share them extensively.[16]

NPS Management of Wildlife Harvest on Alaska Lands

The management of subsistence uses on ANILCA-affected federal lands was initially delegated to the state of Alaska subject to federal review of the state's compliance with the law.[17] (As a general rule, in the United States, states manage fish and wildlife harvest on federal lands.) However, in December 1989, an Alaska Supreme Court decision, *McDowell v. Collinsworth*, found that the laws used by the state of Alaska to provide a subsistence priority for rural Alaskans, consistent with ANILCA, violated the equal protection and common-use clause of the Alaska constitution. In response to this decision, federal agencies took over management of subsistence on Alaska federal lands (largely excluding navigable waters) on July 1, 1990, as required by ANILCA. The result is that the federal government through its various land management agencies manages wildlife over about two-thirds of the state, and the state exercises management responsibilities over the balance including state and private lands. Caufield (1991:28) elaborates:

> In its landmark decision, the court ruled that such a priority violates "equal access" and other provisions of the Alaska constitution. Because the state was no longer in compliance with ANILCA, the federal government stepped in on 1 July 1990 to take over subsistence management on all federal public lands, or nearly 60 percent of the state. . . . As a result, unified subsistence management was replaced by two systems, federal and state, each with its own distinctive legislative mandate and with separate regulatory frameworks.

This decision intensified an ongoing polarized debate between indigenous peoples, nonlocal Alaska hunters, the state of Alaska, and the federal government. Although this debate continues,[18] Bosworth (1995) observes that rural Alaskans generally appear to support federal subsistence management focused on subsistence uses more exclusively than the state fish and game management. The state of Alaska must also consider constituencies of nonlocal Alaska residents, who also want to hunt and fish, and commercial fishermen.

Coevolution of Rural Communities and ANILCA-Established National Parks

As noted above, ANILCA not only provides for the continuation of subsistence uses, it establishes an administrative arrangement institutionalizing a role for rural residents in the management of affected public lands insofar as those uses are affected. Section 801 of ANILCA declares:

> . . . the national interest in the proper regulation, protection, and conservation of fish and wildlife on the public lands in Alaska and the continuation of the opportunity for subsistence way of life by residents of rural Alaska require that an administrative structure be established for the purpose of enabling rural residents who have personal knowledge of local conditions and requirements to have a meaningful role in the management of fish and wildlife and of subsistence uses on the public lands in Alaska.

On lands designated as national parks and monuments within which subsistence uses occur, Sec. 808 of ANILCA established Subsistence Resources Commissions (SRCs). These commissions are composed of people who either engage in subsistence uses in the area or have special knowledge thereof. They have responsibilities for submitting subsistence hunting plans and can legally make recommendations directly to the secretary of the interior. In practice, considerable time has been spent since these commissions were established in 1984 in dealing with issues of eligibility for subsistence uses, access technology issues (e.g., all-terrain vehicles), and other issues such as determining areas where subsistence uses are considered traditional (Caufield 1988, 1991).

Unfortunately, SRCs have had a very mixed record of success partially because the Washington office of the NPS and the Department of the Interior have not responded to many proposals submitted to them—apparently for political reasons. This lack of response has in many cases had a demoralizing effect on the willingness of people to spend their time and energy participating in them. At present, however, there may be reason to be cautiously optimistic that these groups may begin to realize their potential.

Section 805 of ANILCA also established Regional Advisory Councils composed of residents of six regions (now expanded to ten), which have responsibility for reviewing proposals for regulations, policies, and other matters relating to subsistence uses of fish and wildlife on federal lands in the region. These councils provide a forum for the discussion and expression of opinion on any matter related to subsistence uses within the regions. They recommend regulations and management strategies to the Federal Subsistence Board made up of high-level representatives from the federal land management agencies that have final responsibility in adopting regulations. The Regional Advisory Councils were not established until 1993, after the federal government took over management of subsistence. They appear to be working very well and the Federal Subsistence Board generally accepts their recommendations. Not only does the involvement of these councils protect the interests of rural communities as explicitly intended by Congress, the participation of hunters on the councils introduces considerable on-the-ground knowledge into wildlife management discussions.

The extent to which Subsistence Resource Commissions and the Regional Advisory Councils established by ANILCA will successfully link rural communities and NPS managers in the long run remains to be seen. The most intelligent prediction now is cautious optimism. Regardless, the fact remains that this linkage, accompanied by the previously explained legislative mandates, is unique in America. Nowhere else in the National Park System do we have legally mandated procedures designed to institutionalize opportunities for local rural communities to directly influence agency natural resource management decisions of crucial importance to the character and evolution of these communities. In essence, Alaska rural subsistence lifeways are protected under federal law, and elementary mechanisms have been established for rural community representatives to articulate community interests to the NPS and other federal bureaucrats charged with managing lands on which they are dependent. These arrangements will certainly affect the impact of national parks on rural development, but it is too early to conclude how extensive this influence will be and the direction it may take.

An interesting future hypothetical scenario, however, might include an NPS proposal to develop a visitor center catering to nonlocal recreationists in an Alaska community in which residents continue to use the involved park for subsistence purposes. The proposed visitor center would promise economic development that could result in an influx of outside tourists visiting the park. This development might have the potential to set off population growth, which in turn could lead to substantial social change, clouding the area's qualification as a resident zone, and eventually change the character of the community greatly. The desire of nonlocal park visitors to view relatively tame wildlife acclimated to human presence might also affect NPS management policy toward local hunting.[19] NPS managers and planners in ANILCA-created parks in these types of situations will have to more carefully consider the impact of park development on customary and traditional subsistence uses by local rural people and be much more sensitive to the impacts of these decisions on the evolution of rural communities and culture than is characteristic of the agency elsewhere. Many Alaska rural residents may resist dramatic transformations of their communities, if there are apparent quality-of-life trade-offs despite some economic benefits.

An interesting outcome associated with the ANILCA mandate is that evolving local rural communities and their subsistence uses (defined as natural elements of ecological systems but also subject to reasonable regulation) intrinsically contribute to the evolution and character of national park ecosystems (broadly defined as biosocial systems). Even more fascinating is the possibility that the processes of institutionalized interaction between local rural communities and the NPS and the realities of the ANILCA mandate will also affect the evolution of NPS organizational culture in Alaska. This radical departure from the biocentric conception of management of national park ecosystems as static systems ideally free of any human influence, implicit in the Yellowstone model, warrants explanation.

The following case study and interpretation provide insight into how this process might occur through the interaction of federal law and informal community norms, which function together to effect orderly harvest of fur from an NPS-managed area.

Informal Community Norms and National Park Biosocial Systems—A Case Study in the North Additions of Denali NP and Pres (DENA)[20]

The framers of ANILCA intended for formal law and regulations, and informal norms and customs, to operate in a complementary fashion to define many aspects of acceptable behavior associated with customary and traditional subsistence uses generally, and by inference, of trapping and the use of trapping cabins specifically (Johnson et al. 1995).[21] Federal agencies, however, cannot enforce the claims of qualified local residents pertaining to the exclusive use of areas for trapping or the use of cabins built for the primary purpose of harvesting fur against other claims by local residents who may be equally qualified under ANILCA to use or occupy such cabins or land.

Conversely, local American rural communities (including those composed of nonaboriginal people) have traditionally claimed rights for subsistence uses of American public lands.[22] Alaska rural communities also have recognized relatively exclusive individual use rights for trapping areas on lands affected by ANILCA. These customary rights do not focus on legal ownership of the land itself (which resides with the federal government) but on the prerogative of use by individuals (community members) who have "use claims" on cabins, trapping areas, and trapline trails. Local community members articulate these claims as rights traced through a historical stream of "ownership" arrangements that are, and have been for several generations, widely recognized by community members. Such use claims are recognized in the community as coexisting with formal property law. The philosophical basis for their existence is a shared set of values (a collective sense of what is right) within a community, accompanied by an identifiable history of use of the area by members of the community.

Incentives for respect of and compliance with these customary property rights are provided not only by individuals' desires to be members in good standing of the community, but also by the possibility of informal sanctions from the community (e.g., ostracism). People in rural isolated communities are more dependent on the voluntary assistance of the community at large during catastrophic events that are beyond their individual abilities to control. Everyday living is also frequently much easier if one has a network within which work is exchanged, equipment shared, and so on. A person or family that is socially ostracized in an isolated rural Alaska community will probably find life much more difficult.

Individual Use Claims on Trapping Areas and Cabins

A "use claim" for purposes of this example is an asserted individual or partnership right to the relatively exclusive use of a trapline, trapping area, or cabin with corresponding informal restrictions on others' use of that cabin or area. The quote below, from a person who historically trapped in the Nikolai area near Denali NP and Pres, illustrates the use claim concept:

> Respondent: And that's kind of in line with the way . . . cabins are used. Somebody is recognized as owning a cabin, of course you can't own it because you don't [own] the ground, you know, and . . . you've got a use claim to the cabin, I guess, but other people recognize that usually, and will ask you about staying there.

A use claim, similar to legal ownership, has two parts: (1) the relatively unrestricted use of the "property" by the "owner" (hereafter called the "primary user") and (2) the restriction of use of the property by others. Through community norms, primary users have relatively unrestricted use of the properties to which they have use claims. There is, however, explicit acknowledgment that formal government laws do not allow unlimited use.

Trapping area and cabin individual use claims help resolve conflicts between trappers and provide a basis for orderly and peaceful production of goods and services from public resources.[23] Because the primary user of a trapping area receives both the rewards for good management and the damages of depleted fur resources, use claims create strong incentives for conservation according to sustained-use principles by eliminating commons dilemmas.[24] These benefits (i.e., contributing to social order and the conservation of scarce resources), though varying in detail from place to place, have been an acknowledged part of rural Alaska culture in many areas for several generations.

For example, Halpin (1987), writing about a study done in 1984, observes that Tetlin, Alaska (a Native community), has trapping areas where families have recognized exclusive rights to fur populations extending back two or three generations. She quotes an administrator for the Bureau of Education, E. J. Beck, who wrote the following after a visit to Tetlin in December 1929:

> The natives have their own rules and regulations with reference to conservation of the furbearing animals. The chief of the village assigns them to various grounds, and in this way, the fur is not depleted (Beck 1930:31).

Halpin notes further that the protection of these customary property rights was specifically cited in the 1930 executive order establishing the Tetlin Reserve. Subsequently, these trapping areas have been informally passed from generation to generation mostly within families resident to the area.

The Denali Cabin Study is a comprehensive social research project describing traditional use, occupancy, and construction of cabins and shelters associated with fur harvest and other subsistence activities in the north additions of Denali NP and Pres. The design of the study places considerable emphasis on local social norms and customs pertaining to informal use rights associated with trapping areas. The resident-zone communities involved in the Denali Cabin Study (Nikolai, Telida, and Lake Minchumina) recognize use claims pertaining to trapping by individuals who have obtained one of the following: (1) a government permit or official declaration (not available on federal land); (2) legal ownership of the property; (3) establishment of a new trapline or trapping area in an area open for trapline development; or (4) a transfer from someone with a legitimate customary use claim. Our interest here is in (3) and (4), which directly pertain to the vast acreage of public land that comprises the North Additions of Denali NP and Pres and significant acreage managed by the Bureau of Land Management and the state of Alaska outside DENA.

Within the North Additions of Denali NP and Pres are thirteen trapping areas recognized by the community as "owned" by trappers—largely out of the community of Lake Minchumina (see map 7.3). The use and "ownership" of these areas can be traced in an orderly fashion to the 1920s and before. From the perspectives of local rural community members, the "owners" of these areas have exclusive rights to the fur and the cabins built on these traplines that are regarded similar to private property. NPS regulations, as noted above, do not allow for formal designation of exclusively used trapping areas or the ownership of cabins on public land. Legally, trapping cabins located within these areas are the property of the United States, and all qualified users (in this case local subsistence users) have equal access.

A consequence of the federal legal code prohibiting designation of personal trapping areas is that the orderly extraction of fur is dependent on the effectiveness of local social norms in enforcing usufructuary rights.[25] A trapper who "owns" a trapline (perhaps purchased) and who has invested time and money in constructing shelter for wintertime use cannot rely on the federal government to enforce his claim to the area and to cabins associated with trapping activities. Importantly, the exclusive claims of trapping-area owners to fur resources also assign the benefits of conservation practices to those who practice them and thereby provide powerful incentives for conservation that are absent in both federal and state law.

Community Norms and NPS Management of the Construction of Trapping Cabins in Denali NP and Pres

Although ANILCA clearly allows customary and traditional trapping to continue and also provides for the use and construction of cabins for shelter, NPS

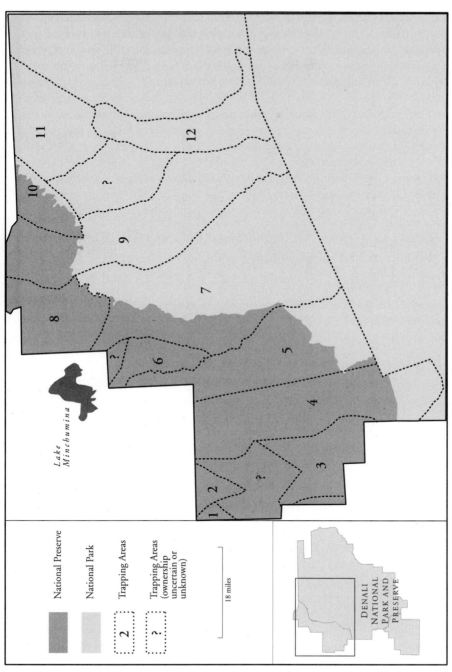

Map 7.3. Trapping Areas in Denali National Park and Preserve

regulations for cabin construction are interpreted stringently. Because of bureaucratic inaction, political pressures from outside special interest groups that
define all consumptive uses within national parks as adverse, and their own
stringent interpretation, the managers of DENA have approved only two permits (as of the summer of 1998) to reconstruct cabins for trapping purposes
since 1980.

The backlog of cabin reconstruction permit applications creates a situation in
which some trappers were and are overreliant on tents for shelter during winter
conditions that can include blizzards and cold below 50 degrees Fahrenheit. The
consequence of this situation is that people who want to continue to trap fur
and who are overreliant on tents are faced with a series of negative consequences
affecting health and safety, profitability of the trapline itself, and, in some cases,
lost opportunities to pass on skills and knowledge associated with this component of traditional living (Johnson et al. 1999).

Johnson et al. (1999) also document the dynamic and fluid nature of rural
community and individual adaptation to the biological systems in what is now
legally defined as Denali NP and Pres. This information is useful to the
DENA SRC as formal documentation of community culture and historical
uses to which NPS managers are supposed to be sensitive. It will assist NPS in
guiding evaluation of future cabin construction permits because it describes
the continual evolution of local customs and traditions associated with fur
trapping, and the use of trapping shelters in the North Additions. The Denali
Cabin Study, however, does not provide a rigid definition of traditional adaptation to the land from which stringent and narrow administrative formulas
can be drawn to guide granting of cabin permits (fixed locations and established construction criteria), trapping-area size, and transportation technology
used for access. To the contrary, the research illustrates how local trappers have
used emerging technologies to strategically adapt their individual situations to
the evolving demands of the external economy and the local ecology and
strongly suggests that if subsistence trapping is to continue, trappers must
retain substantial flexibility to adapt to evolving social and biological conditions.

The Denali Cabin Study thus suggests an interface for local social systems
with biological systems and NPS administration, prompting visions for interac-
tive management of the North Additions as an integrated and dynamic biosocial ecosystem. To be sure, that image by law is grounded in "natural and
healthy" wildlife populations protected by the NPS for enjoyment by future
generations. But this vision also includes moose hunting, dog sleds, snowmobiles, trapping cabins, marten pelts being stretched and worked to bring top dollars, and the persistent presence of local people who, in one way or another, have
used these resources for thousands of years.

ANILCA, Coevolution of Biosocial Systems, and NPS Organizational Culture

I asserted earlier that the ANILCA mandate had the potential to affect the evolution of NPS organizational culture, at least in Alaska. While a thorough discussion of NPS organizational culture in the context of this challenge would be a chapter in itself, I will make some preliminary observations. In 1980, when ANILCA was passed, most managers in the large western parks had been recruited into an organization charged with preserving nature and providing opportunity for selected types of nonconsumptive tourism. Direct benefits of this management flowed disproportionately to tourists who tended to be drawn from outside urban areas, were white, and who were well educated compared to the societal norm and to the business owners who catered to them. One function of management was to keep locals from using the parks in traditional consumptive ways. To many of these managers, national parks were places where hunting, harvesting firewood for personal use, netting fish, and trapping fur were morally inappropriate. Rather, national parks were nature preserves where one went for personal recreation and ideally for religious-like inspiration in wilderness areas. Biological systems were allowed to evolve "naturally." The affects of humans were conceptualized as external to nature and ideally eliminated except for acceptable levels of nonconsumptive tourism and, in some cases, NPS-sponsored biological research.

Some NPS managers in the pre- and early post-ANILCA days predicted that despite what ANILCA said, subsistence uses would gradually decline on national park lands and that these parks would slowly come to resemble their counterparts in the lower forty-eight states. After ANILCA was signed, one also began to sometimes hear the derisive use of the term "soft park"—representing a park which was not "pure" but used traditionally by local people. Soft parks were and are compared to "hard parks." In hard parks, managers are in control, and most consumptive uses including those of local residents have been displaced regardless of prior history or ecological impact.

Of course, some NPS people made intellectual arguments during and after the ANILCA debates supporting the desirability of integrating nature preservation with sustainable use by local people—especially by Native Americans using relatively simple technology. Some recognized that large natural areas could not healthfully survive, surrounded by hostile displaced neighbors, when parks characteristically have low law enforcement budgets and few enforcement personnel. But the facts were in 1980 that the NPS had little experience in working constructively and continuously with local people who viewed parks as their homeland and as the source of their food, who believed it was their right (not a legal privilege) to use natural resources within parks as they were needed, and who had a legal basis for continual consumptive uses of the parks. For their part,

Alaska rural people often resented interference by government bureaucrats and game wardens, and sometimes took indignant exception to outsiders declaring their homeland sanctified wilderness (where, in some Native communities, people claim the legitimacy of thousands of years of occupancy).

I perceived in the early 1980s that most NPS managers were glad to have the state managing subsistence. The management of subsistence was potentially complex and controversial compared to the rather simple but somewhat contradictory management guidelines for national parks in most parks in the lower forty-eight states. Because of intense and persistent political conflict from both internal and external sources, subsistence management was frequently seen by NPS employees as offering little or no career development opportunity. There was little if any attempt to explain to the visiting public the legal framework establishing ANILCA-created park units. (This framework essentially alters the philosophical definition of the national park ecological system by continuing human predation as a perpetual part of the natural system). One could have concluded that park interpreters intentionally avoided the subject of subsistence uses—despite the fact that these uses were continued on more than half of all U.S. national park lands.

After 1990, however, the agency had no choice but to confront the challenges of subsistence management more directly. The first years of more active NPS subsistence management were characterized by a centralized approach based on regulations interpreted rigidly from the Alaska regional office. One observer, with a long history of representing Natives, characterized NPS formal decisions and guidelines as "extremely miserly." My own opinion was that, with some notable exceptions, much on-the-ground subsistence management in the parks was characterized by benign neglect. I visited several resident communities in the early 1990s wherein people did not understand the basic NPS regulations affecting local harvests and visits by NPS representatives for any reason were infrequent. Although local people were afraid that NPS regulation was going to eventually adversely affect them, in reality, they were probably doing things essentially as usual. In other instances, such as the case of the North Additions of Denali reported here, many local people felt that the NPS administration was negatively affecting continuation of traditional subsistence activities, and, therefore, the evolution of local communities through stringent regulations and bureaucratic inertia.

Regardless, some subsistence regulations were changed through federal agency cooperation after 1991, such as the timing of seasons and modifications of regulations designed for recreational hunting developed under state management. (As noted above, federal agencies and especially the NPS can approach subsistence management without political pressure from nonlocal Alaska people who also want to harvest natural resources.) The NPS also initiated several research projects directed toward various aspects of subsistence uses in several NPS-managed areas in the early to mid-1990s.

In 1995, the NPS was reorganized. More power was delegated to the field areas. In Alaska, the Subsistence Division in the Alaska regional office was disbanded and the regional office was designated as a support office. The result of this action was that NPS employees who directly dealt with local people in the parks now had more responsibility and flexibility in the management of subsistence uses.

To successfully carry out its subsistence-related mission with local communities, the NPS needs a different type of employee than it typically recruits to serve in the natural national parks of the lower forty-eight states, if constructive ongoing community-agency linkages are to be maintained. There are now solid indications that the NPS is slowly finding such people, simultaneously as the aforementioned cooperative management processes begin to function. As this is written, a few NPS employees associated with subsistence management have been drawn from rural Alaska. They know and respect the demands and rewards of subsistence living; they appreciate the mythological integration of nature and culture that is characteristic of native villages; and they understand the myths of self-reliance and individualism of Alaska's rural Euro-American residents. They also understand and appreciate the myth of national parks in the outside culture. Some individuals (not necessarily rural Alaska residents), whose views of parks are more consistent with ANILCA, are also entering management positions in Alaska national parks.

As these individuals gain experience and work their way into higher leadership positions, the Alaska NPS organizational culture itself may begin to explicitly reflect ANILCA's enlightened mandate. Park management, however, will be much more complex because it will involve a perpetual examination and consideration of the appropriate integration of evolving local rural social systems and subsistence uses into evolving park biological systems managed for public enjoyment. A continual process of negotiation between stakeholders and the NPS may occur. Although based on enduring principles, park management will be conceptualized as fluid, dynamic, and adaptive as opposed to an effort to re-create a simplified, static, and idyllic vision of the past such as that implicit in the pre-Columbian vignette.

If and when this happens, park visitors will still be exposed to typical interpretations of the wonders of nature. However, they may also hear stories of local culture and history that will not be represented as part of a dead, romanticized past, but as the evolving integration of two of America's most precious assets— some of her most inspirational outdoor places and the diverse cultures of rural Alaska peoples.

Notes

1. In area, Alaska is larger than Texas and the next three largest states combined (586,412 square miles), being about one-fifth the size of the lower forty-eight states. The state has 6,640 miles of coastline. There are more than 3,000 rivers and 3 million lakes in Alaska.

2. About 52 percent of Alaskans lived in the cities of Anchorage (254,849), Fairbanks (31,850), and Juneau (29,813) in 1997. Outside these cities there were twenty-three other municipalities with populations greater than 2,500. Data are from Alaska Department of Labor Research and Analysis Demographics Unit. The U.S. 1990 census is used as a base. Members of the armed services are included.

3. Many informed observers (e.g., Jackstad and Lee 1995) argue that state government spending is currently over $1 billion in excess of what can in the long run be sustained given declining oil production. These are sobering statistics and strongly suggest the importance of sustainable development strategies not only for rural areas but for the entire state.

4. Material in this and several of the following sections has been adapted from the following two reports: Johnson, Gudgel-Holmes, and Levy (1999), and Brandenburg, A., D. R. Johnson, Laurel Tyrell, Mathew Carroll, and Susan Hanson. 1998. "Contemporary and Historic Natural Resource Use Patterns by Rural Residents of the Yukon-Charley Rivers National Preserve Area." Preliminary Draft. Seattle: University of Washington Field Station, USGS/BRD/FRESC, College of Forest Resources.

5. See, for example:
   Johnson, D. R., E. Hunn, P. Russell, M. Vande Kamp, and E. Searles. 1999. "Subsistence Uses of Vegetal Resources in and around Lake Clark National Park and Preserve." Technical Report NPS/CCSOUW/NRTR-98-16 NPS D-19. Seattle: University of Washington Field Station, USGS-BRD-FRESC, College of Forest Resources.

6. Anomie is a social condition characterized by the breakdown of norms governing social interaction (Abercrombie et al. 1994). Here it apparently refers to a hypothetical situation in which rural community values and norms would continue to stress individual responsibility for providing food and sustenance to one's family but without any real opportunity to do so. This dysfunctional condition of the social structure would be expected to lead to pathological individual and group outcomes.

7. Because of the large acreage being considered for inclusion in the National Park System and the fact that a multiplicity of conflicting interests and values were involved in the political compromises worked out in ANILCA, advocates of including large acreages under management of NPS had to choose between reducing that acreage substantially and maintaining national park values in the lower forty-eight states, or accepting subsistence uses on new park and monument lands and the creation of national preserves where sport hunting was legal with a much larger acreage under NPS management. Therefore, ANILCA, Sec. 101b, states that it is the intent of Congress to preserve wilderness resource values and related recreational opportunities including but not limited to hiking, canoeing, fishing, and sport hunting that occur on national preserves.

8. ANILCA did not permit resumption of subsistence uses on National Park System units existing before the Act. It does, however, apply to new lands added to existing

units, with very few exceptions. ANILICA's perspective toward subsistence uses is similar to recent international guidelines such as those from the IUCN Commission on National Parks and Protected Areas of 1994, which remove the basic philosophical obstruction to habitation and subsistence by indigenous people from most categories of protected areas.

9. Sellars (1997), arguing that NPS cannot claim leadership in scientific-based leadership in the preservation of the natural environment, states: ". . . the leadership culture of the Park Service has been defined largely by the demands of recreational tourism management and the desire for the public to enjoy the scenic parks. . . . Overall . . . the dominant Park Service culture developed a strongly utilitarian and pragmatic managerial bent. It adopted a management style that emphasized expediency and quick solutions, resisted information gathering through long term research, and disliked interference from inside or outside the Service" (pp. 283–84). Whether one agrees with this argument or not it is certain that NPS organizational history and culture include little experience with resident peoples who continue to legally use parklands for subsistence purposes.

10. ANILCA, Sec. 803, defines "subsistence uses" as "the customary and traditional uses by rural Alaska residents of wild, renewable resources for direct personal or family consumption as food, shelter, fuel, clothing, tools or transportation; for the making and selling of handicraft articles out of nonedible by-products of fish and wildlife resources taken for personal or family consumption; for barter, or sharing for personal or family consumption; and for customary trade . . . " by administratively designated local rural people.

11. The creation of ANILCA involved multiple compromises among disparate interests, which explains the inconsistent and at times vague language of the Act. Concepts such as "customary and traditional" are in many cases left open for administrative interpretation. See Johnson et al. (1995) for a more detailed discussion of the legislative history pertaining to ANILCA and congressional intent regarding the concept of "customary and traditional."

12. Congress strongly supported the resident-zone concept primarily to spare rural communities and cultures the burden of a complex and potentially culturally disruptive regulatory system. Congress was also aware of the possibility of substantial social change among rural communities that might require evaluation of the resident-zone concept in favor of individual permit systems in specific instances to protect unit values. See Johnson et al. (1995).

13. Priority, however, does not imply that subsistence users have a legal right to harvest wildlife. Allowable harvests are generally controlled with the goal of maintaining "healthy" wildlife populations, or, in the case of national parks or monuments, "natural and healthy" wildlife populations. Should stocks fall too low to allow any harvest, all users may be prohibited from harvesting a particular species, or stocks can be allocated between communities of eligible subsistence users.

14. Generally, all areas outside Anchorage, Juneau, and Fairbanks are considered "rural" in Alaska rural development discussions (Cornwall 1982).

15. Title VIII of ANILCA states that "subsistence uses by rural residents of Alaska, including both Natives and non-Natives . . . [are] essential to Native physical, economic, traditional, and cultural existence and to non-Natives' physical, economic,

traditional, and social existence." We will not here attempt to interpret congressional intent in choosing the word "cultural" for rural natives and the word "social" for rural nonnatives. However, it is apparent that Congress recognized that subsistence uses were essential to Alaska's rural natives and rural nonnatives for somewhat different reasons. It is also evident that one of the principal motives of Congress in Title VIII was to protect the Alaska native subsistence way of life and the Alaska native culture of which subsistence was seen as an integral element (Congressional Record—House; 11/12/80; H29279-80). There is nothing, however, in ANILCA or its legislative history that suggests discrimination for or against either Natives or nonnatives in the administration of this law is appropriate. Title VIII of ANILCA was intended to be interpreted as nonracial, or color blind (Johnson et al. 1995).

16. See Callaway (1995), Robbins and Little (1984), Nelson (1969), and Chance (1990) for discussions of the cultural relevance of sharing in Alaska native communities. Callaway (1995) presents data comparing characteristics of native and nonnative subsistence harvests and uses the Upper Tanana. He observes that some high harvesting households including nonnative households "have much in common including the sharing of resources."

17. See Bosworth (1995) for a more extensive discussion of the history of subsistence management in Alaska.

18. For example, on December 15, 1997, the Federal Subsistence Board released proposed regulations to implement a ninth Circuit Court ruling that the rural subsistence priority should apply on navigable waters on and surrounding federal public lands where the United States has reserved water rights—an action certain to spur controversy throughout the state for the next several years.

19. For example, Catton (1995) states that tourists' desires accompanied by pressures from the concessioner for seals that were easily viewable by tourists in Glacier Bay NM influenced NPS attempts in the 1960s to rescind a decades-old agreement with the Huna Tlingit to continue traditional seal hunting in the monument.

20. The information for this case example is drawn from Johnson, Gudgel-Holmes, and Levy (1999).

21. "In a literal sense, tradition refers to any human practice, belief, institution or artifact which is handed down from one generation to the next" (Abercrombie et al. 1994). Traditions are frequently seen as major sources of social stability. Nonetheless, traditions are not here conceptualized as fixed entities but as constantly evolving and frequently reinterpreted as social and ecological conditions change. Thus, what is seen as traditional today may be considerably different from what was seen as traditional seventy-five years ago, and what is seen as traditional in the future will likely not be what is perceived as traditional today. ANILCA does not explicitly define "tradition." However, its legislative history suggests congressional acknowledgment of the fact that (within limits established by the purposes for which given lands are set aside) it does not freeze subsistence technologies, and, by inference, associated practices at some arbitrary point in time.

22. The term "rights" here does not refer to a legally enforceable right. Rather it refers to "claims of entitlement that are based on customary usage." These are usufructuary rights in that the holder may use a resource owned by another but may not sell or destroy it. See Fortmann 1990.

23. This is not to say that economic concerns are the only factors motivating trapping activities and encouraging conservation-related behavior.
24. A commons dilemma is a situation in which the actions of individuals who utilize a common resource lead to short-term personal gains, but also degrade the total value of the resource. The assumption is made that individuals will act in ways that yield the highest individual short-term return, leading eventually to resource collapse. This result occurs because of operant conditioning. See Lloyd (1833), Edney and Harper (1978), and Platt (1973).
25. "Usufructuary rights" are rights to the use, enjoyment, profits, and avails of property belonging to another.

References

Abercrombie, Nicholas, Stephen Hill, and Bryan S. Turner. 1994. *Dictionary of Sociology.* London: Penguin Books.

Alaska Department of Fish and Game. 1992. *Subsistence Values in Rural Alaska.* Juneau: Alaska Department of Fish and Game.

Beck, E. J. 1930. *Report of Official Visit to Upper Tanana and Copper River Valleys, December 28, 1929 to February 14, 1930.* Anchorage: U.S. Department of the Interior, Office of Education, Office of Superintendent of Central District.

Berger, T. R. 1985. *Village Journey: The Report of the Alaska Native Review Commission.* New York: Hill and Wang.

Bosworth, R. 1995. Biology, politics, and culture in the management of subsistence hunting and fishing: An Alaskan case history. In *Human Ecology and Climate Change: People and Resources in the Far North,* ed. D. L. Peterson and D. R. Johnson, 245–60. Washington, DC: Taylor and Francis.

Callaway, D. 1995. Resource use in rural Alaskan communities. In *Human Ecology and Climate Change: People and Resources in the Far North,* ed. D. L. Peterson and D. R. Johnson, 155–68. Washington, DC: Taylor and Francis.

Catton, Theodore. 1995. *Land Reborn: A History of Administration and Visitor Use in Glacier Bay National Park and Preserve.* Anchorage: National Park Service.

Caufield, R. A. 1991. Alaska's subsistence management regimes. *Polar Record* 28(164): 23–32.

———— 1988. The Role of Subsistence Resource Commissions in Managing Alaska's New National Parks. In *Traditional Knowledge and Renewable Resource Management,* ed. M.M.R. Freeman and L. N. Carbyn, 55–64. Edmonton: University of Alberta, Boreal Institute for Northern Studies.

Chance, N. A. 1990. *The Inupiat and Arctic Alaska.* New York: Holt Rinehart and Winston.

Chance, N. A., and E. N. Andrews. 1995. Sustainability, equity, and natural resource development in Northwest Siberia and Arctic Alaska. *Human Ecology* 2(2): 217–41.

Cornwall, P. G. 1982. Introduction. In *Alaska's Rural Development,* ed. P. G. Cornwall and G. McBeath, 1–4. Boulder, CO: Westview Press.

Edney, J. J., and C. Harper 1978. The commons dilemma: A review of contributions from psychology. *Environmental Management* 2: 491–507.

Fortmann, L. 1990 Locality and custom: Non-aboriginal claims to customary usufructuary rights as a source of rural protest. *Journal of Rural Studies* 6(2): 195–208.

Goldschmit, S. 2000. January 4. Personal communication. Anchorage: University of Alaska, Institute of Social and Economic Research.

Halpin, L. 1987. *Living off the Land: Contemporary Subsistence in Tetlin, Alaska.* Technical Paper No. 149. Juneau: Alaska Department of Fish and Game.

Jackstadt, S. L., and D. R. Lee. 1995. Economic sustainability: The sad case of Alaska. *Society* 32(3):50–55.

Johnson, D. R., D. Gudgel-Holmes, and J. Levy. 1999. "Traditional Use of Cabins and Other Shelters in the North Additions to Denali National Park and Preserve: Introduction, Methodology, Ethno-Historical Context and Background, Ownership and Transfer Norms, and the Choice of Cabins or Tents as Winter Trapline Shelters." Technical Report NPS/CCSOUW/NRTR-99-02 NPS D-290. Seattle: University of Washington Field Station, USGS/BRD/FRESC, College of Forest Resources.

Johnson, D. R., C. Baker, and A. Arvidson. 1995. "Defining Customary and Traditional: Perspectives from Legislative and Case Law Associated with Title VIII of the Alaska National Interest Lands and Conservation Act of 1980." Unpublished report. Seattle: University of Washington, NBS/CPSU, College of Forest Resources.

Kochemer, J. P., and D. R. Johnson. 1995. Demography and socioeconomics of northern North America: Current status and impacts of climate change. In *Human Ecology and Climate Change: People and Resources in the Far North,* ed. D. L. Peterson and D. R. Johnson, 31–53. Washington, DC: Taylor and Francis.

Lloyd, W. F. 1833. *Two Lectures on the Checks to Population.* Oxford: Oxford University Press.

National Park Service (NPS). August 1997. *National Park Service Subsistence Management Program.* Alaska Regional Office, 2525 Gambell Street, Anchorage, Alaska 99503-2892.

———. September 26, 1995. *Draft Rural Residence and Resident Zone.* Alaska Regional Office, 2525 Gambell Street, Anchorage, Alaska 99503-2892.

Nelson, R. K. 1969. *Hunters of the Northern Ice.* Chicago: University of Chicago Press.

Platt, J. 1973. Social traps. *American Psychologist* 28(2): 641–51.

Robbins, L. A., and R. L. Little. 1984. *Effects of Renewable Resource Harvest Disruptions of Socioeconomic and Sociocultural Systems: St. Lawrence Island.* Alaska OCS Social and Economic Studies Program Technical Report 89. Anchorage: Minerals Management Service.

Sellars, R. W. 1997. *Preserving Nature in the National Parks: A History.* New Haven: Yale University Press.

Sloss, C. S. 1991. July 2. Personal communication. As quoted in Johnson et al. 1995. Mr. Sloss at the time of this communication was on the staff of the House Subcommittee on National Parks & Public Lands. He served as an aide to Representative Sieberling during the ANILCA years.

Stevens, S. 1997. The legacy of Yellowstone. In *Conservation through Cultural Survival Indigenous: Peoples and Protected Areas,* ed. S. Stevens, 13–32. Washington, DC: Island Press.

Sumida, V., and D. B. Andersen. 1990. *Patterns of Fish and Wildlife Use for Subsistence in Fort Yukon, Alaska.* Technical Paper No. 140. Juneau: Alaska Department of Fish and Game, Division of Subsistence.

Wolfe, R. J. 1998. Subsistence In Alaska: 1998 Update. Juneau: Alaska Department of Fish and Game, Division of Subsistence.

————. 1983. Understanding Resource Uses in Alaskan Socioeconomic Systems. In *Resource Use and Socioeconomic Systems: Case Studies of Fishing and Hunting in Alaskan Communities,* comp. R. J. Wolfe and L. J. Ellanna. Technical Paper No. 61: 248–74. Juneau: Alaska Department of Fish and Game, Division of Subsistence.

Wolfe, R. J., and R. Bosworth. 1990. *Subsistence in Alaska: A Summary.* Juneau: Alaska Department of Fish and Game, Division of Subsistence.

Chapter 8

Cape Cod: Challenges of
Managed Urbanization

William Kornblum

Cape Cod NS encompasses and preserves the windswept forearm of Cape Cod on the Atlantic shore of Massachusetts (see map 8.1). As in many other urbanizing regions of the continent, the presence of a national park at the region's most spectacular scenic destination has greatly stimulated state and local efforts to ensure more regional environmental preservation and "managed urbanization." This term simply refers to the evolution of ever more effective consensual strategies for understanding and controlling the processes of urbanization. The national seashore, with its traditional bipolar NPS mandate—to "preserve and protect" the Outer Cape, "for present and future generations of Americans"— has ensured that portions of the Outer Cape would remain accessible to the mass visiting public. Here, as elsewhere in scenic America, however, an initial social cost of resource protection and public use is found in the imposition of federal regulations, heightened enforcement and social control, and increased levels of local conflict. The very success of resource preservation and management on Cape Cod contributes to ongoing congestion and urbanization which, in turn, requires continued planning and management. This chapter examines the efforts made in the area of the seashore to mitigate these conflicts and to achieve successes in managing urbanization to preserve a semblance of the area's remote and rural seashore character.

Celebrated in the nineteenth-century writings of Henry David Thoreau (1951) and later in the beautiful images of Henry Beston for its remote beauty, teeming wildlife, and hardy salt hay farmers, Cape Cod and its beaches are now a magnet for vacation travelers and second-home owners from throughout the United States, and especially from the major metropolitan regions of Boston, New York, and Montreal. The remnants of an agrarian environment and the spacious dunes and beaches, however, remain essential economic and cultural features of the Cape Cod landscape, as they were earlier in American history.

Thoreau observed that the city and its busy port had begun to shape the life of this lonely and "natural" barrier beach in ways that were quite evident to concerned observers. All along the beach almost two centuries ago, the hiker or beachcomber found the detritus of a bustling commercial civilization. Such findings might include dead horses and cattle, garbage from the lumbering sailing freighters, beams and pilings from far-off docks and sunken ships, bits of clothing, or the washed-up carcass of a dead whale, its blubber stripped far at sea, tossed up on the sand for its bones to be picked clean by creatures of every phylum. The expanses of sand and dunes and sea are so great that they seemed to absorb these traces of human activity along the tide line. There was plenty of room still for the fox and the beaver, and flights of shorebirds darkened the sky during times of migration. So a wandering man could only imagine that he had turned his back on America; in reality America was even then promising to overwhelm the beaches and the oceans themselves with effluvium. The more fashionable invasions that would occur along all the beaches of the Northeast were

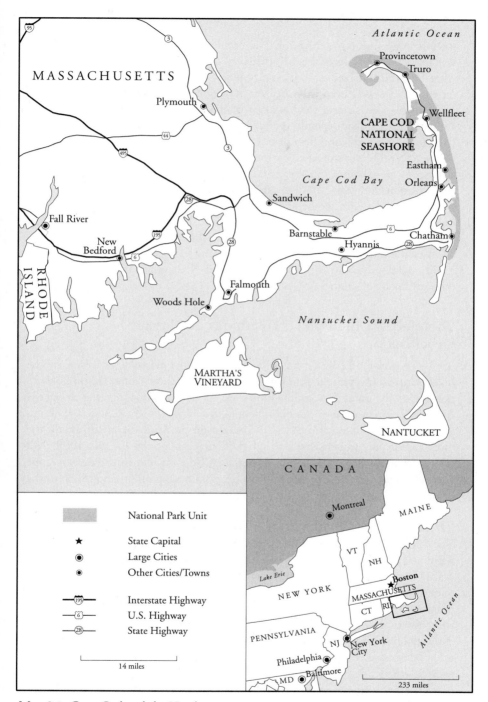

Map 8.1. Cape Cod and the Northeast

still off in an unimagined future. The population of Boston was entirely separate from that of Worcester and other surrounding towns, and New York, with what Thoreau considered its inferior beaches, was a competing commercial center a long trip away even from Boston itself (Thorndike 1987).

The ocean coasts and tidal lagoons of the Northeast are today far different and yet quite similar, depending on what level of reality one enters. Biologically, there is the same ebb and flow of tides, with the same currents of sand, the eternal winds and blooms of life. But socially, the place is changed so that the coast is almost everywhere a congested and settled strand of sand and roadway, with second-home and year-round populations, and commercial village centers interspersed with day and weekend beach users in a complex pattern of symbiotic roosting and private territoriality. Public beach lands comprise only about 10 percent of the shore here and throughout the United States. But with the creation of the national seashores has come a range of growth effects that can be readily documented in the case of Cape Cod NS, even if the causal links are more difficult to untangle.

Shoreline for the Public: Dilemmas of Managed Urbanization

Almost 143 million Americans reside in the counties classified as coastal by the U.S. National Ocean and Atmospheric Agency. Of these, about 62 million (23 percent of the total U.S. population) are in metropolitan regions along the Atlantic Coast. Another 37 million people live on the Pacific Coast, 27 million along the Great Lakes, and about 17 million on the Gulf Coast, at present the most rapidly urbanizing coast of all (U.S. Bureau of the Census 1999). All efforts to preserve coastal environments, as will be evident in the case of Cape Cod, become complex efforts at controlling and managing urban growth in the coastal zone.

The Seashore's Controversial Birth

The federal legislation to create Cape Cod NS and the other ten seashores now within the National Park System was justified during debates at midcentury, primarily as an effort to preserve the fragile barrier beach and bay lagoon ecosystems of major stretches of the nation's ocean shore. Proposals to bring the beaches of the Outer Cape under federal protection and jurisdiction, however, were always extremely controversial (King 1997). On the one hand, regional elites, many with private vacation homes on the Cape, led by the Kennedys and other Massachusetts elected officials, argued that without the creation of a federal park the Cape would continue to experience explosive residential and commercial growth that would efface its rural charm and threaten its natural environment. Boston newspapers often took up this theme:

While Cape Cod cogitates and Washington dallies, motels and beach cottages continue to go up. The longer the decision is deferred, the more expensive it will be, either way. Either Cape Cod will have a national park or it will become another shore resort, such as are to be found from New Jersey to Florida. There is talk now of a Miami Beach type hotel on North Beach (editorial, *Boston Herald,* June 6, 1960).

Local opponents of the legislation, many of whom were year-round residents of the six towns that were to be included as "in-held" enclaves within the proposed park boundaries, made surprisingly similar arguments against the park. They often asserted that creation of the seashore would add to congestion of roadways and beaches, and above all, alter the social ecology of the Outer Cape.

We feel that any uncertain benefits that may be derived from this bill are more than overbalanced by the fact that economic and sociological changes are bound to follow enactment of this legislation which will, for all practical purposes, destroy the identity of the town.

We feel that our present family vacation prototype, who stays from 2 weeks to a month, is attracted by uncrowded beaches, shopping and recreational facilities, and would be discouraged by the crowding of all these which a park would cause. Many of these people buy land and build homes, providing us with work through the winter. We cannot afford to lose them (statement of the Planning Board of the Town of Eastham, Massachusetts, at congressional hearings on a bill to provide for the establishment of Cape Cod National Seashore Park, Washington, DC, June 21, 1960).

Both sides admitted that commercialization and population growth were problems for the Cape, especially at its narrow and more fragile outer reaches, which were under consideration for inclusion in the seashore. But many local voices joined in the chorus of seashore opponents who claimed that local jurisdictions, enforcing local zoning ordinances, could manage land use better than "distant" bureaucrats in Washington. Pro-park advocates denied this assertion. They pointed often to the growing honky-tonk quality of commercialization along Route 6, the major and only arterial road from Eastham to Provincetown. Local opponents often countered this argument by citing the garish gateway effects of towns such as Gatlinburg at the entrance to Great Smokies NP. They claimed that establishment of areas within the seashore for day and weekend visitors would add to commercial pressures along Route 6, which would possibly obliterate the rural quality of small Cape villages such as Truro, Wellfleet, Eastham, and Orleans. One voice of reason in the often rancorous debates was the influential *Cape Codder,* which supported the legislation with clear-headed reservations about the necessity of the seashore and the continuing need for local planning as well:

> Let's face it! Of course the areas not included in the park are threatened by overcommercialization. But Architect Serge Chermayeff of Wellfleet [founder of an extremely prominent Boston urban planning firm] put the problem in focus when he observed that the taking for the park was not a quantity problem but a planning problem. It will not be easy to adopt the planning measures which will be necessary. But it is absurd to be so defeatist as to refuse to accept the fact that we can plan for ourselves. We do not have to allow the area to become a recreation slum (editorial in the *Cape Codder,* June 6, 1960).

These assertions and counterassertions are hardly unique. The creation of every major natural area park leaves some legacy of conflict, often at least superficially captured in the opposing testimonies of cosmopolitans and locals. But with the benefit of hindsight it is clear today that few observers or decision makers at the time came close to adequately anticipating the range of controversies that would follow the actual creation of the park. Assertions that local or even state governments could successfully answer the challenge of urban planning and management outside the seashore boundaries were extremely optimistic. And almost no voices explicitly raised the possibilities of conflict among Cape Cod's existing outdoor constituencies. These conflicts would erupt during the next three decades of the seashore's existence and present extremely difficult challenges to federal park managers and public officials at all levels of government. But these specific cases of conflict must be understood against a background of continuing urbanization in the entire region of Cape Cod.

An Exurban Wave Breaks on a Rural Shore
The story of demographic change on Cape Cod is told through the figures for population growth and urbanization in Barnstable County, which encompasses all eleven townships of Cape Cod east of the canal (of which six townships are within or adjacent to the seashore itself). The actual process of urbanization could more precisely be termed "exurban growth," since much of the population increase is accounted for by retirement migration, second-home construction, and development associated with tourism. These processes create high-growth, suburban-type dispersed settlements, which, however, are not oriented around metropolitan centers to allow for daily commutation (Cape Cod Commission and Land Use Collaborative 1997).

Table 8.1 shows that for an entire half century Barnstable County has been

Table 8.1. Selected Indicators of Urbanization on Cape Cod (Barnstable County, MA), 1950–1990

	1950	1960	1970	1980	1990
Total population	46,805	70,286	96,656	147,925	189,006
% increase	25.5	50.2	37.5	53.0	27.8
Population per sq. mile	117	176	246	370	478
In structures built <10 yr.	28.4	44.2	38.4	39.4	20.1
No. of farms	621	329	116	117	158

Source: U.S. Bureau of the Census 1998

growing at rates far above the national or state average. Between 1980 and 1990, for example, Cape Cod experienced a 27.8 percent increase in residential population, second in growth only to the smaller Dukes County (Martha's Vineyard). The growth of Massachusetts, in contrast, was only 4.5 percent. Estimates of the summer population of the Cape suggest that more than 500,000 persons reside there, about triple the county's official census population (Cape Cod Commission 1994). The residential population of the Outer Cape (Eastham to Provincetown) is estimated at 24,506, or approximately 13 percent of the county's total. The most rapid growth of this population occurs in the townships at the national seashore's southern border (Eastham 28.5 percent, versus 12.9 percent in Wellfleet and 1 percent in Provincetown). Tourists and seasonal residents account for about 44 percent of the region's economic base and retirees for another 15 percent. In consequence, more than 60 percent of all Cape employment is in the retail trade and service sectors (U.S. Bureau of Census 1998).

Between 1950 and 1960, as the debate continued over creation of the national seashore, the Cape Cod region experienced a 50 percent population increase, an alarming growth rate that helped speed the almost sixfold decline in farms in the county between 1950 and 1970. As noted above, this rapid growth has not abated in the county although it has declined somewhat on the Outer Cape, especially within the seashore's designated boundaries. Clearly, however, the fears of municipal leaders and local commercial interests of a drastic decline in home building and commercial development on the Cape were unfounded, at least on a countywide scale. If anything, creation of the seashore has contributed a new growth pole to Cape Cod residential development. Federal land-use controls have largely preserved the rural ambiance and the open dune and beach expanses of the Outer Cape while they have stimulated second-home and retirement-home construction everywhere else on sandy coasts and wooded uplands of the peninsula. By all reports, at this writing, the Cape is experiencing the hottest boom in home building and related construction since the mid-1980s (*Boston Globe,* June 4, 1998). There is no doubt that exurban growth patterns would have accelerated even without the seashore, and it is impossible to exactly apportion the seashore's contribution to this growth. On the other hand, most experts and local observers agree that the seashore has prevented even greater urbanization and commercialization on the great beach between East-ham and Provincetown (Cape Cod Commission and Land Use Collaborative 1997). The NPS itself estimates that creation of the seashore has prevented the construction of as many as 25,000 private homes on the Outer Cape (NPS 1998b).

Much of the residential growth of the Cape's population is accounted for by older adult and retirement migration from the Boston metropolitan region. This is another process that gives the Cape its exurban rather than suburban social ecology. Although the population of the Northeast, and of Massachusetts in particular, is aging faster than that of the United States, we see in figure 8.1 that residents over the age of sixty-five are a far more important proportion of the Cape's population than that of the state, and that this proportion has also been increasing more rapidly than it has for the state. At present, the median age of the Cape's residential population is 39.5, the highest in Massachusetts, for which the median age is about 33.6. On the Outer Cape the contrast is even more marked: the median age of Wellfleet residents is 40.6 and that of Chatham residents, 51.4. About 27 percent of the Outer Cape population is over age sixty-five (NPS 1998b).

Once a region has become established as the destination of retirement migra-

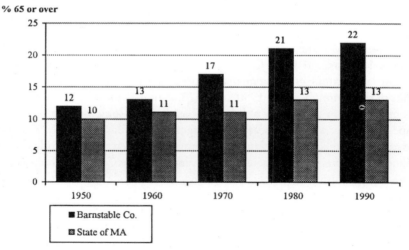

Figure 8.1. Cape Cod's Changing Age Structure (Barnstable County, MA), 1950–1990
Source: U.S. Bureau of the Census 1998

tion, it can be expected to accommodate increased flows of retired-home seek-ers. Indeed, this growth pattern does not yet reflect the large increases in retire-ment among the baby-boom generation. The aging of this massive population cohort and its search for convenient retirement communities may place even greater population pressures on the Cape's already stressed land and water resources.

Concerns about water resources, and especially about runoff from residential properties into the Cape's groundwater table, are high among problems that state, county, and municipal planners are seeking to address (Eichner 1993). So are problems of traffic and labor supply (Brelis 1998; Robertson 1998). All of these are clearly related to the unabated population growth the Cape is experi-encing and none admit to easy solutions. Traffic problems are particularly vex-ing on the Cape. On peak summer and weekend hours, the traffic at the two bridges over the canal can be backed up for over an hour, which vastly con-tributes to problems of air pollution and the spread of the very honky-tonk strip developments along the traffic corridor on which original seashore arguments focused. NPS planners note: "The public often perceives that national seashore visitors are the primary contributors to traffic congestion. However, a 1993 sur-vey of visitors indicates that over 75% specified their primary destinations as particular towns or the Outer Cape region, and not specifically the national seashore" (NPS 1998b:163). Whatever its destinations, traffic on Route 6 on the Outer Cape is a severe problem in the peak season. Robert Mumford, the transportation program manager for the Cape Cod Commission, laments the inability of transportation planning resources to keep up with development. Throughout the county: "It is very frustrating because you are always playing catch-up. You get money and resources to make improvements, and they are very rapidly eaten up by development, which creates more traffic" (quoted in Brelis 1998).

The problem of labor supply, on the other hand, is less obvious to the pub-lic but quite similar to that experienced in most of the nation's major exurban recreation regions (e.g., in the region of Jackson Hole, Wyoming, or in most of the ski regions of the Colorado Rockies). Cape Cod employers in 1998 hired approximately 1,600 nonnational workers, mostly dishwashers and chamber-maids, to do what employers here cannot find locals to do. Importation of out-side labor, often from foreign shores, is increasing by an average of more than 50 percent a year over the past few years. This seasonal labor migration is asso-ciated with severe problems of housing a temporary labor force. Seasonal hous-ing shortages constitute a feature of the exurban, recreation, and vacation-based population change on Cape Cod that is not likely, given the region's popularity, to ease in the foreseeable future (Robertson 1998).

Most planners and policymakers who deal with Cape Cod's growth problems are seeking to institute some form of land banking and regional funding of infrastructure investments (Cape Cod Commission and Land Use Collaborative 1997). There is a growing consensus on the Cape, as on eastern Long Island, and elsewhere in major exurban recreation regions of the United States, that the preservation of existing open space is the only possible way to arrive at population stabilization and reasonable land-use controls (Tin 1995; Farragher 1998). For years, however, efforts to create a land bank or some other effective system of rural land protection on the Cape, in areas outside the seashore, have been frustrated. Nevertheless, it would appear in recent years that innovations by the NPS and its governmental and community allies within the network of seashore advocates are again showing the possibilities of reasonable solutions to what once seemed intractable problems.

Since the seashore's creation there has been a history of extremely active citizen involvement in managing the Outer Cape's resources. The Cape Cod National Seashore Advisory Commission and the larger Cape Cod Commission have been centrally involved with NPS management in developing land-use policies and regulations designed to protect environmental resources. Most of the controversies over land use, and especially those involving implementation of federal regulations over public behavior, have been played out within the context of the cooperating citizen commissions. In this sense, the seashore has helped foster expectations and successes in cooperative planning that appear to encourage similar efforts on a countywide basis. A brief review of social problems that have been successfully addressed at the seashore highlight the challenges and achievements of arriving at consensual social control of public use and exurban development and perhaps suggest solutions to the current situation of runaway exurban sprawl.

With Constabulatory Duties . . . an Unhappy Seashore

The extent to which creation of Cape Cod NS would entail restrictions of traditional recreation activities on the Outer Cape was never explicitly discussed in the legislative history. Hunting, clamming, bass fishing, beach camping, driving on the beach, dirt biking, and nude bathing are all examples of popular activities that have become, at one time or another, the focus of rancorous conflict, contentious rulings, and increased constabulatory responsibilities for seashore rangers. As NPS officials began to exert the resource controls required of land-use managers under federal law, they quickly found themselves in conflict with particular recreation constituencies, many with long-standing traditions of Cape Cod use. Unquestionably, the most difficult and frustrating for resource managers and public constituencies alike has been the controversy over off-road vehicles (ORVs) on the Great Beach from Eastham to Provincetown, the national seashore's prime resource.

Long before the seashore was created, a hardy group of bass fishermen on the

Cape, many of them local residents, had developed a homegrown technology for striped bass surf fishing. This entailed the use of modified step delivery vans, outfitted for camping (long before the advent of Winnebago campers), with oversized tires and surfboats on their roofs. These vans were considered a colorful feature of the summer and fall fishing season. The fishermen drove their vans over the beach until they spotted fish feeding near the shore. At that point they stopped and used their vans to assist in launching the surfboats. At night the fishermen camped on the wide open beaches, sometimes in small clusters of friends, other times alone in a single van. By the 1970s, as the NPS established a presence on the Outer Cape, various environmentalist constituencies were petitioning the NPS to limit ORV use on the Great Beach. They claimed that beach vehicles were destroying vital dune grasses, leaving ruts in the sand, causing various forms of pollution, and threatening nesting birds. This development coincided with the beginnings of commercial production of four-wheel-drive vehicles and mass-produced camper vans, whose users began increasing the numbers of surf fishermen seeking to drive the beach. The protected beaches of the Outer Cape were also becoming increasingly popular among day and weekend visitors: visits to the seashore doubled from about 1.2 million in 1970 to more than 3 million by 1980, and now generally exceed 5 million visits per year. This level of use, which includes repeat visits and visits by one person to more than one area of the seashore on a single day, places the seashore as the ninth most heavily used unit in the National Park System (NPS 1998b). The need for the NPS to adequately develop facilities for the growing user population, and to establish control over the resources placed under its stewardship, made clear the need for a seashore master plan and a special management plan addressed to the use of beach vehicles within seashore boundaries. In 1981, twenty years after its creation, the NPS published its ORV Management Plan, which placed limits on the number of permits it would allow ORV users, designated proper equipment for beach vehicles, and, most controversially, set limits of areas of the seashore where ORVs could be driven.

The 1981 ORV Management Plan was attacked by ORV lobbying groups and environmental organizations alike. Longtime ORV users were particularly incensed over what they regarded as infringements of their traditional rights. Most of this group also recognized that the mass production of off-road vehicles signaled the end of an era of traditional beach buggy use. Many recognized that they would somehow have to make accommodations to the conflicting demands of preservation and off-road vehicle use. But hotheads among them refused to accept the new order of social control. There were many extremely rancorous public meetings about the regulations and numerous acts of violence, including the torching of a national seashore beach visitor center in the early 1980s. Nor were environmentalist lobbying groups more accommodating. Although more equipped to press their claims through administrative and legal channels, environmentalist groups, led by the Conservation Law Foundation, pressed the NPS to eliminate ORV use within the seashore entirely and in 1981 brought suit against the NPS in federal court. Their basic claim was that existing and regulated ORV use was not appropriate for a national seashore. The Conservation Law Foundation also faulted the NPS for never having surveyed park users and Outer Cape residents as to their views concerning the appropriateness of ORV uses and whether they found their enjoyment of the seashore impaired by existing regulated use. In consequence, the federal judge directed the seashore to conduct such a survey, which was then undertaken by this author and his colleagues at the City University of New York (Kornblum and Meyersohn 1984). All parties in the dispute assisted in the design of the study, but when its results were published and it appeared that most beach users were not negatively affected by existing ORV use, the study's adequacy was challenged in the court proceedings as well.

In the meantime, the NPS had already amended its ORV regulations in 1985 such that ORV use was limited to a designated 8.5-mile corridor in the vicinity of Race Point. The suit, however, was not settled or withdrawn. Finally, in 1988 the Federal District Court ruled that:

> ORV use at Cape Cod NS is not inappropriate; that the 1985 amended Plan minimized user conflicts; that the NPS had properly surveyed the sentiments of seashore users; and that ORV use, as managed by the NPS, does not adversely affect the seashore's values or its ecology (NPS 1998a: 9143).

This decision was upheld by the U.S. Court of Appeals in 1989.

By the early 1990s, the existing ORV use policies had become incapable of meeting changed environmental conditions. The population of nesting pairs of piping plover, an endangered species which hatches its chicks on the beach berm above the high-tide line, had increased by about 800 percent in the designated 8.5-mile ORV use zone. To avoid repetition of the rancorous, extremely costly, and demoralizing litigious conflict that marked the earlier round of ORV regulation, the NPS proposed, in the late 1990s, to enter into a process that would seek to arrive at a consensus among all interested parties. The success of this effort represents a model of negotiation and conflict resolution which, in various forms and applications, can point the way toward resolution of many other urbanization issues that are threatening the Cape's future. But successful resolution of the rancorous ORV case would not have been conceivable without the existence and sustained involvement of the Cape Cod Commission, the National Seashore Advisory Commission, and a host of other local and regional planning and advocacy groups, many of which experienced their initial success and early growth through the creation of the seashore itself.

Negotiated Rulemaking: A New Era for Cape Cod?

In the language of the NPS:

> The objective of negotiated rulemaking was to front load the controversy by getting all the interested parties involved in the decision making process from the beginning and acknowledging, if not resolving, all the issues and concerns. The process brings together at the negotiating table the organizations that are interested in the issues and charges them with developing a solution that is acceptable to everyone (NPS 1998a: 9144).

Other federal and state agencies have used negotiated rule making to resolve highly contentious issues, but this is the first instance in which the NPS has used the process to develop a rule that will be incorporated as part of the Code of Federal Regulations.

As a precedent for future negotiations over the complicated issues of land banking, traffic regulation, and aquifer restoration, the NPS-negotiated rule making of the ORV issue is remarkable on a number of counts. First, it offered membership on the negotiating committee to a broad representation of twenty-three discrete entities. These were all agencies, organizations, and interest groups "with long-term interests and involvement" in the ORV issue. Included were national-level organizations, such as the Sierra Club; regional entities, such as the Cape Cod Commission and the Massachusetts Beach Buggy Association; relevant state and federal conservation agencies; and representatives of the six Outer Cape towns. Second, each organization was required to designate one representative for inclusion at the negotiating table and only this representative could put forward the opinions and desires of that particular constituency, although all concerned individuals were invited to comment on the rules once they were published in draft form. Each person at the table had a veto on resolutions so that the committee's work would represent consensus decisions on each issue. Professional negotiators had been contracted to facilitate the sessions, each of which was announced beforehand and was open to the public.

At the end of the long process of discussion, rule making, public review, and comment, the committee's diligent work did arrive at a new and far more flexible set of policies and rules governing the issuance of ORV permits at the seashore. It established a system for the scientific monitoring of ORV impacts and arrived at a complex set of rules for shifting the ORV corridor depending on changing patterns of piping plover nesting on the beaches. An important portion of the cost of administering the ORV-use regulations will be paid by the $60 permit fee levied on the 3,500 annual ORV users allowed by the new regulations. And for the first time since the seashore's creation, NPS managers are enforcing a set of regulations that have been adopted through a democratic process of consensual rule making, which makes their inevitable constabulatory duties far easier if never happy.

Prospects for Managed Urbanization on Cape Cod

How well do lessons like those demonstrated in the process of ORV-negotiated rule making generalize to other issues of social control and land-use management on Cape Cod? At this writing, the paramount issue of preservation of existing open space beyond the seashore appears to be close to resolution after years of debate and conflict. A system of preserving open space for Cape Cod, as noted earlier, is the vital step toward managing the explosive population growth that threatens the future of the region's rural, but essentially exurban, social ecology.

Early in 1998, after ten years of attempts by planners and state legislators to institute a regional tax to fund land banking, Cape Cod voters soundly defeated a proposal for a new real estate tax that would have paid for the preservation of open space on the Cape. A proposal in the referendum would also have funded measures to protect groundwater resources. The defeated proposal would have established a 1 percent tax on all real estate transactions, to be paid by the seller, with the first $100,000 of the sale price exempted. In 1998 money from such a tax would have raised $6 million, which would have been distributed to the fifteen towns and designated for the purchase of undeveloped land. Notably, opposition to the new tax was strongest in the heavily developed towns of the Upper Cape and Mid-Cape. The measure won majorities in the townships within and adjacent to the national seashore, evidence that the environmental ethics that created the seashore are becoming part of the political culture of the Outer Cape. It should also be noted that properties on the Outer Cape are among the most valuable in the region and would have been most subjected to the proposed tax.

Fortunately, the proposed real estate transfer tax was not the only proposal under consideration. In June 1998, the Massachusetts legislature recognized that growth and traffic problems on the Cape were reaching crisis proportions. It therefore passed a bill backed by a coalition of political leaders, environmentalists, bankers, and realtors to save much of the Cape's remaining open space. In place of the rejected real estate transfer fee, the legislators imposed a 3 percent surcharge on all Cape property tax bills. The money would be used to acquire open space in the taxpayer's own community. Because the funds will be collected yearly from all property owners, the individual tax burden is less onerous than under the earlier proposal.

Unquestionably, this legislation marks a crucial turning point in efforts to manage the urbanization of Cape Cod. Even before it was passed, the number of working farms on the Cape was gradually increasing after decades of decline (see table 8.1). But land banking is a necessary but not sufficient measure to preserve the Cape's environment. The costs of funding traffic circulation improvements will be immense. So will proposed solutions to the accelerating pollution and salinization of the Cape's essential groundwater resources. After a generation of struggle to arrive at solutions that would maximize public enjoyment of the Cape's outstanding resources, while somehow preserving its environment and at least a semblance of its rural ambiance, there is hard evidence that creation of the national seashore was a turning point in the region's history. From the inevitable problems of social control and fitful efforts to manage urbanization has emerged an effective regional planning body, the Cape Cod Commission, which has successfully applied many of the environmental lessons gained originally at the seashore.

References

Boston Globe. 1998 (June 4). Consensus on saving the Cape. *Boston Globe,* p. A18.

Boston Herald. 1960 (June 6). In Legislative Hearings, op. cit.

Brelis, Matthew. 1998 (May 31). Getting there (eventually). *Boston Globe,* p. D1.

Cape Cod Commission. 1994. *Cape Trends: Demographic and Economic Characteristics and Trends—Barnstable County, Cape Cod.* 2nd ed. Barnstable, MA: Cape Cod Commission.

Cape Cod Commission and Land Use Collaborative. 1997. *The Outer Cape Capacity Study.* 4 vols. Barnstable, MA: Cape Cod Commission.

Cape Codder. 1960 (June 6). Reprinted in *Hearings Before the Subcommittee on Public Lands.* U.S. Senate, Washington, DC, June 21, 1960, 389.

Eichner, Eduard M. 1993. Watershed protection: A Cape Cod perspective on national efforts. *Environmental Science and Technology* 27: 1736–39.

Farragher, Thomas. 1998 (January 20). Land battle on the Cape: Voters to act on tax plan. *Boston Globe,* p. A1.

King, Seth S. 1997 (January 14). Cape Cod, worried about fresh water supplies, seeks to rein in growth. *New York Times* (late New York edition), p. A10.

Kornblum, William, and Meyersohn, Rolf. 1984. *ORV Use at Cape Cod National Seashore.* Unpublished report to the National Park Service, Cooperative Park Studies Unit. New York: City University of New York Graduate School.

National Park Service (NPS). 1998a. Cape Cod National Seashore: Off-Road Vehicle Use. *Federal Register* 63(38): 9143–48.

———. 1998b. *Forging a Collaborative Future, Vol. 1: Environmental Impact Statement for the General Management Plan.* Washington, DC: U.S. Department of the Interior, National Park Service.

Robertson, Tatsha. 1998 (May 23). Longing for labor. *Boston Globe,* p. B1.

Thoreau, Henry David. 1951. *Cape Cod* (reprint ed.). New York: W. W. Norton.

Thorndike, Joseph Jacobs. 1987. Thoreau walks the Cape. *American Heritage* 38: 70–75.

Tin, Annie. 1995. Coastal management grants OK'd by subcommittee. *Congressional Quarterly Weekly Report* 53: 3204.

United States Bureau of the Census. 1999. *Statistical Abstract.* Washington, DC: U.S. Department of Commerce, Bureau of the Census.

————. 1998. *County and City Data Book.* Washington, DC: U.S. Department of Commerce, Bureau of the Census.

Chapter 9

Development by Default, Not Design: Yellowstone National Park and the Greater Yellowstone Ecosystem

Dennis Glick and Ben Alexander

> We regard the passage of this act [the creation of Yellowstone Park] as a great blow struck at the prosperity of the towns of Bozeman and Virginia City which might naturally look to considerable travel to this section, if it were opened to the curious but comfort-loving public.
>
> *Helena Rocky Mountain Gazette,* 1872

> If the people of Gardiner cannot refrain from slaughtering the game of the park, then it is time for the American people to summon the town of Gardiner before the bar of public opinion to show cause why the town should not be wiped off the map.
>
> *Naturalist William Hornaday,* 1913

When Yellowstone NP was created in 1872, it was a wilderness surrounded by more wilderness with few political or administrative boundaries crisscrossing the landscape. Today, the 2.2-million-acre park sits on the northwest corner of the state of Wyoming with a sliver of Montana and Idaho forming its northern and western borders. Seven national forests encircle the park and twenty state counties further define the 18-million-acre region known as the Greater Yellowstone Ecosystem (GYE; see map 9.1). This chapter examines the relationship of the park to its larger ecosystem and the continuing struggle to find balance between protection and development.

From its inception, Yellowstone NP has been viewed as a treasure trove of natural wonders on the one hand, and as a cash cow on the other. The popular account of the founding of Yellowstone, the world's first national park, holds that the idea was conceived by one of the early exploratory parties. In fact, an agent for the Northern Pacific Railroad Company who recognized the enormous tourism potential of this "wonderland" passed on to Washington the suggestion, "Let Congress pass a bill reserving the Great Geyser Basin as a public park forever" (Sax 1980:6). The Northern Pacific Railroad later became the principal means of access to Yellowstone and its first concessionaire providing services for tourists (Sax 1980). [*Editors' Note:* For additional discussion, see chapter 3.]

With the campfires of the early Yellowstone explorers still smoldering, the area was already locked into its duel role as wildlife sanctuary and income generator. The controversies resulting from this schizophrenia are as legendary as the geyser basins themselves. They have not abated in the past 125 years. At the beginning of the twenty-first century, the inability of the NPS and the communities that surround Yellowstone to resolve these issues threatens the well-being of both.

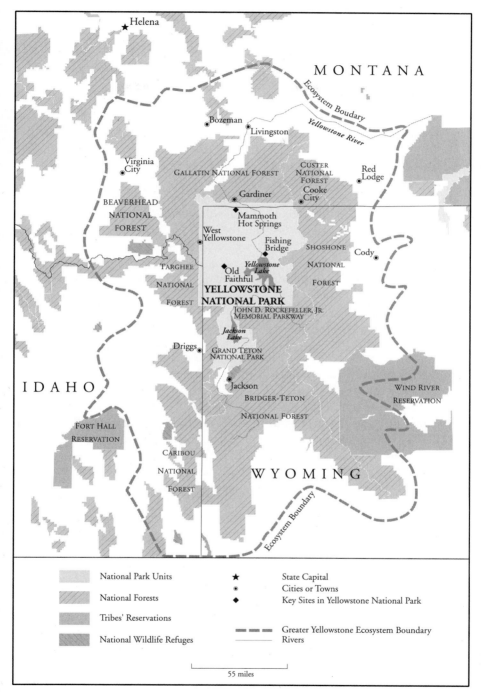

Map 9.1. Greater Yellowstone

A Historical Perspective

To understand the current role that Yellowstone plays in rural development, it is helpful to know the colorful and often conflict-ridden history of the park's relationship to regional economies and communities. Unlike most national parks, Yellowstone was created before the establishment of the surrounding gateway towns.

Scattered bands of Shoshoni Indians were observed by white fur trappers of the early 1800s, such as Jim Bridger and John Colter (Haines 1977). Their tales of "wonderful fountains that project a column of boiling water to a height of more than one hundred and fifty feet" (Phillips 1940:257–58) began to filter out of the region. It was the prospect of gold, not geysers, that attracted the next wave of visitors in the 1860s. Some of these prospectors established camps in or near what is now Yellowstone NP, and their activities stimulated commerce in the recently established communities of Bozeman and Virginia City, in Montana Territory.

Government-sponsored expeditions in the 1870s confirmed many of the fabulous tales of boiling mud and exploding geysers. Talk of protecting the region as an area that "ought to be kept for the public in some way" (Cook 1922:22) resonated with eastern politicians. Railroad promoter Nathaniel Langford, the former governor of the newly created Montana Territory, realized that this spectacular area and its natural curiosities could be just the carrot needed to gain financial support for the construction of the Northern Pacific Railroad through the region.

Debate in Congress over the bill that proposed "to conserve for public use this country for a public park" was relatively brief and tame (Haines 1977:169). The initial bill was introduced in December 1871 and signed into law by President Ulysses S. Grant on March 1, 1872. Though the concept was generally supported, early political opponents such as Senator Cornelius Cole of California, chair of the Senate Appropriations Committee, protested, "I do not know why settlers should be excluded from a tract of land forty square miles in the Rocky Mountains or any other place" (Haines 1977:170). Locally, the *Helena Rocky Mountain Gazette* editorialized that creating a park would "keep the country a wilderness and shut out travelers for many years. . . . A great blow struck at the prosperity of the towns of Bozeman and Virginia City which might naturally look to considerable travel to this section, if it were thrown open to the curious but comfort-loving public" (*Helena Rocky Mountain Gazette* 1872:1).

Such a contemptuous view of the national park concept by some regional and national politicians and press has been a recurring theme since the founding of Yellowstone NP. Even early proponents of preservation were, for the most part, keenly aware of the potential economic benefits this "wonderland" could provide. The *Helena Herald,* which promoted the creation of the park, sagely predicted that park establishment would be "a means of centering upon Montana the attention of thousands heretofore comparatively uninformed of a Territory abounding in such resources of mines and agricultural and of wonderland as we can boast, spread everywhere about us" (*Helena Herald* 1872:1). The writer understood early on that the park would serve as a magnet, drawing people and businesses into the entire region.

The official designation of Yellowstone as the world's first national park by no means guaranteed its protection. Initially it was hoped that the Northern Pacific Railroad would arrive bearing tourists who, in turn, would support concessionaires. The concessionaires, through their franchise fees, would finance park protection and development (Haines 1977).

Following the depression of 1873, insolvency halted railroad construction for six years. Tourists were few and far between and little progress was made installing visitor services. Regional communities were quick to voice their displeasure: "What has the national government done to render this elephant approachable and attractive since its adoption as one of the nation's pets? Nothing!" (*Bozeman Avant Courier* 1874:2). Already, regional communities were developing a sense of entitlement toward the potential benefits of the park.

The first visitor facilities consisted of a crude log hotel and bathhouse built at Mammoth Hot Springs in the early 1870s. But isolation and incidents like the kidnapping of park visitors by Nez Perce kept tourist numbers, and concessionaire franchise fees, low. Infrastructure development and resource protection languished. Finally, in 1878, Congress appropriated the first federal funds ($10,000) for park development.

Still, progress in opening the park to tourism seemed to local business interests to be moving at a snail's pace. The editor of the *Bozeman Avant Courier* in particular frequently attacked the character and accomplishments of then Superintendent Philetus Norris. The *Courier* speculated that Norris favored Virginia City businesses over those of Bozeman by cooperating in the development of a mail route between Virginia City and the park. Bad press and political pressure resulted in Norris's being replaced by a succession of three civilian superintendents over a period of four and a half years. Norris would not be the last park superintendent skewered by the local press.

During this period the so-called Yellowstone Park Improvement Company attempted to secure a contract as the sole park concessionaire. This position would have included exclusive development rights on several square miles of parkland. The ensuing scandal, coupled with the continued destruction of park features, resulted in the arrival in 1886 of soldiers from the First United States Cavalry, who managed the park for thirty two years until the creation of the NPS.

In 1883, the Yellowstone Park Improvement Company announced its intention to construct a railroad linking the northwest corner of the park to the northeast corner. Several bills related to railroad construction were introduced into both the Senate and the House. Though eventually defeated, this incident underscored the fragility of the national park ideal and the strength of local and national business interests in manipulating park management to meet their economic aspirations.

While the principal economic activities of regional communities were varied—agriculture in Bozeman, railroading in Livingston, ranching in Jackson Hole, mining in Cooke City—the park and its growing number of tourists helped to diversify and expand these economies. These communities were also varied in their views on park protection issues. On the one hand, the illegal slaughter of wildlife was decried. The *Bozeman Avant Courier* warned, "If Yellowstone National Park is to be reserved and preserved from despoliation, then the grass subsisting, inoffensive game which may be found therein, or can by any means be induced to take up its abode there, should be sacredly preserved from wanton destruction" (*Bozeman Avant Courier* 1883:1). On the other hand, the perpetrators of many poaching problems resided in these same communities and received a certain amount of local sympathy. This infuriated park personnel such as naturalist William Hornaday, who insinuated that the town of Gardiner be "wiped off the map."

By the turn of the century, with railroads now serving the area, tourism began to increase. Before 1877, no more than 500 visitors entered the park in any given year (Haines 1977). Towns such as Livingston to the north and Cody to the east, while not gateway communities per se, still served as jumping-off points for eastern tourists anxious to see the wonders of Yellowstone. Improved roads and the construction of large, comfortable hotels such as the Canyon Hotel completed in 1911, the Lake Hotel built at the turn of the century, and the Old Faithful Inn completed in 1904 met a growing demand.

Visitor services continued to improve over the next several decades. In 1911, the Gallatin Automobile Association in Bozeman attempted to organize an automobile tour of the park as part of a movement to force revocation of the rule excluding automobiles from Yellowstone (Haines 1977). Their efforts led to Senate Resolution 275, which called on the War Department to study the costs of making the Yellowstone road system suitable for automobile traffic. In 1913 a section of park road was opened to vehicular traffic. The park would never be the same.

As both Yellowstone and the surrounding regions developed, park managers realized that while the park was large (approximately 2 million acres), its boundaries did not encompass sufficient habitat to preserve much of its wildlife. As early as 1882 General Sheridan suggested doubling the size of Yellowstone to make it a better game sanctuary. In 1918 legislation was introduced into Congress proposing the addition of 1,265 square miles of wildlands to the existing park (Yellowstone National Park 1919). Initially receiving widespread support, the bill eventually died largely because of opposition by Jackson Hole cattlemen.

At a 1919 public meeting in Jackson, proponents of the extension, including Senator Kendrick of Wyoming and Park Superintendent Horace Albright, were "hooted off the platform by the enraged citizens" (Ross 1927:8).

North of the park, the editor of the *Livingston Enterprise* commented that national public opinion on the extension "is powerful enough and overlooks local interests to such extent that the park authorities can appeal to the nation and obtain results which will work hardships on communities close to the park" (*Livingston Enterprise* 1920:1). Though local communities felt the park was running roughshod over their interests, in fact, national conservation goals were often derailed by local economic interests.

This failed effort to enlarge the park and the animosity it engendered set the stage for the twentieth century's often stormy relationship between the NPS and its neighbors. The struggle for control of park resources continued in the 1920s. Idaho politicians attempted to capture Yellowstone's water resources by proposing reservoir construction in the basins of the Falls and Bechler Rivers within the park to supply water for Idaho potato farmers. William Gregg, a member of the recently formed National Parks Foundation, a nongovernmental conservation group, explored the area proposed for development and declared it "a camper's paradise, with good fishing and an abundance of wildlife" (Gregg 1921:474). As a result of this trip, Gregg formulated a set of guidelines for parks and the interested public. They included the following:

- National Parks are created for the whole public.
- No commercial project—for private advantage—must be permitted.
- Park extensions should be advocated only after careful and unprejudiced study of reasons for and against them.
- The motives of plausible persons who express great devotion for the parks they wish to exploit are always to be suspected.
- Persons living near a national park who feel themselves harmed by their situation must bear their burden cheerfully (Gregg 1921:474).

This was one of the first interventions by a nongovernmental conservation organization in a park development issue. Despite these recommendations, the assaults continued. For example, a bill was introduced into the Sixty-sixth Congress (later defeated) to allow the state of Montana to build a dam on the Yellowstone River within the park for downstream flood control.

Succeeding decades saw increased tourism-related construction along park boundaries and entrance roads. By the second half of the century, Yellowstone-related tourism was no longer a business, it was an industry. Not only was visitation growing (by 1950, annual visitation had topped 1 million), but the seasonality of tourism was also changing. In 1949, snowplane tours were conducted between West Yellowstone and Old Faithful, allowing thirty-five people to experience the park in winter (Yellowstone National Park 1989). By the winter of

1993–1994, the number of winter visitors had risen to 143,000, most of these individuals traveling on snowmobiles or in snow coaches (Yellowstone National Park 1997). Communities such as West Yellowstone and Cody became enthusiastic promoters of snow machines as a means of generating tourist dollars during what had been the long, lean winter season.

By the time the park had celebrated its 100th birthday in 1972, "recreation and tourism had surpassed the agricultural and livestock industries as the economic base of the region" (NPS 1972:5). In that year, the park issued a new master plan that addressed some of the growing concerns about the impacts of tourism within the park and the affects of increasing development outside park boundaries. The plan stated, "With the nation and the park facing an environmental crisis, it should be apparent that to have both [i.e., a pleasuring ground and preservation] is to have neither . . . " (NPS 1972:2). It went on to suggest that the park should "perpetuate the natural systems within the park in as near pristine conditions as possible for their inspirational, educational, cultural, and scientific values for this and future generations" (NPS 1972:2).

Reflecting a growing national concern for the environment and a clearer understanding of the relationship between the ecological health of the park and the environmental quality of the surrounding landscape, the new master plan recommended a number of bold initiatives. For example, the plan stated that regional and local planning and zoning (on private lands) be established and "vigorously enforced." It also called for restructuring visitor use, including scaled-back overnight facilities and revised park transportation systems. It could be argued that many of these ideas, such as using regional communities to assume a greater role in providing visitor services, could have benefited gateway economies. Nevertheless, many of the more progressive recommendations, like turning Old Faithful into a day-use-only facility, were met by local opposition and never implemented.

More recent park controversies are, to a great degree, variations of the same conflict between preservation interests and business interests, with the NPS caught in the crossfire. One of the proposed actions in the 1972 master plan called for removal of campgrounds and associated visitor facilities at Fishing Bridge, on the north end of Yellowstone Lake. The array of services coupled with the attraction of lakeside camping made this a popular destination, especially for tourists arriving from Cody and the park's east entrance.

In the early 1970s, it became clear that Fishing Bridge was also popular with grizzly bears. Spawning cutthroat trout and other habitat features attracted bears to this busy area, often resulting in human-bear confrontations. More than fifty bears had to be "removed." Park biologists and environmentalists demanded elimination or relocation of these facilities as per a recommendation in the master plan. However, opposition by Cody businessmen, who feared that removal of visitor services would reduce traffic through their town, hobbled these plans.

Park Superintendent Bob Barbee noted that "the National Park Service under-estimated the political bottom line" (Greater Yellowstone Coalition 1987:9). That bottom line related to the profit margin of gateway community businesses. Business owners' ability to mobilize their congressional delegation to intervene at the highest levels of the NPS was a vivid display of local interest shaping national park policies.

The massive Yellowstone NP fires of 1988 brought into sharp focus the con-flict between restoration of ecological processes and pursuit of economic devel-opment goals. The release of the so-called Leopold Report in 1963, which rec-ommended that national parks be managed using ecological principles, resulted in a greater tolerance for wildfire (Sellers 1997). During the summer of 1988, record heat, drought, and wind churned up the wildfires of the century in Yel-lowstone, ultimately affecting 1.4 million acres of the park. The tempers of regional residents were as hot as the conflagrations that nearly overran the towns of Cooke City and West Yellowstone.

Park managers were denounced in the press, in local coffee shops, and on the floor of Congress. Wyoming Senator Alan Simpson declared that "the incinera-tion of Yellowstone is a startling, devastating and dramatic disaster. Let me tell you colleagues, the ground is sterilized. It is blackened to the very depths of any root system within it" (Williams 1989:64). Though scientists were nearly uni-versal in their support of this "let burn" policy, regional residents believed that the fires had destroyed their multimillion-dollar tourism industry (although the following year the park saw record visitation). Yellowstone Superintendent Bob Barbee took the brunt of the criticism. In hindsight, he said, "I now realize fully that when the stakes are perceived to be high, trying to hang on to the fundamental values of parks and wilderness areas becomes more difficult" (Ekey et al. 1990:104). Again, those "stakes" related more to perceived mone-tary losses associated with lowered visitor numbers than to the loss of natural treasures.

In the 1990s, not only did recreation grow in and around the park, but resource extraction on the public lands of the region and development of rural private lands continued to erode the ecological integrity of what had become known as the Greater Yellowstone Ecosystem (GYE). On the national forests of Greater Yellowstone, more than 7,500 miles of forest roads had been built, bil-lions of board feet of timber had been cut, and half the public lands were open to grazing (Glick et al. 1991). A building boom on the private lands was trans-forming farms and ranches into leapfrog subdivisions, ranchettes, and trophy homes.

Recognition by scientists and environmentalists that Yellowstone NP was but a piece of a much larger ecosystem spawned the concept of a GYE that encom-passes approximately 18 million acres, including Yellowstone NP and Grand Teton NP, seven national forests, three national wildlife refuges, approximately

3 million acres of private land, and more than a dozen communities with nearly 300,000 residents. Though ecologically connected, administratively and politically the area is highly fragmented. More than twenty-five different resource management agencies and committees hold jurisdiction over various parts of the ecosystem. And the region itself encompasses portions of three states (Idaho, Montana, and Wyoming) and twenty counties (Glick and Clark 1998).

Conflicts between the U.S. Forest Service and the NPS (as exemplified by the hundreds of square miles of clear-cuts on the Targhee National Forest on Yellowstone's western boundary) spurred the creation of the Greater Yellowstone Coordinating Committee (GYCC). This body includes the superintendents of Yellowstone NP and Grand Teton NP, the supervisors of the seven national forests, and other regional officials from both agencies. Among its goals is the desire to improve communication and coordination between land management agencies (Greater Yellowstone Coordinating Committee 1987).

In the late 1980s and early 1990s, the GYCC crafted what became known as the GYCC vision document. This precedent-setting initiative sought to identify shared management goals and strategies for national parks and national forests of Greater Yellowstone. Initially, vision goals stressed the desire to "conserve the sense of naturalness and maintain ecological integrity" (Greater Yellowstone Coordinating Committee 1990). The other two principal goals related to economic concerns, and community relations and coordination. They included the desire to "encourage opportunities that are biologically and economically sustainable" and "improve mechanisms to cooperate and coordinate with federal agencies, state and local governments, private land owners, and Greater Yellowstone area users" (Greater Yellowstone Coordinating Committee 1990).

This initiative was significant in many ways. First, it signaled an acknowledgement by land managers that Greater Yellowstone represents an interconnected ecosystem that is being degraded, in part, because of their own management activities and conflicting mandates. The vision document also seemed to imply the end of business as usual for the extractive industries (timber, mining, oil and gas development, and public land grazing) and a fostering of more environmentally benign development strategies. Finally, the emphasis on conserving naturalness and ecological integrity supported the claim of environmentalists that the highest and best use of these public lands is the protection of their natural values.

Advocates of the vision stressed both the ecological and economic benefits that would accrue from its implementation. However, many regional businesses and elected officials, and nearly all of the extractive industries, organized in opposition to the plan. With the aid of most of the congressional delegates from the states of Montana, Idaho, and Wyoming, the GYCC was forced to scrap its original, relatively bold vision. Several high-level agency personnel who had defended the "unedited" vision, such as NPS Rocky Mountain Director Lorraine Mintzmyer, were summarily transferred out of the region. Eventually the GYCC adopted a significantly watered-down version that has had little impact on improving resource management and coordination.

Yellowstone and Greater Yellowstone at the Close of the Twentieth Century

The GYCC vision document, though gutted of many of its progressive recommendations, acknowledged that Yellowstone is larger than its boundaries. The linkages between watersheds, wildlife migratory patterns, and geothermal activity inextricably link the park with the surrounding region. These interconnections are mirrored in adjacent human communities as well. None of these towns is a self-sufficient economic entity. Proximity to protected lands, cross-county commuting, and overlapping newspaper circulation all contribute to their interconnectedness. Local economies, in turn, are linked to the region's parks and forests.

Recent studies have documented the dramatic demographic and economic changes sweeping this region. There is growing evidence that the natural wonders associated with Yellowstone and the surrounding wildlands play an important role in driving these changes.

While communities in Greater Yellowstone experienced generally steady growth since the establishment of the park, these rates have skyrocketed in recent years. The population of Greater Yellowstone grew by an average annual rate of 2 percent between 1990 and 1996, more than double the national average. The fastest-growing counties during this period were Teton County, Idaho (8.4 percent per year), Teton County, Wyoming (3.6 percent per year), and Gallatin County, Montana (3.3 percent per year; U.S. Bureau of the Census 1997). Many believe that growth in the 1990s is caused largely by the desire to escape urban environments, decreasing locational constraints on services and other industries, relatively favorable real estate opportunities, a steady increase in early retirement, and abundant recreation and tourism. Economists and demographers have concluded that these trends are likely to increase in the coming years, especially in high-amenity areas such as Greater Yellowstone (Cromartie and Beale 1996).

In the past, economists used to describe the process of development as "jobs first—then migration." The popular belief, which is still held by many in the business community in Greater Yellowstone, was that the opening of a factory, a mine, or a lumber mill would create a demand for labor, and people would migrate into an area to fill jobs. Today, much of the population growth can be explained instead by "immigration first—then jobs." People first decide where they want to live, and then either look for a job, create jobs for themselves, or live off investment and retirement income.

Teton County, Idaho, southeast of Yellowstone NP, appears to follow these trends. County population grew by 57 percent between 1990 and 1997 (U.S. Bureau of the Census 1997). In 1995, nonfarm proprietors (the self-employed) accounted for 30 percent of county employment and 10 percent of county personal income. If only earned income is counted, then nonfarm proprietors earned more than a third of all the income in the county. During that same year, nonlabor income accounted for 39 percent of total personal income, and over half the growth in new income from 1970 to 1995 (Bureau of Economic Analysis 1997).

Driggs, Idaho, located in Teton County, is a good example of the changes occurring in gateway communities in Greater Yellowstone. Part of its growth is stimulated by tourism. Driggs has become a bedroom community for service workers who commute to the resort town of Jackson, Wyoming. But most of the growth is stimulated by retirement, and by people telecommuting to flexible jobs in distant urban and suburban areas, which in turn is driven by people's desire to live in remote, charismatic settings (Riebsame et al. 1996). In other words, retirees and modem cowboys are replacing farmers and real cowboys in many Greater Yellowstone communities. Tourism acts as a stimulus to new forms of economic development (with many people first learning about the attractiveness of Greater Yellowstone as tourists) but it is not the dominant form of economic growth.

Rapid growth and immigration in Greater Yellowstone have already resulted in the subdivision of over a million acres of private lands into sections no longer large enough to farm or ranch (Glick et al. 1991). This is of particular concern to rural communities historically reliant on agriculture for their livelihood and to conservationists concerned about ecosystem health. The rural private lands in Greater Yellowstone, which make up approximately 20 percent of the ecosystem, are generally valley bottoms that encompass riparian corridors, wetlands, and winter ranges where much of the region's biological diversity is found. Efforts to manage growth at the community and county level have generally been ineffective because of state and local resistance to land-use planning. Many river valleys once known for their pastoral agricultural landscapes have become classic examples of suburban sprawl (Greater Yellowstone Coalition 1993).

The sheer scale and pace of development make for a growing number of conflicts between wildlife and humans. For example, 25 percent of Yellowstone's northern elk herd leaves the park and resides on privately owned land during the winter, while 90 percent of Grand Teton NP's mule deer winter outside park borders. Grizzly bears and wolves regularly den and roam outside the park, and dozens have died as a result of human confrontations associated with rural development and increased human presence (Harting and Glick 1994).

The most recent and striking example of the importance of private lands to the ecosystem was the wholesale slaughter of bison as they left Yellowstone NP in search of forage during the harsh winter of 1996–1997. Fears of brucellosis transmission to neighboring cattle (which has never been documented but could cause cows to abort their fetuses) prompted the Montana Department of Livestock to shoot or ship to slaughter nearly 1,100 bison, reducing the remnant population to 1,700 in 1998 (Souvigney, pers. comm., February 2, 1999). At issue is whether Yellowstone will be managed as a ranch with rigid boundaries or as an ecosystem that transcends administrative and political boundaries. Park Superintendent Michael Finley aired his perspective at a heated public hearing on bison management in Gardiner, Montana, in 1997: "Yellowstone never was, is not now and never will be managed like a ranch. It is a national park" (Finley, per. comm., March 23, 1997). Finley's comments notwithstanding, the jury is still out on whether natural processes will be allowed to run their course with little manipulation by park managers.

The challenge of maintaining a natural ecosystem that includes private holdings will most certainly endure into the foreseeable future. In 1996, a 320-acre parcel of private land on the border of Yellowstone NP was proposed for a golf course community with some commercial development. Park officials expressed deep concern about the potential spillover impacts on park wildlife, particularly migrating grizzly bears, elk, and bison that regularly occupy the area. Park personnel, sensitive to ongoing local concerns that the NPS has plans to enlarge the park, are reluctant to try to resolve this problem through direct purchase of the parcel. Nongovernmental conservation groups have stepped in and are attempting to negotiate with the landowner (Greater Yellowstone Coalition 1996a).

Rural subdivision is a sign of the shifting regional economy which, along with the population, has grown, diversified, and changed substantially in the last twenty-five years. The popular belief that the economy of Greater Yellowstone is primarily based on resource extraction or tourism could not be farther from the truth. From 1970 to 1995, 51 percent of all growth in personal income was from nonlabor sources, 41 percent from service and professional industries, 11 percent from government, 6 percent from construction, and 3 percent from manufacturing not related to resource sectors (Bureau of Economic Analysis 1997). During this period resource extractive industries contributed 1 percent of new personal income, while income from agricultural employment declined, both in relative and absolute terms.

In 1995, the largest sources of personal income were service and professional industries (38 percent), nonlabor income (37 percent), government (12 percent), construction (7 percent), and manufacturing not related to resource sectors (4 percent). Resource extraction and farm and agricultural services each contributed 3 percent to total personal income in 1995 (Bureau of Economic Analysis 1997). This decline in the number of resource-damaging industries is welcomed by park officials. Rural communities have had a harder time adjusting to the new economy. Although strong growth in new economic sectors has helped to offset declines in resource extraction, not everyone has the skills and knowledge to make the transition to a new economy.

Perhaps the most striking aspect of this economy is the growth of nonlabor income. In the past twenty-five years, nonlabor income, which consists of dividends, interest, rent, and transfer payments, has been the largest new source of income in the region. Dividends, interest, and rent are often referred to as money earned from past investments. Transfer payments are primarily retirement related (pensions and Medicare), but also include disability insurance, income maintenance programs (i.e., welfare), and payments to nonprofit institutions. As the nation's overall population ages, wages for most Americans fail to keep pace with inflation, and if the stock market remains strong, the relative importance of nonlabor income to Greater Yellowstone will continue to increase—as will the ability of Americans to relocate to the region.

The influence of nonlabor income can be seen in rising per capita income. While average earnings per job in Greater Yellowstone declined between 1980 and 1995, per capita income increased. If an area is attractive to a retirement-age population with substantial investment incomes, there is a greater likelihood of finding relatively high and growing per capita income figures. For example, Teton County, Wyoming (town of Jackson), which is the southern gateway to Grand Teton NP and Yellowstone NP, has experienced a dramatic growth (in constant 1995 dollars) in per capita income from $26,195 in 1980 to $39,134 in 1995.

In most of Greater Yellowstone, despite a major shift away from a resource-based economy to one based on services and professions, there was no aggregate growth in poverty between 1980 and 1990 (Bureau of Labor Statistics 1999). The significant exception to this general finding is Fremont County, Wyoming, where the poverty rate jumped from 9 to 19 percent between 1980 and 1990. Several ore and uranium mines in the county closed during this decade. The local economy simply could not absorb the loss of so many jobs in such a short period. However, the simultaneous increase in per capita income and population between 1990 and 1995 in this county suggests a new vitality. Income from resource industries has not recovered from mid-'80s declines, while service and professional and nonlabor income are growing steadily and currently account for 72 percent of all total personal income (Bureau of Economic Analysis 1997). The question remains whether old-timers have been able to take advantage of new opportunities or whether newcomers, who often bring with them their own businesses and independent sources of nonlabor income, are driving this resurgence.

Although traditional resource industries are either in absolute or relative decline, they still have an impact on the region. Farm and ranch employment in 1995, for example, accounted for only 2 percent of all personal income in Greater Yellowstone (Bureau of Economic Analysis 1997). Yet these industries maintain most of the remaining open space on private lands. Failing agricultural enterprises are a major concern as rural sprawl degrades habitat essential for the survival of species generally associated with national parks and other public lands. Ranchers who manage their land well can be compatible with wildlife, but their general dislike of large predators such as wolves has greatly affected efforts to protect or restore these species.

After years of contentious debate, the formerly extirpated gray wolf (*Canis lupis*) was reintroduced into Yellowstone NP in 1996. The NPS and the environmental community believed that restoration of the wolf would help to maintain ecological integrity and would benefit local communities through increased tourism associated with the wolves. Many in the agricultural and ranching communities, however, fought reintroduction. In 1997, a federal judge ruled in favor of a Farm Bureau–initiated lawsuit charging that reintroduction of the wolves was illegal. That decision has been appealed and for the time being this program, which has been very successful from an ecological perspective, will not be dismantled. Still, the lawsuit has driven the wedge even deeper between the NPS and farmers and ranchers.

Wolves have, in fact, been a boon for tourism, which is a subset of the second-fastest-growing division of the economy over the last twenty-five years, and in 1995 constituted the largest source of personal income: services (Bureau of Economic Analysis 1997). For some people the "service" economy suggests that all people do anymore is change sheets at the Old Faithful Inn or sell wolf T-shirts at Lake Hotel. Actually, services are a mix of industries, lumping together chamber maids, physicians, computer programmers, entertainers, and architects. They include low-paying and high-paying occupations. On average, the salaries in the service industries in Greater Yellowstone are 20 percent higher than the average wages for all industries combined (Alexander and Rasker 1997).

To understand the wide range of employment within the services category, it is helpful to break it into producer, consumer, social, and government services (Beyers 1991). Jobs in consumer services, for example, are generally low paying. These include jobs in amusement and recreation, hotel and lodging facilities, repair shops, household services, and personal services often associated with employment with park concessionaires. Producer services, on the other hand, are defined as part of goods production. They include some of the higher-paying sectors, such as finance, insurance, real estate, legal and business services, membership organizations, and engineering and management services. Producer services are of growing importance in Greater Yellowstone. For example, in 1995 more money was earned in Gallatin County, Montana, by people working in producer services ($46 million) than in consumer services ($29 million). The three largest service sectors in 1995 were health, business, and engineering and management services, all relatively high-wage industries. The fourth- and fifth-largest service sectors are hotels and other lodging services, and amusement and recreation services, both of which tend to be low-wage industries (Bureau of Economic Analysis 1997).

Tourism, although only a portion of a much more diversified economy, is nevertheless still important. Visitation to the park has grown steadily and dramatically since the end of World War II. In the last twenty-five years, visitation has risen from around 2 million in 1972 to more than 3 million in 1997. The current average annual rate of growth in visitation is almost five times that of the previous decade (3.9 percent versus .8 percent). The largest growth has been in the so-called off seasons, which increasingly means that the park is becoming a year-round attraction. From 1973 to 1995, for example, winter visitation, which is mainly snowmobile use, grew by almost 6 percent annually, three times the summer growth rate for the same period (Souvigney, pers. comm., October 27, 1998).

Tourism in Greater Yellowstone is no longer just focused on the park. The combination of two national parks, seven national forests, and three wildlife refuges provides world-class wildlife viewing, scenic, and recreational opportunities. Tourism in the region is quite varied, ranging from higher-impact activities such as resort skiing and motorized backcountry travel, to lower-impact activities such as bird-watching and hiking. The sheer number of visitors, however, most of whom drive their cars to the area and through the park, results in overcrowding, air and noise pollution, the spread of noxious weeds, excessive pressure on fisheries, and human-wildlife conflicts (Glick 1991).

The NPS's dual mandate to conserve natural resources while providing for the enjoyment of the American public, as set out in the 1916 Organic Act, is an increasingly difficult balancing act, as evidenced by the fate of the 1972 park master plan and the subsequent emasculation of the GYCC vision document. Despite phenomenal growth in visitation, the NPS has not been given the resources to cope with additional management responsibilities. Between 1970 and 1995, the base budget for the park increased less than 19 percent, while visitation in the same period increased 36 percent. Traditional areas of responsibility—resource management, research, and interpretation—have been neglected in favor of basic maintenance (Rasker et al. 1992). In 1996, Congress authorized Yellowstone NP to raise its entrance fees. The park is now allowed, on an experimental basis, to keep 85 percent of the increase in revenue it takes in at the gate to address its maintenance backlog and management duties.

Because the U.S. Department of Commerce does not have a Standard Industrial Classification for tourism per se, it is hard to quantify its financial impacts. Some local studies indicate significant revenues. Data collected in Livingston, Montana, indicate that tourism generated approximately $54 million in direct and indirect revenues in 1996 (Park County Conservation District 1998). Another important indicator of tourism is the bed tax, which is in place in

Idaho, Montana, and Wyoming. In Wyoming, for example, bed tax revenues in Greater Yellowstone account for about 84 percent of Wyoming's total bed tax revenues. These revenues have increased 75 percent in Greater Yellowstone counties in the last five years alone.

In Montana, all revenues from the 4 percent bed tax go directly back into promoting more tourism. This promotional feedback loop takes the short-term perspective that more visitation is better and makes no attempt to use tourism revenue to mitigate tourism impacts. West Yellowstone, Montana, implemented a 3 percent resort tax to generate additional revenue for the municipality. Because Montana has no statewide sales tax and relies almost entirely on property taxes for general expenditures, communities such as West Yellowstone have a hard time keeping pace with growth without a way to tax nonresident tourist traffic. The resort tax helps to offset the costs of new infrastructure and the ongoing service demands of the community. Only small communities meeting several tourism-related criteria can levy this tax.

There are a number of reasons for economic growth in Greater Yellowstone. They all work in tandem in some fashion and many are related to the natural amenities in and around Yellowstone NP. But even the regional economy is subject to outside influences. Globalization of production is one of them. No longer are goods produced in one location, where everyone from the blue-collar assembly worker to the accountant and engineer work under the same roof. Today the assembly line is more commonly scattered, with the engineering subcontracted from one location, the small components purchased from another, and the owner or manager living in yet a different location. Some people in these professions can work in a rural setting, using modern telecommunications and delivery services such as the United Parcel Service and Federal Express, even though the clients may be at opposite ends of the world.

A nationwide survey of businesses to determine why they had located in a rural setting found that the most frequently cited reason was "quality of life," which includes proximity to unspoiled natural areas. In contrast, fewer than 2 percent of respondents felt traditional economic reasons (lower local tax rates, presence of low-cost labor, lower energy/occupation costs, government assistance) were important considerations for business location (Beyers 1994). A study in the northern portion of the Greater Yellowstone area found similar results. The study revealed that the most important reason for people's decisions to locate or retain a businesses in the area had to do with scenic amenities, rural character of towns, low crime rates, and proximity to wildlife-based recreation (Johnson and Rasker 1995).

Environmental quality is therefore an economic asset and a comparative advantage of the Greater Yellowstone region. Transportation and telecommunications infrastructure, taxes and education, international price trends, and national business cycles also play a role. However, it is clear that damaging the environment—whether from too much development in the park or on its boundaries, too many tourists inundating small towns in the area, fragmentation of private lands from low-density sprawl, or high-impact resource activities—in the long run degrades a community's ability to compete economically.

Recognition of this new reality played an important role in stopping a proposed gold mine near the northeast boundary of Yellowstone NP. The proposed New World Mine would have established a large-scale industrial mining complex just a few miles from the park border. Local environmentalists led a spirited campaign to convince governmental agencies and the nation that threats posed by this operation were not worth short-term monetary gain. The superintendent of Yellowstone NP, Michael Finley, became a vocal opponent of the mine. At the ceremony announcing the $65 million buyout of the mining leases, President Bill Clinton commented, "This agreement, which has been reached with Crown Butte to terminate this project, altogether proves that everyone can agree that Yellowstone is more precious than gold" (Greater Yellowstone Coalition 1996b:1). Though the killing of this mine was a significant chapter in the history of the conservation movement, a number of factors helped environmentalists win. Besides mounting a well-organized campaign, the facts that the mine would sit at the edge of America's best-loved national park, that it was proposed by a foreign-owned company, and that it would negatively affect an established tourism industry and the recreational pursuits of thousands of people all helped in this victory. Private land issues are proving to be much more difficult to resolve because they often involve local citizens, neighbors, and sometimes the very people who oppose resource-damaging activities on public lands.

In summary, many economists agree that "the main producers of wealth have become information and knowledge" (Drucker 1993:183). Yellowstone NP and the surrounding mosaic of private and public lands that make the region a magnet for tourism are also one of the best assets for attracting people with means and skills in the information economy. From the point of view of rural development, communities, land managers, businesses, and development agencies should be thinking about how to invest in knowledge and human resources, in infrastructure, and in creating a setting that is conducive to entrepreneurship. The flip side of this logic holds as well: the fastest way to kill new economic opportunities would be to destroy what makes the region attractive.

A decline in extractive industries and an increase in other sectors of the economy do not imply sustainable development, improvement in the quality of life, or development that is light on the land. Uncontrolled growth can have significant detrimental effects on the region's communities, and on the health of protected wildlands. The scale, pace, and location of new development and resource activities in Greater Yellowstone will have a critical effect on the region's long-term sustainability. Clear-cuts that denude mountainsides and mines that pollute are simply bad for the economy, regardless of the number of jobs they produce in the short term. The same can be said for residential development, resorts, or recreational facilities in important wildlife habitat. The major challenge facing Yellowstone NP and Greater Yellowstone in the twenty-first century is how best to accommodate growth.

Conclusions and Recommendations

In the 125 years that Yellowstone NP has been in existence, it has played a major role in the creation and evolution of the region's economy. In the past decade, however, the nature of this role has changed. Initially, the park served as the catalyst for a burgeoning tourism industry that affected in-park concessionaires, gateway communities, and other towns that could be described as "gateways to the Greater Yellowstone Ecosystem." In recent years, with an impressive expansion and diversification of the regional economy, the popular belief that tourism, extractive industries, and agriculture are the area's financial backbone no longer holds true. In fact, these activities make up a relatively small portion of the overall economic picture.

Nonlabor income and the diverse service sector dwarf tourism and extractive industries. The engine driving this growth appears to be Greater Yellowstone's unique quality of life, which includes the area's wildlands and wildlife. Ironically the very growth stimulated by this quality of life may ultimately destroy it.

With this in mind, maintaining a robust regional economy depends on preservation of the ecological integrity of Yellowstone NP and the surrounding GYE. With rampant subdivisions gobbling up important, privately owned wildlife habitat and vocal (if not widespread) support for continued resource extraction on public lands, the long-term prognosis for the park, the ecosystem, and ultimately the communities does not look good.

Despite the important role that Yellowstone has played in spurring regional development, much of this has occurred by default, not design. Such a piecemeal and parochial approach may have been appropriate in the era of the Wild West, but those days have gone the way of mountain men and cattle drives. The present challenges call for effective relationships between public land managers and outside partners including regional residents and national stakeholders. Without proactive, collaborative planning Yellowstone NP will most likely become an island of seminatural habitat surrounded by a sea of development. Ultimately, the park will lose many of the wild qualities it was created to preserve. The precedents of the park's master plan and GYCC vision document indicate that future partnerships and planning efforts must have real support in the communities that are outside the park but have a stake in its future—communities of place (e.g., Jackson Hole) and interest (e.g., snowmobilers)—in order to be effective.

Fortunately, a growing number of individuals and organizations are recognizing these problems and actively seeking solutions. Several Greater Yellowstone communities and counties have embarked on local "visioning" or comprehensive planning processes (Howe et al. 1997). In some cases, representatives of Yellowstone NP, the U.S. Forest Service, and other land management agencies have participated in these efforts. In Gallatin County, Montana, collaborative planning between the county and public land managers, including Yellowstone NP, has been institutionalized through a memorandum of understanding that defines a process for collaborative county planning. These fledgling efforts show progress toward more cooperative and environmentally benign land use and development strategies on both public and private lands (Swanson, pers. comm., November 3, 1998).

Unfortunately, not all collaborative planning is entered into with a positive spirit of cooperation. For example, a number of regional counties and state agencies recently gained "cooperator status" in the preparation and review of Yellowstone NP's Winter Use Environmental Impact Statement. In this case, regional interests are attempting to exert a local veto on a process and issue of national importance. As new relationships and partnerships are formed, participants will have to learn to consider interests beyond their own immediate agendas. The most important lesson learned in the past 125 years is this: the park and the region need and can benefit from increased emphasis on and skill in developing partnerships that support the mission of the NPS and prosperity in local communities.

Perhaps the best approach is to move forward with efforts to develop integrated conservation and development plans. These could ultimately help to sustain wildlands and wildlife, as well as communities and regional economies (Glick and Clark 1998). Some communities and public land managers are already pioneering efforts that reflect these goals. It is appropriate that as Yellowstone NP celebrates its 125th anniversary, residents and managers of Greater Yellowstone join together to prepare for its next 125 years.

Recommendations for Communities

1. Many communities in Greater Yellowstone lack community or county development, land-use, or growth management plans. To begin the process of planning for community sustainability, shared community visions and development plans need to be created. These blueprints should be drafted with a solid understanding of local and regional environmental, economic, and social trends. They should include an inventory of local assets (natural, cultural, and economic) identified by the community. An action plan that includes the tools and strategies for achieving these goals should be part of this vision.

Residents of Red Lodge, Montana, just northeast of Yellowstone NP, came together in the early 1990s and developed a shared community vision for their scenic but changing community. Representatives of public land management agencies participated in but did not dominate this process. This effort spawned the Beartooth Front Community Forum, which, in turn, led to implementation of recommended actions. These have included development of a new master plan for the town, establishment of water quality monitoring projects, and protection of thousands of acres of ranchland through conservation easements, among other accomplishments. Perhaps most important, this initiative has created a forum for civil dialogue of complex and often conflictive issues.

2. In collaboration with local, state, and federal officials, communities need to develop a regulatory framework bolstered with market incentives and other nonregulatory tools for guiding development while protecting local and regional assets.

In Gallatin County, Montana, which abuts portions of the northern and eastern sides of Yellowstone NP, county commissioners have established an Open Lands Board to address the loss of agricultural lands, wildlife habitat, and open space on private land. The board is currently implementing a tool kit—voluntary, market-based, and regulatory—to protect open space for environmental, economic, and recreational benefits.

3. Relations with public land managers should be formalized through the drafting of memorandums of understanding (MOUs) or other mechanisms for sharing information for more effective management of both public and private lands.

Created in 1991 by citizens concerned about the environmental and aesthetic impacts of logging practices in the watershed of Bozeman, Montana, the Bozeman Watershed Council has matured into a productive and effective vehicle for resolving resource-use conflicts. The group includes representatives of public land management agencies, resource users such as forest industry representatives, local government officials, and concerned citizens. The group has crafted a vision of the watershed for the next century and is moving forward in making that vision a reality. It recently completed a study of alternative actions the city of Bozeman could take to delay the need for constructing a reservoir and dam in the watershed.

4. Nongovernmental efforts to assist in achieving integrated development and conservation goals should be created or supported.

In Teton County, Idaho, southeast of Yellowstone NP, citizens have initiated a number of efforts to support county economic and environmental goals. The

Teton Valley Economic Development Council has drafted a sustainable eco-nomic development plan that, for example, identifies strategies for adding value to the valley's agricultural products (especially the rapidly disappearing dairies). A local land trust has been created to help preserve farm and ranchland. And a grassroots, nongovernmental conservation group known as Citizens for Teton Valley serves as a watchdog for monitoring and, where necessary, intervening in inappropriate private or public land development.

Recommendations for Yellowstone National Park and Other Public Land Managers

1. Resource protection or restoration should become the shared overarching management objective of Yellowstone NP and the surrounding public lands.

Yellowstone NP is in the process of developing a winter-use plan and is long overdue for the revision of its master plan. Most of Greater Yellowstone's national forests are also gearing up for their forest plan revisions. These planning initiatives represent a golden opportunity to phase out environmentally destruc-tive management activities (related mostly to visitors in the national parks and to extractive industry in the national forests). These plans should institutional-ize the transition to ecosystem protection and ecological restoration as overar-ching management goals.

2. More effective and inclusive means of coordinating management activities on public and private lands that are ecologically interconnected need to be developed and implemented.

While the GYCC vision document was scrapped, its intent is as relevant today as when the document was proposed. The NPS may be learning that develop-ing policy behind closed doors and presenting it to the public as a fait accompli earns more animosity than support. In 1996 Yellowstone NP managers, in col-laboration with other public land managers, state agencies (such as the Montana Department of Highways), and the community of West Yellowstone, organized a workshop called "The Greening of Yellowstone." The workshop explored how activities such as infrastructure development could be planned and carried out in a more environmentally benign fashion. A follow-up to this workshop was held in conjunction with the 125th anniversary of Yellowstone NP.

3. Visitor carrying capacity should be determined with appropriate modifica-tion of current visitor use in Yellowstone NP.

The NPS has lately begun to modify visitor management in some park units such as Yosemite NP and Grand Canyon NP. Public transportation systems are being developed and some facilities removed or moved. Yellowstone NP is in desperate need of data on visitor carrying capacity and a revised visitor use and transportation plan. Initial work on a new transportation plan for Yellowstone that is more regional than local in focus is a step in the right direction.

4. A mechanism needs to be devised by the park and surrounding landowners and communities for improving and streamlining communication and cooperation on regional development issues.

In the past decade, Yellowstone NP technicians have developed geographic information system (GIS) capabilities and are amassing considerable data. This information is extremely relevant to land-use planning and management efforts on adjacent private lands and in communities. Some information is now being shared between the park, nearby counties, and national forests. Accelerating this process of data collection, analysis, and sharing could build a technological bridge and lead to better communication and cooperation.

References

Alexander, B., and R. Rasker. 1997. *The New Challenge: People, Commerce and Environment in the Yellowstone to Yukon Region.* Washington, DC: The Wilderness Society.

Beyers, W. B. 1994. *Producer Services in Urban and Rural Areas: Contrasts in Competitiveness, Trade and Development.* Unpublished paper presented at the Forty-first North American Regional Science Meeting, Niagara Falls, Ontario, November 1994.

———. 1991. Trends in service employment in Pacific Northwest counties: 1974–1986. *Growth and Change* 22(4): 27–50.

Bozeman Avant Courier. 1883. "Slaughtering Game." January 25, p. 1. Bozeman, Montana.

———. 1874. July 31, p. 2. Bozeman, Montana.

Bureau of Economic Analysis. 1997. *Regional Economic Information System.* Washington, DC: U.S. Department of Commerce.

Bureau of Labor Statistics. 1999. *Local Area Unemployment Statistics.* Washington, DC: U.S. Department of Labor.

Cook, C. W. 1922. Remarks of C. W. Cook, last survivor of the original explorers of the Yellowstone Park region, July 14. Official transcript. Mammoth, WY: Yellowstone National Park Archives.

Cromartie, J., and C. Beale. 1996. Rural population rebounds in the 1990s. *Agricultural Outlook* November: 18–21.

Drucker, P. 1993. *Post Capitalist Society.* New York: Harper Business.

Ekey, R., B. Mayer, and J. Woodcock. 1990. *Yellowstone on Fire!* Billings, MT: *Billings Gazette.*

Finley, M. 1997 (March 23). Personal Communication. Superintendent, Yellowstone National Park, U.S. National Park Service.

Glick, D. 1991. Tourism in Greater Yellowstone: Maximizing the Good, Minimizing the Bad, Eliminating the Ugly. In *Nature-tourism: Managing for the Environment,* ed. T. Whelan, 58–74. Washington, DC: Island Press.

Glick, D., and T. Clark. 1998. Overcoming Boundaries in a Managed Landscape: The Case of the Greater Yellowstone Ecosystem. In *Managing Beyond Boundaries,* ed. Richard Knight and Peter Landres, 237–56. Washington, DC: Island Press.

Glick, D., M. Carr, and B. Harting. 1991. *An Environmental Profile of the Greater Yellowstone Ecosystem.* Bozeman, MT: Greater Yellowstone Coalition.

Greater Yellowstone Coalition. 1993. The Land Rush Is On: Greater Yellowstone Bursting at the Seams. In *Greater Yellowstone Report, Winter 1993.* Bozeman, MT: Greater Yellowstone Coalition.

———. 1996a. Golf and Housing Development Proposed Next to Yellowstone Park. In *Greater Yellowstone Report, Summer 1996.* Bozeman, MT: Greater Yellowstone Coalition.

———. 1996b. Victory for Yellowstone: Historic Agreement Stops New World Mine. In *Greater Yellowstone Report, Summer 1996.* Bozeman, MT: Greater Yellowstone Coalition.

———. 1987. No Freeboard for Yellowstone Grizzlies. *Greater Yellowstone Report, Fall 1987.* Bozeman, MT: Greater Yellowstone Coalition.

Greater Yellowstone Coordinating Committee. 1987. *An Aggregation of National Park and National Forest Management Plans.* Billings, MT: National Park Service and U.S. Forest Service.

———. 1990. *Vision for the Future: A Framework for the Coordination in the Greater Yellowstone Area (Draft).* Billings, MT: National Park Service and U.S. Forest Service.

Gregg, W. 1921. The Cascade Corner of Yellowstone Park. *The Outlook* 129: 474.

Haines, A. 1977. *The Yellowstone Story.* Yellowstone National Park, WY: Yellowstone Library and Museum Association.

Harting B., and D. Glick. 1994. *Conserving Greater Yellowstone: A Blueprint for the Future.* Bozeman, MT: Greater Yellowstone Coalition.

Helena Herald. 1872. "Our National Park." March 1, p. 1. Helena, Montana.

Helena Rocky Mountain Gazette. 1872. "Yellowstone Expedition." March 1, p. 1. Helena, Montana.

Hornaday, W. T. 1913. *Our Vanishing Wildlife.* New York: Scribner's.

Howe, J., E. McMahon, and L. Propst. 1997. *Balancing Nature and Commerce in Gateway Communities.* Washington, DC: Island Press.

Johnson, J., and R. Rasker. 1995. The role of economic and quality of life values in rural business location. *Journal of Rural Studies* 11(4): 405–16.

Livingston Enterprise. 1920. April 30, p. 1. Livingston, Montana.

National Park Service (NPS). 1972. *Yellowstone National Park Master Plan.* Yellowstone National Park, WY: National Park Service.

Park County Conservation District. 1998. *Upper Yellowstone River Cumulative Effects Investigation.* Livingston, MT: Park Conservation District.

Phillips, P. C. 1940. *Life in the Rocky Mountains.* Denver: Old West Publishing Company.

Rasker, R., N. Terrell, and D. Kloepfer. 1992. *The Wealth of Nature: New Economic Realities in the Yellowstone Region.* Washington, DC: The Wilderness Society.

Riebsame, W. E., H. Gosnel, and D. M. Theobald. 1996. Land Use and Land Change in the Colorado Mountains: Theory, Scale and Pattern. In *Mountain Research and Development.* Boulder: University of Colorado, Department of Geography.

Ross, T. 1927. *Outdoor America* (December) 8.

Sax, J. 1980. *Mountains without Handrails.* Ann Arbor: University of Michigan Press.

Sellers, R. W. 1997. *Preserving Nature in National Parks.* New Haven: Yale University Press.

Souvigney, J. M. 1998 (October 27). Personal Communication. Program Director, Greater Yellowstone Coalition.

———. 1999 (February 2). Personal Communication. Program Director, Greater Yellowstone Coalition.

Swanson, T. 1998 (November 3). Personal Communication. Former Mayor of Bozeman, Montana.

United States Bureau of the Census. 1997. *Census of Population and Housing.* Washington, DC: U.S. Department of Commerce.

Williams, T. 1989. Incineration of Yellowstone. *Audubon* 91(1): 38–85.

Yellowstone National Park. 1989. *Existing Winter Use Management Guidelines, Inventory and Needs.* Yellowstone National Park, WY: National Park Service.

———. 1997. *Environmental Assessment: Temporary Closure of a Winter Road.* Yellowstone National Park, WY: National Park Service.

———. 1919. *Annual Report for Yellowstone National Park 1919.* Yellowstone Park, WY: National Park Service.

Discussion

The case studies included in part two were deliberately chosen to reflect the wide range of possible relationships between national parks and regional rural development. They vary in geography, from Alaska wilderness to Pacific Northwest temperate forest to the urbanized ocean shore of Cape Cod. They vary in level of park use, from high visitation sites (such as Grand Canyon NP, Yellowstone NP, and Cape Cod NS) to relatively low visitation sites (such as North Cascades NPS Complex and the Alaska national parks and preserves). And they vary in regional context, from national parks surrounded by other federal lands and natural resource extraction activities (such as the Alaska units) to those surrounded by a longtime fully urbanized economy (Cape Cod NS).

The case studies reported here provide perspective on the differing state of affairs among parks and neighboring communities. Some parks and communities are only now realizing the potential benefits to mesh planning efforts regarding public land protection and rural development. Others are forced into post-development planning, spurred on by the rapid growth of residential populations at the boundary of a park.

Nevertheless, several convergent themes emerge. The first is that surrounding land tenure and land use directly influence the relationship between national parks and rural development. Federal lands, such as national forests, make different neighbors than private ranches, suburban housing developments, or small-scale tourism enterprises. Hence, the case studies emphasize the importance of land-use history as a necessary foundation for regional planning, rural development, and park management.

A second theme is the recognition that rural development adjacent to parks has more often than not taken place without concerted planning on the part of either the benefiting community or the host park. In the Pacific Northwest, the economies of communities dependent on timber production have grown or declined resulting from forestry issues external to and independent of protected areas. The same can be said for Alaska native communities with established traditional lifestyles on lands later to become parks. On the other coast, the pattern is similar. The establishment of the Cape Cod community preceded Cape Cod NS. A well-established New England community, lifestyle, and historical land-use pattern forces natural system planning by the park into a reconstructive mode. In both cases, postdevelopment planning places park managers and community leaders in a somewhat defensive posture to reclaim common ground.

A third theme is the differential interdependence of neighboring communities and parks. In Alaska, the sharing of tenure rights on parklands for subsistence hunting and fishing provides different challenges than the entrepreneurship of residents who are merchants in an accelerating tourism economy. Both kinds of local residents rely on the park, but the results are different. At Grand Canyon NP, private rights to common resources—the airport, water supply, and accommodations—describe unique mutual dependency. At Cape Cod NS and the GYE, housing growth results in fragmentation of lands and isolation of the parks' natural systems. While exurban growth might be defined differently in these examples, amenity values remain of constant importance.

A related theme is the volatility of tourism as an engine of rural development. In several of the cases, park use has "extreme seasonality"—code words for spikes in visitation, local employment, economic prosperity, and resource impacts. The impact of such socioeconomic cycles may be profound, as local communities seek to maximize the economic benefits of the tourist season and buffer against unused capacity during off times.

The implications of these case studies are significant. The history of local land tenure can define the relationship between a park and its region. The socioeconomic cycles of tourism, unique among contemporary service industries, help govern the ebb and flow of gateway communities. Hence, collaborative planning and management are inevitable and essential.

Part Three

ESSAYS

The history of national parks has been deeply influenced by the interrelationship between parks, neighboring communities or adjacent regions, and rural development (primarily economic). The emerging NPS and its first director, Stephen Mather, set the precedent for considering economic benefits of a national park as a critical rationale for its establishment. Mather, in attempting to build constituency support for this fledgling park system, openly promoted economic development.

Successors to Mather have both praised and condemned economic development associated with the national parks. For example, NPS professionals during the 1960s and 1970s sharply questioned the unbridled development around national parks and conflicting land uses on park borders. To emphasize the integrity of natural and cultural resource management within parks, the NPS of the period chose to define and solve resource issues separate from rural development strategies. In recent years, such isolationism (and in extreme, a fortress mentality) has been reduced.

The essays in this section present strongly held and personal opinions about this complex issue. The authors provide different viewpoints regarding the role parks should or should not play in rural development, the relationship of park management to neighboring lands, and the responsibilities of national park managers and community leaders for conservation and economic development.

Don Field begins the section with an analysis of the relationship between parks and their neighbors. He suggests parks are not cultural or biological islands. Rather, parklands and associated resources (such as wildlife) are intertwined with land-use practices within the region in which a park is located. He further argues that the implementation of ecosystem management and integrative resource management on public lands will draw the NPS into the larger arena of land-use planning at a landscape scale. He is largely optimistic about a shift in national park management that can include conservation and rural development in a mutually collaborative strategy.

This shift toward collaboration and integrated management is a key responsibility of the NPS, according to Destry Jarvis. In his essay, the importance of local communities to the NPS is described. The author suggests park managers break out from hiding behind statutory "invisible walls," and become ambassadors of rural development. In doing so, the NPS becomes a proactive stakeholder influencing the direction of rural development on neighboring lands and a practitioner applying Leopold's land ethic. Jarvis includes instructive examples of rural economic development around parks that have had very different results. In addition, he outlines specific steps the NPS can take—and in some cases, is taking—to increase its involvement in rural development.

Rick Smith is a champion of promoting the integrity of park resources and protecting the borders of parks. He views parks as places where visitors can experience a "different life's course," if only for a moment; places where the conventions of the outside world are left behind. He presents the view that continued development is a threat to the integrity of the national parks, and the first responsibility of the NPS is to protect resources within its bounds. He places much of the responsibility for controlling development with community planners and decision makers, and envisions an active role for the NPS in solving transboundary issues and assisting gateway communities.

The final essay outlines an international experience integrating parks and rural development, a partnership in place in many developing countries for some time. In his essay, Jim Tolisano underscores cultural connections to land. Human communities, he notes, are part of the natural condition, and local or participatory decision making is essential to successful protection and development options. He discusses how "integrated conservation and development projects" (ICDPs) have been used to balance both conservation and development needs at local and regional levels. He presents lessons learned from the field, from the Chocó forests of northwestern Ecuador, the Río Plátano Biosphere Reserve in southeastern Honduras, and numerous other locales. Importantly, he shows how these lessons could be beneficially applied within the United States.

Chapter 10

Symbiotic Relationships between National Parks and Neighboring Social-Biological Regions

Donald R. Field

In his book *National Parks: The American Experience,* Alfred Runte (1979) presents a historical picture of the emergence and development of a national park system. Central to his thesis about this uniquely American venture is the argument employed by politicians and park advocates alike who spoke on behalf of additions to this system of parks. The arguments as Runte notes are couched in the terms of the day reflecting "images of parks." These images helped to define what places should be set aside as parks, what such places are, represent, or could become.

Images such as scenic wonders and worthless lands helped to set in motion the establishment of Yosemite NP, Yellowstone NP, and Mt. Rainier NP; images such as economic value helped to buttress support for a fledging system and for the creation of Glacier NP; and finally images of ecological integrity helped to preserve Everglades NP and sustain Grand Canyon NP.

Runte suggests that images employed to establish or defend parks have changed over time. I agree. Elsewhere I have noted the dynamic nature and change in such definitions, values held, and rhetoric offered about parks as the people who argue for them, use them, work within them, manage them, and live around them change (Field and Machlis 1981).

Runte's historical account of America's national parks ends with the decade of the 1960s. The purpose of my presentation is to introduce the next chapter and suggest a new image of national parks is emerging in the world community and American society. The image is sustainable development. Parks—the institution, parklands, park landscapes—are an essential ingredient for sustainable development throughout the world and the relationships parks have with their neighbors is a critical factor in achieving a sustainability goal. There is, in other words, a symbiotic relationship between parks and their neighbors—a growing mutual dependence. I will develop my thesis in the following manner. First, I will suggest the NPS embrace a broader image for the resources it manages and the importance of those resources to the larger society. And second, I will note several trends in resource management that inextricably link parks with neighboring social-biological regions. These trends will alter park management philosophy in the twenty-first century.

A Growing Dependence

Parks at one time were argued to be self-contained systems. The emphasis in management, research, resource management, and interpretation was "within"—the protection, management, and interpretation of resources natural and cultural contained within the bounds of a preserve. At one time perhaps this philosophy made sense. After all, we have yet to complete a natural resource inventory on major parklands, let alone establish parameters to monitor change in those resources overtime. Further, remote parks were often thought to be immune from the encroachment of economic development and human settle-ment. One prevalent and successful strategy to protect resources was to mark the boundary in word and deed and stand sentry at the doors of a park, reminding those who entered of the differences in the place they visited from the sur-rounding lands.

Such a philosophy (if ever completely embraced in the NPS) has been super-seded. Today, without question, parks managed as independent biological or cultural islands will fail to achieve their goals. Ecosystem requirements, espe-cially for ungulate populations and free-ranging predators, clearly show parks alone are too small to accommodate their needs. Recent discussion of global issues such as biodiversity, air and water pollution, and restoration of plant and animal species reinforces a premise that parks are interdependent with a larger world; such areas shape and are shaped by resource activities bordering the park and social-biological region in which a park is located.

Vigilance, understanding, and protection of natural and cultural heritage within a park should be maintained. The public demands strong custodial care of such resources. But now, and in the future, much more is expected of the parks and the National Park System. Parks are more than a place for preserving and protecting vignettes of our biological and cultural heritage. They are reser-voirs for genetic plant material for local ecological restoration, for plant and ani-mal populations to reinhabit local environments. Parks are partners with forests and private lands providing habitat for endangered species and wide-ranging ungulate populations. Parks are sources for new foods to feed a growing world population and for genetic materials used in medicines. These are places that provide aesthetic vistas on mountaintops, along river corridors, and the urban fringe, places for human contemplation and recreation. Parks are likewise viewed as components of regional landscapes as part of sustainable resource development and soil and water conservation.

Overlay tourism-ecotourism on parks and the complexity and diversity of expectations further unfold. Parks are becoming backyards for human settle-ment and play. They are more often than not scenic vistas for development, and economic generators for rural revitalization. Never has so much by so many been focused on these public lands.

A New Management Era

The NPS, whether it wants to or not, is being drawn into a new conservation era that simultaneously promotes economic viability, social integrity, and envi-ronmental quality. The diametrically opposing paradigms for resource manage-ment of preservation versus utilitarianism are being amended to include an envi-ronmental paradigm encompassing the above factors (National Research Council 1990). Traditional environmental coalitions are now being joined by farm groups, hunting clubs, and consumer groups to outline a much broader and diverse environmental–natural resource management agenda that includes parks. The agenda directly links issues of protection of endangered species and food safety, acid rain and deforestation, agricultural production and groundwater quality. We are seeing, in other words, a convergence of environmental interests that have not always been together in thought or action and a convergence of groups that have traveled along different paths. As many have noted, environmental organizations were central players in the final version of the 1990 farm bill—and in the Midwest, the Sierra Club is as interested in agricultural production issues as in park or forest management issues.

This convergence in the environmental communities suggests a park manager must be equally comfortable defending park preservation principles and supporting sound agricultural and forestry practices. Such debates for the past ten years surrounding the 1985 and 1990 farm bills have in part brought the federal land management agencies together to help define a common course of action and reinforced several resource management principles—principles that will guide us all into the twenty-first century. These principles are integrated resource management, ecosystem management, regional systems, and restoration of human and biological characteristics. It is to these principles I will turn next.

Integrated Resource Management Planning

Managing for the integrity of natural and cultural resource requirements in concert with other resource mandates will become a prerequisite in resource management policy and planning. Who would have ever thought that the NPS and U.S. Forest Service would plan together? Who would have thought that either or both would invite the Bureau of Land Management and state and local agencies to participate in this process? They are doing so, and from a self-preservation perspective, they must. Do not assume this egalitarian thinking arises from complete mutual trust among these organizations. There remains much mistrust. Rather, convergence arises from a desire to maintain divergent land-use planning goals, and the only way such goals can be accomplished is by planning together. Integrated resource management includes the incorporation of social and biological sciences, appropriate scientific concepts from several disciplines woven into a conceptual framework embracing a systems perspective.

Ultimately, the desire to sustain independence leads to greater interdependence and common planning goals. Park proponents are finally beginning to understand that to preserve they must support resource development, and vice versa. For the developer to sustain resource extraction, it is important to maintain preserves as genetic reservoirs for future seed stocks, to maintain diversity in ecosystems, and to provide for diverse human requirements. Convergence in integrated planning will embrace four general themes: (1) resource preservation;

(2) resource management and restoration; (3) maintaining habitats for the safety and health of plant and animal populations, including humans; and (4) economic development. These are the same basic principles underlying sustainable development. (See Dixon and Fallon 1989 for a detailed discussion about the concept.) [*Editor's Note:* For additional discussion, see chapters 1 and 5.]

Ecosystem Management

Agriculture—like forestry, fisheries, mining, tourism, and the protection of natural resources—can no longer pursue a resource policy in isolation. Forestry at the expense of agriculture, or agriculture at the expense of fisheries, or any primary resource production process at the expense of resource protection, ignores the systemic relationships that exist. Conversely, as noted earlier, few parks and preserves in the nation and world are of sufficient size to protect the species within their bounds. Such enclaves are dependent on the resource management practices around them to achieve their goals. The twenty-first-century forester, farmer, government warden, and park manager will need to recognize the interdependence of all forms of natural resource management. To succeed, resource management will have to be considered in an ecological systems context in which the totality of resource development, conservation, and protection is considered simultaneously. Competition for resources will give way to cooperative management strategies wherein conservation and resource management are linked together in sustainable resource systems (Field and Burch 1988).

Ecosystem management is outlined by James Agee and Darryll Johnson in *Ecosystem Management for Parks and Wilderness* (1988:7). The authors note:

> Ecosystem management includes, within a given geographic setting, the usual array of planning and management activities but conceptualized in a systems framework; identification of issues through public involvement and political analysis goal setting, plan development, use allocation, activity development (resources management, interpretation), monitoring, and analysis. Such coordinated management is a process by which goal-oriented management can effectively occur; it is not an end in itself. Success in ecosystem management is defined by achieving goals, not by volume of coordination.

New forestry or new perspectives in forestry acknowledge ecosystem management as a basic premise. New perspectives likewise incorporate diversity of age structure in plant communities and a diversity of species. While they are emphasized in some of the initial descriptions of new forestry, the perspective also includes diversity of human populations and diversity of human economic activity. Ecosystem analysis recognizes that diversity produces systems that are potentially sustainable in contrast to monocultural systems. This is as true for parks as for managed forests, agriculture, and aquatic systems. Achieving such diversity, however, is often beyond a single land management agency's lands and waters, thereby calling for a larger frame of reference as a region, or landscape.

Regional Systems: Managing Landscapes

Landscape at present is perhaps an elusive concept. "Landscape" is defined as a heterogeneous land area, composed of a cluster of interacting ecosystems, where conservation principles are followed and sustained simultaneously with resource development (Forman and Godron 1986). Landscapes can be as large as a multistate region or as small as a watershed. Landscapes include patches and corridors of distinct plant communities that through connection provide pathways for animal movements. Water systems, both flowing and stock, provide additional threads linking land forms into viable landscapes. It is at this macrosystem where parks are thrust into regional development and become partners in the resultant resource management practices.

Much has been written about resource-dependent communities and the ebb and flow of the economy or employment tied to resource cycles. Parks, while acknowledging relationships to single communities, will be asked to assist multiple communities simultaneously. At the landscape level, parks have the opportunity to construct ecotourism and more compatible forms of development consistent with resource preservation. Within a landscape, individual communities can search for a unique niche within a cluster of communities. Cluster communities is an evolving concept whereby communities together plan for a collective future. The implications are that individual communities may not be able to sustain a diverse economy or social structure but can, by planning together, develop a region diverse in structure and economy to survive, grow, and potentially sustain itself biologically and socially. Parks, as noted earlier, can be a contributor to a viable regional system.

Restoration in Human and Biological Characteristics

Few systems remain as natural and diverse ecosystems. Even parks at times have pursued a monocultural practice—protecting or managing for a species at the expense of the habitat where a group of species coexists. Restoration principles are couched in a community ecological context—community of plants, animals, and people. Restoration provides both biologists and social scientists a unique opportunity to adopt a strategy enhancing reconstruction of plant and animal materials in concert with reconstruction of human living requirements. When such a strategy is adopted, the pattern of landscape biodiversity can be set in motion.

Restoration has been an art and principle of the National Park System. The NPS needs to export its expertise beyond the boundaries of a park to assist other public and private entities to incorporate such knowledge into their management practices.

Summary

I have been altogether brief on specifics. Mutual dependence has been the underlying theme, with a call for integrated resource management based on ecosystem principles enacted at a regional or landscape level and implemented through restoration principles.

We must capture the enthusiasm of the time—whether it is perceived as a thrust of regulatory action (a perceived negative action undermining individual legal rights) or as the enlightened maturity of progressive national environmental thought on land use (society's collective wisdom to preserve and conserve for sustainable systems)—to integrate, to consolidate, and to act. But to do so means we must clarify our management and planning processes. We need public acceptance, participation, and enthusiasm for the mature, interdisciplinary, ecosystem planning processes that are necessary in land-use planning and that will be required to handle twenty-first-century resource conflicts and requirements.

Scholars of land-use management and planning have a unique opportunity before them. Never before have so many with such diverse perspectives sought common ground. Never before have we witnessed intellectual and scientific discourse among so many with such diverse backgrounds. And never before have so many come together recommending interdisciplinary efforts to solve resource problems and recommending a systems approach to those problems. The management challenge is to contribute understanding of the changing patterns of human and natural systems in rural and urban regions, linking park systems with other resource systems in new arrangements of thinking (theory) and action (applied strategies) that complement natural and global resource policies.

Our faculty remind me that I am a resident in "Leopold country" and I am proud to be. Let us not forget Leopold's legacy. He was a champion of ecosystem management. He was an advocate for wildlife management, preservation, and stewardship of resources—a mosaic of land uses bound together in one. Leopold was a teacher of sustainable resource systems.

The NPS must assume an assertive posture in this process. We must be an active player defining the goals and the collective benefits of preserving a heritage for mankind, while we recognize the human requirements for an abundant, safe food system and a secure living environment. If the NPS does not act, others will take the lead and the environmental torch will pass to a new generation of visionary natural resource stewards.

References

Agee, James, and Darryll Johnson. 1988. *Ecosystem Management for Parks and Wilderness.* Seattle: University of Washington Press.

Dixon, John A., and Louise A. Fallon. 1989. The concept of sustainability: Origins, extensions and usefulness for policy. *Society and Natural Resources* 2(2): 73–84.

Field, Donald R., and Gary E. Machlis. 1981. *People and National Parks: An Ecological Perspective.* Unpublished paper presented at the National Recreation and Park Association annual meetings, Minneapolis, October 25–29.

Field, Donald R., and William R. Burch. 1988. *Rural Sociology and the Environment.* Middleton, WI: Social Ecology Press.

Forman, Richard T. T., and Michael Godron. 1986. *Landscape Ecology.* New York: John Wiley.

National Research Council. 1990. *Forestry Research: A Mandate for Change.* Washington, DC: National Academy Press.

Runte, Alfred. 1979. *National Parks: The American Experience.* Lincoln: University of Nebraska Press.

Chapter 11

The Responsibility of National Parks
in Rural Development

T. Destry Jarvis

In his 1949 classic of conservation ethics, *A Sand County Almanac,* Aldo Leopold observed:

> all ethics so far evolved rest upon a single premise: that the individual is a member of a community of interdependent parts. His instincts prompt him to compete for his place in that community, but his ethics prompt him also to co-operate (perhaps in order that there may be a place to compete for). The land ethic simply enlarges the boundaries of the community to include soils, waters, plants, and animals or collectively, the land (Leopold 1966: 239).

These expressions of Leopold's are analogous to the situation the NPS must face:

- it, too, is an interdependent part of a community, consisting not only of a park's natural ecosystem or cultural landscape, but also the surrounding small towns and rural residents outside the park;
- education of and by the community is required of the NPS; and
- while struggling for resource preservation and appropriate uses, the NPS must also cooperate with its neighbors on issues that do not compromise its core purpose.

For the natural and cultural elements of a national park to be sustained for future generations, each park must function as a part of its community. To make matters more complicated, and perhaps serving as the NPS's excuse for having ignored or resisted reaching out to its neighbors, many of these communities still largely ignore, or struggle to identify with, the land ethic as reflected in Leopold's vision and the NPS mission.

The NPS presumably has sufficient biological knowledge and ethical perception to want to preserve parks' resources, but has mistakenly felt that it could do so within the invisible walls of its statutory boundaries. Time and again, events have shown that that approach will not work. For the parks to survive, and for the NPS to truly reflect Leopold's land ethic, the NPS must accept the responsibility to reach outside its boundaries and work with adjacent rural communities.

From a historical perspective, the effect of national park establishment and the ensuing growth in visitation on rural communities has been poorly understood and even more poorly responded to by the NPS. In some cases, for instance, the New River Gorge National River (NR) in West Virginia and several of the national seashores and lakeshores, the stimulating effect of national parks on rural development has been nearly instantaneous. Since the 1960s, tourism has emerged as a leading industry, with the national parks serving as a major magnet for tourists, while the communities around them provide a land base and political support for associated commercial development. Even though in a few cases, such as Redwood NP in California and Voyageurs NP in Minnesota, parks established more than twenty years ago have not yet resulted in much development in the surrounding rural areas, it is likely that such development will occur in the future.

Why Adjacent Communities Are Important to Parks

Development—good, bad, and indifferent—has followed the establishment of national parks in rural areas. However, the NPS has done little affirmatively to play a role in channeling this inevitable development. For at least three good reasons, the NPS should take responsibility to influence this development.

First, a nearby community can be the best location for supporting visitor services, such as hotels, restaurants, gift shops, gas stations, and automotive service garages, as well as for homesites for NPS employees. Such a community also incorporates small businesses with which the NPS can contract for various maintenance services including carpentry, plumbing, electrical work, and trash collection and removal. When such services can be provided in a neighboring community, little or no land within the park needs to be devoted to them. Contracting more services in the community reduces the number of federal workers needed in the park, and puts federal dollars to work in these towns.

Rocky Mountain NP's primary gateway, the town of Estes Park, has turned itself into a terrific partner of the NPS in recent years. More than a decade ago, the town made a major commitment to compatibility with the park through zoning ordinances, sign control, and landscaping. More recently, the NPS hired a community planner, formerly employed by the adjacent county, specifically to coordinate town and county government land-use decisions.

Second, to get adjacent development done in a manner that is not in conflict with preservation and interpretation of a national park's resources, the NPS must step outside the park and take its expertise to the community in a cooperative spirit. Often the specific location of a certain type of facility, its visual effect on the setting, its scale, color, and architecture can have either a positive or negative effect on the park. Unless the NPS steps outside its boundaries, there is no chance that it can influence what goes on there.

Within the past two years, Rocky Mountain NP, led by Superintendent Randy Jones, has secured legislative approval for a financial partnership with a private developer to construct a visitor center in downtown Estes Park, in which the NPS will lease space for staff and exhibits and the developer will run food service and sales areas. The NPS will have final approval of all design and landscaping to assure compatibility with its mission and public image. Both the town and the park will benefit.

Third, the NPS has an affirmative role to play by working with community leaders, assisting them in preserving the overall character and lifestyle of adjacent rural areas while maintaining opportunities for planned growth to provide good jobs for local residents. Helping the community to grow, or to stabilize, sustainably is key to Leopold's land ethic—only then can the NPS truly be part of the community. When the NPS steps outside its boundaries into gateway communities and rural neighborhoods, it must not be solely to enhance what the community can do to serve the park's interests, but in the true spirit of partnership.

Community cooperation is a two-way street, and while the NPS cannot legally and should not morally compromise its core values or the quality of its resources to meet a neighboring community's demands, it should realize that numerous things can be done to simultaneously enhance the park and the community. As an example, during the government shutdown of 1996, Zion NP Superintendent Don Falvey and his staff volunteered in the gateway town of Springdale, Utah, to assist with community projects, including refurbishment of the town park.

The Best and the Worst of the Great Smoky Mountains

At the time of park establishment, advocacy for national parks has often come from residents and businesses in surrounding communities, who most often cite the economic benefits to the community that a new national park would bring.

A 1925 promotional booklet published by the Swain County, North Carolina, Chamber of Commerce concluded with the optimistic and cheerful note that "every trade and business associated with tourist life would plant itself on the park border and thrive. Real estate values would double, triple, quadruple, multiply indefinitely. The mountain counties of far Western North Carolina would emerge from obscurity and become gems in the old State's crown" (Kephart 1925:14).

The present-day contrast between Gatlinburg/Pigeon Forge and Townsend, Tennessee, is perhaps illustrative of the worst and best that happens outside the boundaries of a major national park attraction. First Gatlinburg, and more recently Pigeon Forge, grew seemingly without plan or limit, offering park visitors approaching from the west every conceivable choice of tacky gift shop, recreational pastime (hillbilly golf), amusement park (Dollywood), fast food, and roadside motel. Not far to the south, and still adjacent to the park, Townsend's residents have invoked a land-use plan, zoning ordinance, local land trust, and other land-use planning tools to resist the uncontrolled growth and loss of community character and rural lifestyle that Gatlinburg has capitulated forever. It is instructive that the NPS has not lifted a finger in the past fifty years to assist *or* resist the type, location, and scale of adjacent development in either town. Had it done so, or were it to do so in the future, things could be different and both the park and either town could be beneficiaries.

National Land-Use Planning and the National Parks

In one of the most comprehensive early treatises on the need for application of a variety of professional skills to the problems facing the earth's environments, ecologist Raymond F. Dasmann (1959:339), in *Environmental Conservation,* noted:

> Planners have not traditionally been educated in ecology nor have they necessarily been exposed to conservation philosophy in the course of their training. It is not surprising, therefore, that plans are made with due regard to engineering, architecture, and economic factors, but with a great disregard for ecological principles and conservation values. Since many planners are only too willing to give consideration to ecology and conservation, *it becomes an important duty of those with such training or interest to work with their local planning agencies* [emphasis added].

NPS professionals, the ranks of whom have been dominated for decades by landscape architects and planners, have an affirmative responsibility to take their knowledge outside park boundaries to assist rural communities, some of which do not even have a local planning agency.

In 1973, the U.S. Congress engaged in a vigorous, but ultimately ill-fated, debate over national land-use planning assistance. This debate was stimulated by two very different controversies—energy facility siting decisions and land development adjacent to national parks.

The late Senator Henry M. Jackson, chairman of the Committee on Interior and Insular Affairs (today the Committee on Energy and Natural Resources), was the major sponsor of a bill known as the Land Use Policy and Planning Assistance Act, which represented the first serious national debate over the rampant development and urban sprawl that was (and still is) consuming rural lands across the nation. Upon the successful passage of the bill from committee to the full Senate, the authors of the committee report (93–197) noted that "decisions of more than local concern should also enjoy the contribution of members of the public who would be affected by the results of the decisions but who are not represented by and cannot vote for local decision makers."

In further making their point that no level of government was adequately dealing with the complex questions of land-use planning, the report's authors stated:

> Of course, the most flagrant example of lack of coordination between levels of government, and one of the most difficult to correct, involves the planning and management of federal lands. In the Western states where lands owned or held in trust by the Federal government constitute anywhere from 29% to 95% of each State's

land mass, planning for or regulating non-Federal land under present law is made very difficult by the inability of local and state governments to obtain sufficient knowledge or, much less an input in, Federal land management decisions. . . . By the same token, the quality of federal lands, particularly the national parks, wildlife refuges and the wilderness areas, can be and is often threatened by unplanned or poorly planned land use patterns on the periphery of those lands—patterns which could be avoided with better intergovernmental cooperation and coordination . . . the failure to coordinate either on an intragovernmental or intergovernmental basis is usually unintentional. The decision makers are simply unaware of the land use impacts of their decisions.

In an April 1972 letter to Senator Jackson about the proposed Land Use Policy Act, President Richard Nixon stated:

As a Nation we have taken our land resources for granted too long. We have allowed ill-planned or unwise development practices to destroy the beauty and productivity of our American earth. Priceless and irreplaceable natural resources have been squandered . . . the country needs this legislation urgently.

This important bill passed the Senate by a wide margin, but was ultimately killed in the House by conservative western congressmen who feared a federal intrusion into what they believed should be exclusively local decisions. Without Senator Jackson, Congress has never again taken up a similar bill.

If the ensuing twenty-five years have taught us anything about land-use decisions, it is that no land-use decision around a national park is exclusively local *or* national, but always has implications for or effects on both. The NPS should realize its affirmative responsibility to actively participate in local land-use decisions, and should similarly be aware of the effects of its decisions on its neighbors, allowing them to be involved in the process of arriving at those decisions.

Despite the failure of Senator Jackson's farsighted legislative proposal, the NPS still has tools to assist adjacent communities in land-use planning that will be compatible with the national parks' mission.

One excellent means for the NPS to build cooperation with gateway communities is by providing technical assistance. Under the National Recreation Policy Act of 1965, the NPS, through its recently established National Center for Rivers, Trails and Conservation Assistance, has extensive technical assistance authorities that it regularly utilizes at the request of communities all across America. [*Editor's Note:* See appendix II for additional description of these and other federal programs.] However, traditionally these employees, hugely talented in community cooperation and team-building skills, as well as in land-use coordination, are rarely employed in park gateway communities, but instead focus on the thousands of other communities in the country.

These other communities unquestionably benefit from the technical assistance supplied by the NPS, but so too could the park gateway communities. The artificial barriers the NPS has erected over past decades, separating its park staff from its technical assistance staff, should be torn down and the two blended together seamlessly.

Civil War Battlefields Lead the Way

Until quite recently, virtually all of the successful models of the NPS's cooperation with its neighbors were concentrated in the East. Most of the best examples, for reasons associated with emotions left over from the American Civil War, are found in the communities around the national battlefields that preserve the hallowed grounds from that tragic, but ultimately progressive, period of our history. Antietam National Battlefield (NB) may be the very best example of local and state government, together with the NPS, achieving more than any one of these levels of government could have done alone.

The battle of Antietam was fought on farmland, and so it is appropriate that that battlefield remain as farmland today. Both the NPS, with funds appropriated from the Land and Water Conservation Fund, and the state of Maryland, through a combination of transportation enhancement funds and its own Project Open Space, have purchased hundreds of acres of easements over the lands where the battle occurred. These easements leave the farmland on the tax rolls, in private ownership, but assure that they will remain as farmland in perpetuity, and provide cash payments to the landowners for the acquisition of these rights. Everyone wins.

Furthermore, the surrounding Washington County, including the historic town of Sharpsburg, Maryland, has passed a zoning ordinance that keeps the typical tourist-town pressure for development to serve visitors at a minimum, and development located to avoid intruding on historic battle sites. In fact, the town proper, which saw street-to-street fighting during the battle, has entirely residential zoning. Visitor services are provided across the Potomac River in Shepherdstown which, while also quite historic, did not see action during the battle.

None of these beneficial results would have occurred without several park superintendents, most notably Rich Rambur, working cooperatively outside the park's boundaries. It is well worth noting that Antietam is administratively within the NPS's National Capitol Region; the NPS regional director during these critical years was Bob Stanton, who strongly supported his superintendents in their work outside park boundaries. Today, Mr. Stanton is the NPS's fifteenth director, having been appointed to the post in the summer of 1997 by President Clinton.

In their helpful handbook titled *The Dollar$ and Sense of Battlefield Preservation,* Frances Kennedy and Douglas Porter note that:

> A protected battlefield can be a dynamic partner with both residential and nonresidential development. The balance between preservation and development requires planning: creating an economic development policy that builds on community strengths, one of which is the protected battlefield. Planning must involve the community and then be honored by those authorized to enact the plan through zoning and other governmental actions (Kennedy and Porter 1994:22).

The National Park Service Takes On the Challenge of Gateways

For the past ten years, the NPS's *Management Policies* manual, the pre-eminent statement of all NPS policies, has included a small section titled "Park Planning in a Regional Context," which has given rise to the progress the NPS has made in committing to work effectively with its neighbors. This subsection states, in part:

> Recognizing that parks are integral parts of larger regional environments, the National Park Service will work cooperatively with others to anticipate, avoid, and resolve potential conflicts, to protect park resources, and to address mutual interests in the quality of life for community residents, considering economic development as well as resource and environmental protection (NPS 1988:9).

At the time this book went to press, the NPS was in the midst of a once-a-decade review of *Management Policies,* with the expectation of extensive revision and expansion of text to reflect evolving policy development on a number of subjects, including its work outside park boundaries with surrounding communities.

Roger Kennedy, the NPS director from 1993 to 1997, began this review internally before he left office in early 1997. With his highly intellectual and dynamic personality, Director Kenney led the NPS in its first serious recognition of the need for field superintendents to work effectively outside NPS boundaries. Some, again most notably in the East, did so with success.

When Barbara West reported for duty as the new superintendent of Voyageurs NP, Minnesota, in 1996, one of her first acts was to call the chairman of the Koochiching County Board of Supervisors for a meeting and get acquainted. The chairman's first reaction was shock: he had been chairman for a dozen years, and West was the first park superintendent ever to call him.

Through the mid-1990s at Shenandoah NP, Virginia, then-Superintendent Bill Wade waged a very visible and effective campaign against the impact of outside air pollution on the park, generally by means of effective communication with local and state officials.

At Cape Cod NS, Massachusetts, Superintendent Maria Burks spoke out more frequently, using a more intense communication style, coupled with a sense of humor, to begin to overcome years of local animosity toward the park. Her efforts settled decades-old disputes over a solid waste transfer station, water wells, and a small airport.

Through the cooperative leadership spirit of Mammoth Cave NP's then-superintendent Dave Mihalic, the level of trust and cooperation between the park and neighboring town and county governments over land-use practices became sufficiently strong that the adjacent counties sought to expand the International Biosphere Reserve designation of the park to include private lands of the two counties around it.

Given the high degree of fear of international designations that has developed in other parts of the country, it is a remarkable testimony to the cooperative spirit of Mammoth Cave's staff and leaders from surrounding communities that this happened. Adjacent towns see the designation both as recognition of the region's international significance, and thus as an added draw to tourists, and also as a means of attracting increased federal funding for infrastructure enhancements, such as an expanded regional waste treatment plant. This waste facility benefits both the towns and the park, since the highly porous karst geology of the region otherwise directs the sewage from septic systems directly into the park's underground rivers and through the caves.

A series of training conferences for NPS personnel on working effectively with surrounding communities were held in 1996 at Director Kennedy's direction. An excellent summary of the results of the two training sessions, *National Parks and Their Neighbors,* was developed by the NPS and distributed to all park superintendents by Director Stanton in late 1997. Among the more important contents of this report are a set of "Lessons Learned from Partnership Experiences" (Sonoran Institute 1997:8–9). The core message of these lessons bears repeating:

- communicate on a consistent basis;
- link park and county planning efforts;
- mend poor communication quickly;
- talk like a local business;
- create cooperative positions/rethink traditional job descriptions;
- build credibility through informed leadership;
- get involved in the community;
- invest the community in the park;
- get the word out to the community about resources at stake.

In his cover memorandum transmitting the report to the field, Director Stanton noted, "we must develop a regular means of engaging in a two-way dialog with neighboring communities, civic and business leaders and residents . . . we cannot succeed in carrying out our vision without working closely with park neighbors; certainly to listen but also to inform them of the purposes and policies for which each park was established and must be managed."

In a somewhat more negative tone, the news headline following a February 1998 Conference on the Future of Federal Lands, held at Boise State University, Idaho, blared, "Westerners Demand a Say in Land Restoration." During his keynote speech at that conference, NPS Director Stanton cited his recent decision to ask the adjacent states of Wyoming, Montana, and Idaho to be "cooperating agencies" in the development of a winter-use plan for Yellowstone NP, noting, "We cannot succeed without working with park neighbors."

The Greater Yellowstone region is a perfect example of the interdependency that exists between agencies and neighboring communities and the failure to capitalize on it through cooperation. Adjacent, tourism-induced development reduces critical habitat for grizzly bears, elk, bison, wolves, and other key species while the very presence of the two national parks, Yellowstone and Grand Teton, creates enormous development pressures for visitor accommodations, restaurants, houses, and a wide variety of related land uses that are cumulatively developing every available private parcel. Much to the chagrin of many ranchers in the region, prime grazing lands are being converted to housing subdivisions or commercial services developments. Alone, neither the NPS nor the towns and states involved can deal effectively with the situation; but perhaps by working together, a viable solution can be found.

Conclusion

One of the most cherished principles on which American society was founded is the right to individual freedom. But rights appropriately exercised in such a democratic society carry with them a heavy burden of responsibility—to our neighbors, our community, our nation, and future generations. The National Park System is the special heritage of all Americans, and each American has both a right to use these parks and a responsibility to pass them on, unimpaired, to his or her grandchildren and others of future generations. These mutually shared rights and responsibilities associated with the NPS's special places must be exercised together.

NPS professionals and community residents are interdependent components of the parks' ecosystems, cultural landscapes, habitats, and special recreation spaces. Only by working together can the goals of park preservation, sustainable and compatible community growth and development, and harmonious relationships be achieved. We've got a long way to go, but I have hope that the strong commitment of NPS leaders to achieving this end will be successful.

References

Dasmann, Raymond F. 1959. *Environmental Conservation.* New York: John Wiley.

Kennedy, Frances H., and Porter, Douglas R. 1994. *The Dollar$ and Sense of Battlefield Preservation: A Handbook for Community Leaders.* Arlington, VA: The Conservation Fund.

Kephart, Horace. 1925. *A National Park in the Great Smoky Mountains.* Bryson City, NC: Swain County Chamber of Commerce.

Leopold, Aldo. 1966. *A Sand County Almanac.* New York: Oxford University Press.

National Park Service. 1988. *NPS Management Policies.* Chapter 2. Washington, DC: National Park Service.

Sonoran Institute. 1997. *National Parks and Their Neighbors.* Tucson, AZ: The Sonoran Institute.

Chapter 12

Saving All the Parts

Richard B. Smith

It was the early 1970s when I first saw them: huge, ugly billboards planted on Highways 180 and 64 as one approached the Grand Canyon. "Only 17% of Arizona can be bought and sold," the signs proclaimed, an invitation to passing motorists to stop at the nearby real estate office to purchase their piece of that 17 percent. Although that decade's monkey wrenchers sawed the signs down repeatedly, the developers reerected them, first placing metal sleeves at the bottom of the posts and then substituting complete metal posts for the wooden ones that the chain saws had so easily cut through. While it was mildly amusing to watch the battle between the saws of Edward Abbey's disciples and the persistence of the land company, it was scary to contemplate the last 25 miles of the highway to Grand Canyon as an extension of Tusayan, with houses and development changing the whole experience of coming to the canyon. For me, the approach to the canyon along the largely undeveloped road had always been a rite of passage. As Flagstaff or Williams faded in the rearview mirror, I could feel the artifacts of the twentieth century slipping away. I knew that once I got to the canyon and away from the development of the South Rim, there would be no more living by my watch, no more urgent meetings, no more rigorous schedules. I looked forward to the solitude in the 90 percent of the canyon that was still wild.

This chance to leave behind the factors that controlled most of my daily life was enhanced by the largely undeveloped character of the roads leading to the canyon. I had experienced the same feeling during my approaches to other parks. I began to understand that this is what motivated a certain segment of visitors to come to parks, the chance to spend some time at a pace a bit less frantic than that which governed their normal existence. While the park was the ultimate goal, the approach to it underscored the fact that one was leaving the normal behind and going toward an experience that promised to be different.

Although a few lots were sold and a few houses built, the vision of a suburban-type development stretching from the park to the current Flintstone Amusement Park at the junction of 180 and 64, and beyond, was never realized. Perhaps the lack of water and other amenities doomed the developer's dreams. But the threat of development near the borders of our nation's parks is a reality in many places and a growing threat in many others. Much of this development has been, and still is, unplanned and uncontrolled, a product of forces in society and the country's political landscape that have not been clearly defined or analyzed by policymakers responsible for decisions in either our rural communities near the parks or in the parks themselves. The future of our parks depends, at least in some degree, on our willingness to address this issue. This future is important, not only because Yellowstone is the world's first national park, but also because, as observers such as environmental historian Roderick Nash (1970) claim, the national park idea is America's landmark contribution to world culture.

Nash's observation about the importance of the national park idea might be considered by some to be hyperbole, but it is difficult to overstate the role that parks play in our society. In the first place, parks are embodiments of civilization's capacity to restrain itself, what Nash has called "planetary modesty" (Nash 1997:59), a recognition that humans share the earth with millions of other species. America's Endangered Species Act gives legal status to the concept that these species have a right to exist. Parks are also reservoirs of natural processes, processes that began millions of years ago. In a world that is changing rapidly, one in which humankind is able to shape the direction of evolution, we need national parks, if nothing more than as a point of comparison. For Professor Joseph Sax, the parks stand as an external standard against which we can measure the pace of change. "It is not that we are necessarily going too fast, but that we risk losing contact with any external standards that help us decide how fast we want to go" (Sax 1976:19). Modern science, moreover, has still not found a way to duplicate or replicate these natural processes. Their preservation, therefore, is an imperative. If we allow these processes to end, we end the evolutionary sequences that are responsible for all life, including our own.

Parks are also one of the most honest reflections of our culture. Not only have we preserved the sites on which great events of the nation's history have occurred—the battlefields, the landing sites, the theaters—we have also kept the houses where great figures were born or raised, the homes and libraries where they did their greatest work, and, finally, as commemorative sites, the places where they were buried. These areas all help us understand who we are as a people and what past events bind us together. Our National Park System is also an excellent representation of what each generation of Americans has considered important. As sites are added to the system, as chaotic and unpredictable as the process may seem, they are reflections of the people's will, an indication of what the majority considers significant at that moment of the park's establishment.

It is important, therefore, to take a look at the history of the creation of our parks. Outside of Alaska, our natural parks were primarily established for reasons that cannot be considered ecological. Everglades NP, established for environmental reasons, was our first national park that did not contain the tallest trees, the deepest canyons, the highest waterfalls, or some other spectacular expression of nature. This tendency has been characterized by environmental author Al Runte (1982) as "monumentalism," putting extraordinary displays of nature inside national park boundaries. These boundaries were almost never designed to follow ecological or topographical features. Instead, the park borders were drawn along political boundaries—township, section, county, or property lines. Significant components, then, which were absolutely critical to the environments in which these features existed, were left outside the park. At first this wasn't much of a problem, as many of our early parks were carved out of the public domain in areas that were essentially isolated. Now, of course, many of the conflicts between parks and their surrounding communities relate to how to preserve and protect the ecologically significant areas, central to the future health of park ecosystems, which are beyond park boundaries.

This situation is a bit different from, although similar to, what has occured in our historical or cultural parks, now representing almost 60 percent of the National Park System. For example, the Civil War parks, established by the War Department following the conclusion of the conflict, were designed to commemorate the battlefields on which so many had died. The lands around the battlefields, which are so necessary to tell the story of the battles to visitors generations removed from the time of the engagements, were not protected. What is lost is not, as in the case of the natural parks, critical components of a healthy functioning ecosystem; it is historical context, the ability to relate the events of the battlefield to their surroundings. It is difficult to inspire and educate visitors, at least two of the goals of historical interpretation, by relating that the general started his charge at the nearby Burger King and engaged the opposing army in an initial skirmish near Kinney's Shoes.

In an ideal world, the decision makers would sit around a table, invite the public in for consultation and comment, and make decisions based on the greatest good for the greatest number. There are certain demographic, technological, economic, and political trends, however, that make this kind of conflict resolution extremely difficult. If rural and national park policymakers wish to increase the possibilities of collaborating to protect parks while appropriately managing rural development, they must consider these trends and plan for their eventual outcomes.

It is almost a cliché to say that the fastest-growing segment of the U.S. population is that over fifty years of age. The baby-boomer generation, on retirement, is going to represent a significant challenge to rural America. At the rate they are saving—many economists claim that baby-boomer investment for retirement is what fueled the eight-year expansion of the American economy in the 1990s—boomers will have the ability to move out of the cities to their dream retirement sites in the country. Ads in retirement magazines extol the pleasures of country living, complete with golf courses, hiking trails, campgrounds, and trout streams and lakes. This population shift will place enormous pressure on landowners to sell extensive holdings and on rural planning agencies to approve additional subdivisions with their corresponding demands for water, sewer, and other utilities.

Many observers have noted that this shift will be accelerated as the "virtual" office becomes more of a reality. People will not have to go to their offices. They will be able to work anywhere they can connect their computers, faxes, and telephones. It is certain that one of the places they will want to work is outside the cities, farther away from crime and congestion, places where their children can attend schools and not be subject to the temptations of modern urban life.

This trend represents an enormous threat to our national parks. Ecological components outside park boundaries, but critical to park ecosystems, and therefore to their survival—wetlands, riparian zones, habitat for park species, aquifers—are likely to be destroyed or fragmented under the relentless pressure for additional housing developments and their related infrastructure. The resulting loss of habitat and ecosystem components will make the world less safe for the species with whom we share the planet. Moreover, resources responsible for much of the parks' ability to give sustenance to the human spirit are likely to fall victim to this same tendency. To contemplate vast panoramas of undeveloped land, central to the experience of parks in the West, depends on areas outside the parks that will not exist if development is allowed to creep up to park boundaries. Similarly, to observe the night sky as the Plains or Pueblo Indians once saw it is an enduring resource in many of our parks. This vision will be spoiled by the intrusion of ambient lighting from streetlights, strip malls, and houses. There will be increasing pressure on our historical or cultural parks to serve purposes quite apart from the values for which they were established. Development on the borders will invoke calls for these areas to serve as open spaces, sites for fun runs and other community activities. The opportunity to contemplate what happened there years, decades, or centuries ago will be diminished as the park staff is forced to spend more time as recreation managers and less as historical interpreters.

Also occurring are economic changes that represent challenges to those interested in preserving and protecting our national parks, yet promoting sustainable activities in the communities around these parks. Perhaps the most profound is the globalization of our nation's economy. One of the products of this trend is the gradual decrease in the ability of rural communities to continue resource-consumptive activities that were the cornerstones of the economic lives of many of their residents. America's rural landscape is dotted with boarded-up sawmills, gated mines, and abandoned or subdivided farmland. These once-thriving businesses have fallen prey to the relentless pressure to compete on a scale that exceeds their ability to remain economically viable.

There is a tendency, often generated by groups or individuals whose agendas are purely political, to blame the environmental movement for these changes, accusing public-land preservation advocates of crippling these businesses by working for environmental regulations that, opponents claim, make it unnecessarily difficult or costly to do business. This has led to an unfortunate "us versus them" attitude that characterizes many of the relationships between local communities and nearby parks. This attitude makes cooperation and collaboration between park managers and local leaders to mutually address these issues extremely unlikely. Parks can simply not exist without some reservoir of support from local residents.

Increases in rural property values contribute to the economic realities that local residents face. As new people come to these communities and build their trophy homes, property values are sure to rise. In so-called gateway communities, those at the entrances to many of our nation's larger national parks, property values have skyrocketed as enterprises that serve visitors compete for scarce lands upon which to base their activities. Families that have lived for generations in these communities are forced to sell their properties to meet rising tax burdens. What is lost—a sense of community—is irreplaceable. An area without community spirit is vulnerable to a breakdown in local political and planning processes, a situation that often leads to uncontrolled or inappropriate development because the community lacks the will to resist or manage it.

It is not only local political processes that are at risk; the national dialogue regarding environmental issues is becoming increasingly shrill. Among the issues that divide us, several are extremely important to the interface between park boundaries and the lands that are contiguous. The first is the debate over grazing. There is no doubt that grazing, especially as it has been practiced in the West, is in danger of becoming extinct. It is very difficult for western ranchers to compete with eastern feedlots for raising beef cattle; it has been economically possible to do so only because of the subsidies ranchers receive for grazing their cattle on public lands. The fees they pay for their use of public lands have been kept artificially low through the efforts of western politicians. Environmentalists have, with little success, sought to have these fees raised to something close to market value, charging that cattle production in the West has produced generations of "welfare ranchers."

Whichever side of this debate one favors, there are serious implications for parks if western ranches are forced out of business. Many of the lands adjacent to our parks are managed by families who have been in the business for generations. The parts of these ranches that are owned in fee are maintained in their rural, seminatural state by these families. They are part of the view sheds that give these parks their expansive vistas. If these same families are forced to sell and subdivide their ranches, the 5-acre ranchettes that are likely to replace them will not provide the same buffering effect that the original ranches did for generations.

The sensitive development of these ranchettes, and, for that matter, all rural housing developments—their siting, densities, sewage disposal systems, water supplies, lighting plans, and traffic control patterns, all of which are critical to nearby parks—will depend, to a great degree, on county and local development and zoning ordinances. Many of these ordinances are being challenged by property rights activists or "takings" groups, another contentious issue in the nation's environmental dialogue. The argument put forward by these groups is that individual property rights are supreme over the common good. They claim that land-use ordinances, regulations, or special designations constitute a "taking" of the value of private property and that just compensation is required by the Fifth

Amendment of the U.S. Constitution as a remedy. This position, of course, puts the attempts by local governments to control development at risk. The high cost of compensation, of defending local zoning ordinances against court challenges, or of the legal counsel required to develop "litigation proof" ordinances has brought the local-control-of-development efforts to a standstill in many communities.

This makes the management of rural development much more difficult, especially since almost all attempts to control activities near park boundaries involve some kinds of measures that limit, in one way or another, an individual's unfettered right to do whatever he/she desires with the property owned. Historically, they have been based on the assumption that resource stewardship contributes to the general welfare and that individual property owners cannot exercise their property rights so as to injure others. Moreover, while a property owner does have a right to a reasonable return on the use of the land, the Constitution does not guarantee the most profitable use. It is clear that the issues surrounding attempts to manage development will continue to be explored in the nation's courts and in the U.S. Congress and local statehouses.

It would be easy to be discouraged about the future of the lands surrounding National Park System areas, and, therefore, become discouraged about the future of the parks themselves. Establishment of parks with boundaries not drawn with ecological or historical sensitivity is a fact; at this point in our nation's history, there are limited opportunities to legislatively redraw boundaries that would more accurately reflect the environmental or cultural significance of adjacent lands. Moreover, the trends examined above suggest that some segments of society are content with a future in which parks could become cultural or natural islands that have little chance of maintaining their ecological or historical integrity. The advocates of national park preservation, however, see ample opportunities to address these issues and are becoming increasingly impatient about the failure to do so. It is worth looking at the measures they suggest as ways to mitigate or influence the existing tendencies.

In 1991 the NPS celebrated its seventy-fifth anniversary by convening a conference in Vail, Colorado. Attendees, representing a broad spectrum of American society, including employees of the agency, made recommendations to the NPS on a wide variety of issues. The results of their deliberations, commonly known as the *Vail Agenda,* addressed the issues of adjacent lands. Although implemented unevenly across the National Park System, the recommendations contained the genesis of a proactive approach to the problems surrounding rural development around parks. These recommendations also highlighted the failures in the NPS's approach to adjacent-land development.

The Vail Conference participants noted, for instance, that the NPS had provided little guidance and almost no training to park managers on the authorities they currently possessed to influence or challenge development proposals that were incompatible with park values. The Resources Stewardship Working Group reported:

> . . . most park managers receive little or no training on the laws, strategies, or policies that might be used to address resource issues which transcend park boundaries. As a result, some park managers are reluctant to involve themselves in external affairs, expressing concern or confusion about their authority to do so. Others may feel that they lack the requisite skills to work with external groups and the media, particularly in confrontational situations. These concerns can also hamper a park's ability to cultivate public understanding and support for its own resource preservation and management programs (NPS 1992:126).

The Working Group went on to recommend that the NPS should:

> initiate an intensive training course and develop appropriate training aids for managers that explain existing federal, state and local authorities, mechanisms and strategies for addressing transboundary issues, and to help managers to view park management in an ecosystem and historical context. The course should be a requirement for new superintendents and be a mandatory part of any managerial development program. It should also be a component of the resources management specialist training program (NPS 1992:126).

Without such an effort, and this recommendation has not yet been implemented, NPS efforts to successfully address adjacent-land issues will depend, as they have in the past, on the individual interests and talents of park superintendents. Some park managers have been very successful in this area; many others have not. This is far too important to leave to chance. Park superintendents are selected from a wide variety of occupational and academic backgrounds. While the ability to communicate park values to others has long been among the selection criteria, managers have also been commonly selected for their administrative or supervisory skills. If the new manager has not come from a resources management background, it is unlikely that he/she will have sufficient knowledge of the authorities, laws, and mechanisms available to be a fully participating member at the table where decisions about adjacent land issues are considered and made.

The Resources Stewardship Working Group also addressed another significant problem that hampers the ability of the NPS to address transboundary resource issues. The group defined the problem as follows:

> The Secretary of the Interior should clarify existing authorities, ensure their appropriate and consistent use, and seek additional legislation necessary to protect park resources from external threats.

The Secretary should encourage Department of the Interior solici-
tors and the Department of Justice attorneys to be more aggressive
and supportive in the use of existing authorities (NPS 1992:127).

The Department of the Interior has traditionally been very reluctant to become
involved in adjacent-land issues, often leaving individual park managers to fight
battles without appropriate counsel and advice. Many park observers question
the department's hesitation, for instance, to utilize the 1978 amendments to the
Redwoods Act that amended the NPS authorities legislation. It directs that
within the National Park System:

> . . . authorization of activities shall be construed and the protection,
> management, administration . . . shall be conducted in light of the
> high public value and integrity of the National Park System and
> shall not be exercised in derogation of the values and purposes for
> which these various areas have been established . . . (PL. 95-250, 92
> Stat. 163, as amended, 1978).

This seems like a clear call for the NPS to afford the highest standard of care and
protection for park resources; no decision can compromise these resource values,
unless specifically authorized by law. Why could this clause not be invoked to
try to prevent the most egregious threats to park resources?

Moreover, these same observers have wondered why the department has not
been more aggressive in asking Congress to insert so-called federal consistency
clauses to laws that affect development in rural areas. These clauses would
require that in projects where federal money will be involved or federal permits
required, park managers be afforded the opportunity to comment on potential
adverse effects of the projects and offer options or suggest mitigation efforts.
Park managers have used a similar section of the Clean Air Act to successfully
lobby against the establishment of new polluting sources near park boundaries.
For example, Superintendent Bill Wade successfully used the authorities of the
Clean Air Act to argue against the proposed siting of additional power plants in
the Shenandoah Valley.

Not even the most well-trained park managers, armed with a broad array of
legislative and regulatory authorities, can alone resolve the complexities of adjacent-land development issues. There are a host of additional stakeholders and
groups—landowners, local politicians, park neighbors, advocacy groups, developers, and other economic interests—whose voices must be included in the dialogue about the amount and nature of adjacent-land development.

Together, they must attempt to create the climate in which the parties can
agree that some kinds of control are appropriate and necessary. The focus of
such attempts should be on rural conservation, protecting the communities that
local people have managed to build over the years (Stokes et al. 1997). The

National Trust for Historic Preservation has outlined the following principles on which to base a rural conservation program:

1. Rural conservation should integrate natural resource conservation, farmland retention, historic preservation, and scenic protection.
2. A successful rural conservation program is linked to the social and economic needs of the community.
3. Rural conservation programs will be more sustainable if local governments and private nonprofit organizations cooperate.
4. Rural conservation programs will be more effective if they rely on more than one technique.
5. The public should be involved at *all stages.*
6. Sustainable rural conservation requires a long-term commitment (Stokes et al. 1997:3–5).

Local park managers should actively participate in all stages of the process. They should make the resources of the NPS planning and external assistance offices available to their neighbors. Too often, park officials tout only the economic benefits that accrue to local communities from tourism. Edward Abbey objected to the marketing of parks on economic terms some thirty years ago (Abbey 1968). The planning and external assistance programs that the NPS has at its command are often far more important to assure productive relationships with its neighbors than the dollars park visitors spend at local businesses. Park managers should aggressively seek to maintain the viability of the communities that surround their areas. The key goal of these efforts must be to promote a local sense of community identity that allows people to determine their own destinies. Such communities will be the NPS's strongest allies in the struggle to manage development on adjacent lands appropriately.

In the United States at the beginning of the twenty-first century, civilization is rapidly closing in on our remaining wild places and is increasingly careless about our cultural heritage. Our national parks are evidence that the American people believe that some areas are so important, some values so eternal, that they must be part of the legacy we pass on to future generations. To compromise this legacy to meet the needs of the current generation would be to abuse our trust responsibilities to our children and to the species that share the planet with us. It would also violate the spirit of intergenerational equity that has characterized the national park movement in the United States. One of the reasons so few parks have ever been deauthorized after being established is that current generations are hesitant to pass judgment on the wisdom of their predecessors. If, through the lack of a coordinated approach to resolving the issues of rural development, we allow our parks to become environmentally or historically impoverished, we will be guilty of not exercising appropriate stewardship of the legacy we received from previous generations. We simply must find a way to satisfy the needs of the current generation without squandering our legacy or abusing our trust responsibilities for the beings, including our children, who inhabit, or will inhabit, this land.

Aldo Leopold observed that the first law of intelligent tinkering is to save all the parts (Leopold 1949). That ought to be our goal in managing development around our national parks, to save all the parts so that, within parks and in adjacent lands, environmental processes can continue and historical context be maintained. We now understand enough ecology to know that parks cannot exist as islands surrounded by a sea of development. Nor can we fully understand our past if the development around our cultural parks robs us of the opportunity to know the rest of the story. Saving parts will require practicing self-restraint and cooperating together to assure some are not lost. The cost of this protection is not inconsiderable, but the benefits are incomparable.

References

Abbey, Edward. 1968. *Desert Solitaire: A Season in the Wilderness.* New York: Ballantine Books.

Leopold, Aldo. 1949. *A Sand County Almanac.* New York: Ballantine Books.

Nash, Roderick. 1970. The American invention of national parks. *American Quarterly* 22: 726–35.

———. 1997. Why Wilderness? *Plateau Journal* Summer: 55–62.

National Park Service. 1992. *National Parks for the 21st Century: The Vail Agenda.* Post Mills, VT: Chelsea Green.

Runte, Alfred. 1982. *National Parks: The American Experience.* Rev. ed. Lincoln: University of Nebraska Press.

Sax, Joseph. 1976. America's national parks: Their principles, purposes, and prospects. *Natural History* Summer: 19.

Stokes, Samuel, Elizabeth A. Watson, and Shelley Mastran. 1997. *Saving America's Countryside: A Guide to Rural Conservation.* 2nd ed. Baltimore: Johns Hopkins University Press.

Chapter 13

Bridging Culture and Nature: An International Perspective to National Parks and Rural Development

James Tolisano

It cannot be either elephants or people. It must be both.
—Comments offered by a group of Sri Lankan farmers

The crux of the challenge in international conservation is working to save spectacular species under trying circumstances, in the context of host peoples and nations who daily confront staggering issues of poverty and development.
—Amy Vedder, Wildlife Conservation Society

People working with the management and conservation of parks and protected areas in the United States and other developed-nation contexts can greatly benefit from the recent experience of protected-area personnel in developing nations, which emphasizes a participatory planning and management strategy that includes surrounding rural communities. Some of the keystones of this approach include establishing partnerships among *all* interests, reforming policies, building institutions, promoting environmentally sound economic enterprises, supporting environmental education, providing training opportunities, and introducing ecologically responsible production technologies. The foundation of the work being carried out in developing-country contexts is based on integrating the development needs of rural communities outside parks with the conservation needs within the parks. While developing-country park managers work in areas with less infrastructure and fewer financial and institutional resources, the social and economic conditions they are addressing are only slightly different from those facing management personnel in the United States and other developed-nation settings. As a result, these experiences incorporating local communities into park planning and decision making may prove to be very relevant and appropriate for parks in the United States to adapt to their own social situations. The chapter outlines some of the lessons learned by park managers outside of the developed nations, and identifies key principles from these experiences that should be universally applicable.

Parks in the Midst of People

The Río Plátano Biosphere Reserve in southeastern Honduras includes more than 300,000 hectares of lowland rain forest, mountainous cloud forests, expansive wetlands, lagoons, pine savannas, and empty white sand beaches. The area is largely unknown terrain to the scientists who like to name, categorize, and interpret the mystery of such wild places. Cataloging birds from my canoe, I am overwhelmed by the wildness around me, and I ask Gabriel Swanson, my Miskito guide and counterpart, to indicate on our map of the mountains separating the Río Plátano from the adjacent Río Patuca the location of trails that can get me across the divide. After carefully inspecting the map he comments, "There are none." This vast, last unknown expanse of Central America's wilds seems to get more and more intriguing the longer you linger. In so many ways it would seem to fulfill perfectly our vision for a protected park: a designated national or international landscape that protects an area of great scenic or unique ecological significance and wildlife species, and provides opportunities for public access to experience this scenery and significance (Mackintosh 1991).

However, as isolated and minimally disturbed as the Río Plátano Biosphere Reserve remains, and as much as it would fulfill any criteria of great scenery or ecological significance, it is still home to some 40,000 indigenous members of the Miskito and Pech tribes and Garífuna communities. These groups live within the boundaries of the reserve, and continue to ply their traditional uses of the surrounding forests, rivers, and sea, leaning heavily on hunting, fishing, and complex gardens to build a multifaceted economy to match the scenery. As such, the Río Plátano joins a multitude of parks that still serve as the source for critical resources or perhaps even home base for rural communities.

The conditions in the Río Plátano provide an important lesson for managers of protected areas in both developing and developed nations: any successful protected area management plan will include measures that integrate and balance conservation and sustainable land-use objectives inside and adjacent to parks. Some of the keystones of this approach include (a) establishing partnerships among *all* interests, (b) reforming national and local policies, (c) building institutions, (d) promoting environmentally sound economic enterprises, (e) supporting environmental education, (f) providing training opportunities, and (g) introducing ecologically responsible production technologies (Larson et al. 1998). People working with the management and conservation of parks and protected areas in the United States and other developed-nation contexts can greatly benefit from the several decades of experience obtained by protected-area personnel in developing nations who are readily applying these keystone methods. Initially, we need to identify some of the similar social realities being faced by park and conservation organizations in both developed and developing nations and determine why it is ecologically essential for park managers to include adjacent human landscapes disturbed by humans in strategic plans for parks and protected areas. We can then use these observations to identify possible constraints and risks in working with the neighbors, and outline some basic principles evident from the international experience of park managers and conservation organizations.

The Invisible Line Separating Human and Natural Communities

Throughout the world, and particularly in the tropical ecosystems of the less developed nations, many people live within the boundaries of designated parks, or so close to the boundaries that in their own minds there is little distinction between inside and outside the park. This creates some challenging management needs for often understaffed and minimally equipped national park agencies that are charged with the mandate to protect the biological, ecological, and aesthetic values of these areas. On the one hand, these rural communities on the borders of parks and protected areas may be making demands on the resources in the ecosystem that could threaten the long-term conservation goals of the park. On the other hand, these people are not likely to be living anywhere else soon. The use of stringent control and enforcement measures to limit what impacts these communities may have on the park is usually beyond the financial and jurisdictional capabilities of most parks. Such top-down, centralized measures will also only heighten any local or regional opposition to protected-area objectives.

However, innovative management tactics that attempt to integrate biological conservation measures with controlled economic development are being widely tested throughout the developing nations in an effort to give rural residents a stake in the conservation of their areas, and a role to play in park and protected-area management. Linking economic activities adjacent to parks with the long-term conservation objectives of the parks themselves has proven to be an essential tool for protected-area managers in developing nations, who must balance the goals of parks and their human neighbors (Larson et al. 1998; Margolis and Salafsky 1999). A recent comprehensive global survey by the World Wildlife Fund of practitioners of integrated conservation and development approaches has confirmed the necessity for managers to integrate the social and economic needs of adjacent human communities in park and protected-area management strategies, and outlined eight key lessons for managers to use as guidelines in developing strategic plans for conservation agendas (Larson et al. 1998; table 13.1).

The social and economic conditions being addressed by these developing-country park managers are only slightly different from those facing management personnel in the United States and other developed-nation settings. As a result, their experiences in incorporating local communities into park planning and decision making may prove very useful for U.S. park managers, who can adapt them to their own social situations.

Ecologically and socially, the complex culture and nature conflicts being confronted by park personnel in these less developed environments often differ from situations we find in the parks of our more developed nations only in terms of income levels and available infrastructure. For example, Miccosukee tribal lands in southern Florida are surrounded by Everglades NP and Big Cypress NPres. In the western United States, the Cochiti Pueblo reservation borders Bandelier NM, and Cochiti residents still engage in ceremonial rituals in the Bandelier backcountry to rely on lands that have been integral to tribal culture for centuries. Farther to the north up the spine of the Rocky Mountains, a mix of ranching communities, tribal reservations, and growing rural economies is

Table 13.1. Lessons Learned from Conservation and Development Projects Worldwide

Lessons Learned	Recommended Actions
1. *Integrating conservation and development needs is an essential tool wherever human pressures affect natural systems.*	• Identify national and local-level collaborative institutions. • Conduct rapid ecological assessments, identify threats and risks, and set conservation priorities. • Define local natural resource management practices, values, and social organizations. • Evaluate stakeholders: strengths, constraints, visions, relationships, resource-use practices, linkages, and participatory capabilities. • Interpret and evaluate policies, laws, and standards that affect local resource-use patterns and management options.
2. *Establish detailed and measurable conservation and protected-area management objectives that show regional ecological and socioeconomic linkages.*	• Incoporate four fundamental goals for biological conservation: (a) represent all distinct natural communities; (b) maintain ecological and evolutionary processes that create and sustain biological diversity; (c) maintain viable populations, (d) conserve large enough blocks of habitat to accommodate disturbance. • Build conservation strategies around biological and ecological threats and risks, particularly habitat loss or degradation and wildlife exploitation. • Build monitoring indicators into conservation management: sensitive species, habitat integrity, ecological processes.
3. *Seek stakeholder consensus on conservation agendas, and build collaborative management capabilities into park and protected-area strategic plans. Agencies and organizations responsible for park and protected-area management should work in strategic partnerships with local communities and organizations, and should act more as facilitators than as implementers.*	• Identify principal stakeholders. • Define land- and resource-use practices, existing conflicts, and tenure issues. • Carry out organizational strengthening among stakeholder groups. • Establish conflict mediation and resolution measures. • Develop and publicize collaborative management agreements. • Set up a collaborative management institution, if appropriate, including roles, responsibilities, and rights of stakeholders. • Monitor activities and results, and modify strategic plans as needed. • Recognize and work with local rights and use practices.

continues

Table 13.1. *Continued*

Lessons Learned	Recommended Actions
4. *Address and respond to external policy and institutional factors.*	• Map the institutional and policy landscape to show interrelationships, opportunities, conflicts, and risks. • Identify political, economic, administrative, and legal policies and institutions affecting the viability of a regional strategic plan. • Define management needs and responsibilities at the local, regional, national, and international levels. • Select the institutions most appropriate to undertake rigorous policy analysis, effective campaigning for policy changes, and policy implementation. • Establish the criteria to measure the impacts of policy work on park and protected-area strategic plans.
5. *Provide technical, financial, and institutional commitment over the long term.*	• Form strategic alliances and partnerships and help build local capacity to manage, monitor, and evaluate results. • Actively promote a supportive policy environment, including legislative frameworks. • Diversify funding sources and develop sustainable funding mechanisms to support recurrent and developmental costs. • Avoid subsidizing community development activities.
6. *Plan, monitor, learn, and adapt.*	• Begin with measurable objectives and indicators of success. • Identify key indicators to monitor achievement. • Determine who will collect data and analysis tools. Keep this process as participatory as possible, including extensive participation among local communities. • Communicate results in easily assimilated formats (lots of graphics), particularly to decision makers.
7. *Use local and traditional knowledge to build on what already exists.*	• Work with existing institutions that include local users or at least have achieved mutual trust and accountability with local users. • Ensure that planning, decision making, and conflict resolution include broad representation and effective communication among stakeholders. • Involve traditional authorities without abdicating full responsibility. • Involve a wide range of community members and local organizations to avoid domination by elite groups.

8. *Generate economic benefits for local people.*	• Determine how rural livelihoods are earned in target areas and how economic incentives and disincentives affect the behaviors of individual resource users. • Provide training opportunities for local residents in business management and administration, entrepreneurship, marketing, and commercialization. • Work creatively with private-sector firms, financial institutions, and local stakeholders to develop effective financing and business strategies.

Source: Modified from Larson, Freudenberger, and Wyckoff-Baird 1998

pressing against the border of Yellowstone NP. In these and many similar developed-nation contexts, the tactics being tested in less developed nations may prove to be essential lessons for national parks to mimic and apply.

Why Worry about the Neighbors?

In many cases, the landscapes or seascapes protected by a park may not be large enough, or may not provide the habitat composition and vertical and horizontal diversity necessary to meet the reproductive, dispersal, or feeding needs of some species. In these cases, the park may exist as an island that actually isolates species from traditional movement and dispersal routes (Quammen 1996). The biological trend inside the park may be toward the creation of population sinks, where death rates exceed birth rates and population density is maintained only by immigrant individuals, or possibly even toward local extinctions through loss of genetic diversity in the population (Meffe and Carroll 1998).

This limitation becomes compounded when we consider that the biological values of some lands *outside* the park boundary, in terms of habitat types and condition, could, in some cases, equal or exceed those within the park itself. From a landscape perspective, species and ecosystem diversity may increase when buffer-zone lands surrounding a particular park are included in the overall mosaic of biological communities that occur in a particular location. In Amazonian Brazil a significant longitudinal species richness gradient is evident for fish communities ranging from headwaters to downstream reaches (Peres and Terborgh 1995). However, this biodiversity gradient has not been incorporated into existing parks and reserves. In other areas, the unique features of buffer-zone communities may result in lower species richness, but may incorporate other factors (such as the presence of rare or endemic species) that ultimately make these areas more valuable than others with higher diversity (Heywood 1995).

This principle may be most easily recognized in species that move across biological community boundaries, such as neotropical migratory songbirds (NMBs). Research has indicated that the reproductive success of many NMB species is significantly reduced in landscapes where the available habitat has been fragmented (Donovan et al. 1995). In small fragmented habitats many bird species experience increased nest predation and decreased pairing success. The evidence suggests that the long-term viability of these species depends on maintaining large tracts of forest throughout the breeding range. Although we lack the data to determine the spatial scale necessary to ensure this long-term population viability, it is likely that existing parks and protected areas will not provide sufficient space to meet the reproductive needs of some species. A regional landscape analysis of suitable habitat to support expanding wolf habitat in the northern Great Lakes region of North America has reached similar conclusions, indicating that public lands and surrounding private industrial forestlands are *both* essential to meet the reproductive and dispersal needs of the endangered eastern timber wolf (*Canis lupus lycaon;* Mladenoff et al. 1995).

Thus, the conservation biology goals inherent in national park designation force us to look to the lands outside the park, and to work with residents to cocreate a land-use vision for these buffer-zone areas that can accommodate people and biodiversity (Warshall 1989). Park and protected-area managers in the less developed nations have perhaps made the most ambitious and creative strides toward fostering this sort of land-use vision, mostly because they have had little choice. With extremely limited or nonexistent budgets to manage their parks, these managers cannot hope to successfully patrol park boundaries and enforce strict protection mandates. They often need the moral and physical support of surrounding human communities, and their physical presence, just to keep more serious threats such as colonization or illegal logging at bay. However, none of this has occurred without first overcoming some significant social opposition.

Traditional Attitudes to Wildlands: An International Perspective

The designation of parks and other protected reserves does not always motivate cheers and impulses of gratitude among local residents living on the perimeters of these areas. Loss of access to traditional resource use and extraction areas, combined with a stronger government presence and an ever-increasing influx of visitors, often builds resentment toward protected areas among buffer-zone residents. This attitude is due, in part, to the fact that many designated parks and protected areas totally excluded local people from consideration when they were initially established (Wells and Brandon 1992). Park management efforts have been oriented toward enforcement of mandates that incorporate little, if any,

local input, and have typically been unsympathetic to the needs of local populations. In many cases, people living inside the parks were forcibly evicted, or, if
allowed to remain within park boundaries, were still denied access to traditional
resource use areas.

The resentment expressed by traditional residents inside and surrounding
designated parks is further compounded by the opportunism of immigrants
moving into buffer-zone areas. An assessment of parks and protected reserves
in Brazil indicated that 40 to 100 percent of the area of all existing nature
reserves in Brazilian Amazonia are directly accessible via navigable rivers or
functional roads (Peres and Terborgh 1995). This accessibility facilitates the
illegal harvest and conversion of forest resources, and the limited resources of
protected-area staff leave them largely unable to monitor or control the
threats.

My own experience in working with rural communities in a wide variety of
tropical settings suggests that residents are not necessarily opposed to the idea of
protecting wildland areas (Tolisano 1994). In fact, I have worked with many
communities in developing-country contexts who include the concept of "protected reserves" in the vision of the uses for their own traditional lands. These
are places they do not visit, or visit sparingly based on spiritual, physical, or biological criteria. The Imbongu tribe in the Southern Highlands of Papua New
Guinea have large areas in their traditional land base they do not visit for fear of
disrupting delicate balances in the spirit world. The Afro-Ecuadorian communities in northwestern Ecuador similarly leave certain upland forested areas off-
limits to protect watershed values. Even here in the United States the Zuni
inhabiting west-central New Mexico have allocated what amounts to a form of
protected status to various traditional lands that serve important cultural or natural resource needs (Enote 1999).

Ethnobiologists working worldwide have also recognized extensive and
diverse conservation values inherent in indigenous land-use practices (Alcorn
1995; Nabhan 1998). Miskito communities in the Río Plátano recognize the
need to avoid certain wildlife-rich areas to encourage the reproductive success of
some species and thus ensure good hunting.

These experiences suggest that rural communities are not by nature opposed
to the idea of parks and protected areas. On the contrary, they can see the benefits. However, they consistently and often vehemently oppose decisions that do
not include their input or recognize their needs, or that constrain the prospects
of maintaining their traditional economic, social, or spiritual practices, even if
these decisions are aimed at landscapes outside the customary or private lands
used by these people. Protected-area planning and management efforts must
incorporate ways to draw out and reinforce any inherent conservation values,
and enable rural residents to apply their own awareness and emotions in the creation of a conservation agenda.

Integrating Conservation into Surrounding Human Communities

The conflicting challenge of managing complex natural and social environments for both optimal biological and ecological conditions *and* the needs of surrounding human communities appears at first glance to give park management agencies an ambitious challenge. In the first place, the purpose of a park typically requires us to ensure that human disturbance of the natural environment will be minimal and hopefully insignificant. This task is further complicated when we acknowledge that land-use practices on the borders of parks can have significant biological and ecological impacts inside the park. Add to this the fact that people living on the borders, or perhaps even inside the boundaries, of a park are generally looking to better their lives, or at least maintain what they've got. Such people usually will not tolerate stringent restrictions imposed by government agencies aiming to achieve global conservation objectives.

As a solution, many government agencies in the developing nations are working closely with national and local conservation nongovernmental organizations (NGOs) to implement park and protected-area management plans that integrate conservation and development projects (ICDPs). The conservation side of this equation generally involves recognizing and acting to protect the biological, ecological, and geologic systems and their components. The development side of the equation is a more complex challenge for planners and managers. What range of human uses and interactions with the surrounding biological and ecological systems is acceptable? Jim Enote, former director of the Zuni Conservation Project in New Mexico, articulates this best by referring to the development quotient as "lessening the burden" of those who bear the weight of conservation actions (Enote 1999). This lessening of the burden will hopefully include the support of measures outside parks and protected areas that enable human communities to live well and sustain their cultural and economic traditions, while adapting to an ever-changing economic world. However, these development measures should not be made at the expense of biological or ecological values, but rather some means should be found to balance the interests of both.

Typically, these ICDPs are implemented through partnerships between park and protected-area management agencies and local community organizations, often with significant input from local or national environmental groups or other NGOs. The communities will assume an important role in defining conservation agendas outside the parks or reserves, and will balance their own economic activities so they do not compromise these conservation objectives. Additionally, the communities or NGOs will begin to have a stronger voice in the management practices within the parks and begin to recognize more of the social and ecological benefits that can accrue from the parks' presence. The goal of these community-based conservation (CBC) projects is to carry out measures that can ensure the conservation of biodiversity while simultaneously stimulating economic activities in the buffer zones of parks and protected areas that will improve human living standards. The conservation objectives become framed in a context that recognizes the *social* limitations of the place, and the development objectives are based on the *ecological* limitations of the ecosystems present.

There is little question that encouraging economic development activities on the perimeters of designated protected reserves increases risks to the integrity of biological systems, and probably guarantees some loss of biological diversity and system functions, particularly in the surrounding buffer-zone areas (Robinson 1993). ICDPs and CBC projects accept these risks and work to encourage economic and land-use practices that aim to minimize the damage (Soulé and Terborgh 1999). The alternative to the ICDP or CBC approach could be far more devastating biologically and culturally (Alpert 1996; Kremen et al. 1994; Glick and Wright 1992; Robinson 1993; Wells and Brandon 1992; Western and Wright 1994).

Any use of the ICDP or CBC approach requires complex social and institutional arrangements designed to link and balance the management of national parks and other protected areas with the subsistence and economic needs and land-use practices of the rural communities surrounding the park. These social, economic, and institutional mechanisms aim to provide local people with environmentally sound, economically sustainable alternatives to destructive land use.

There are no set formulas for designing ICDPs or CBCs. However, a few important principles have emerged to guide planners and decision makers responding to social and economic threats to parks and protected areas. In particular, the following parameters appear to be important elements in the design of programs that seek to integrate social and economic development outside parks with the conservation of ecosystems within and adjacent to protected areas (modified from Stallings, pers. comm., August 18, 1998; Wells and Brandon 1992):

Planning measures must recognize and respond to local, regional, national, or international laws, policies, resource-use patterns, social changes, and economic forces that are directly or indirectly acting on a park. Such constraints could include:

- uncertain political commitments to a project;
- legislation conducive to the achievement of ICDP objectives;
- realistic institutional arrangements that will support *local* project management and minimize the role of distant national or international management entities;
- social disorder, such as civil disturbances, energy shortages, commodity price collapses, or refugee situations;
- systematic attention to land ownership and other resource access rights of intended beneficiaries;

- technical, organizational, and planning skills among local participants that will enable them to assume responsibility for carrying out, monitoring, and evaluating project component activities;
- component activities that are compatible with other regional development initiatives; and
- clear, mutually agreeable conflict resolution mechanisms.

Protected-area managers may not be able to directly influence these conditions. However, the existence or predicted occurrence of such conditions must be incorporated into any short- or long-term planning efforts.

ICDPs and CBC projects must work at a geographic scale that is broad enough to encompass the physical, ecological, social, and economic threats they are trying to address. However, this should not encourage planners and managers to take on too much responsibility initially, nor should it discourage smaller projects that can demonstrate quick, replicable results.

ICDPs and CBC projects must be designed and implemented through collaborative partnerships that include the participation of local and national government agencies, conservation- and development-oriented NGOs, local community organizations or representatives, and donor agencies. A key factor will be ensuring that local communities feel they have a voice and sense of ownership for the initiatives to be proposed.

Not every park or protected area is suitable for the ICDP or CBC approach. Site conditions that can best support these kinds of initiatives include:

- relatively low or at least stable population densities, including little risk of immediate large-scale in-migrations or resettlement plans;
- widespread use of or demonstrated enthusiasm for low-impact resource extraction practices;
- parks or protected areas with effective management programs in place;
- well-defined community organizations, local leadership, and local and national government agencies demonstrating a commitment to both ecologically sustainable economic development *and* biological conservation objectives;
- a clear linkage of suitable partnership organizations;
- local or national policies and legal frameworks that will support project initiatives, or are flexible enough to consider modifications;
- existing or proven potential markets for ecologically sustainable income-generating initiatives; and
- demonstrated community-level and regional mechanisms for resolving conflicts.

ICDPs and CBC projects must recognize that they will typically have high start-up costs for small outputs, and that funding needs will increase continuously over time. It is unrealistic and threatening for ICDPs or CBC projects to set overly ambitious achievement goals, or to assume that even with well-endowed budgets they can hope to enact large-scale significant changes quickly. Such rapid scaling efforts can often overwhelm the absorptive capacity of implementing agencies or the intended beneficiaries. Also, the gradual achievement of project objectives will warrant greater investments in these activities to expand and replicate the results.

It is unrealistic for ICDPs or CBC projects to anticipate rapid financial self-suffi-ciency or even coverage of recurrent costs. For some projects, where monitoring and maintenance costs are necessarily high because of geographic or social con-straints, it may be unrealistic for an ICDP or CBC project to ever anticipate financial self-sufficiency. Assuming the conservation objectives for the project are of significant national or international interest, it could be fully appropriate for national or international agencies to recognize the need to provide ongoing financial support for such projects.

The long-term sustainablity of ICDP or CBC benefits is largely dependent on the effective participation of local people. This must include the direct participation of local people in problem identification, project design and implementation, deci-sion making, data collection, monitoring, and evaluation. Effective local partic-ipation can enable ICDPs and CBC projects to overcome the failure or poor results of some project activities, and can instead turn these poor showings into lessons to guide improved decisions.

Motivating Participation in Rural Communities

Incorporating the economic, social, and ethical interests of rural residents sur-rounding protected areas into the reserve's conservation agenda usually involves trade-offs. However, this "softening" of some of a protected area's conservation demands to support controlled development in the surrounding buffer zones may be essential simply to get surrounding residents to participate in the process (Soulé and Terborgh 1999). Not surprisingly, many protected-area neighbors who might only endorse the park's existence begrudgingly will eagerly come to the discussion table when they start to recognize benefits that can accrue from the process.

For example, the imminent threat of colonization and massive influx of non-resident outsiders who almost certainly would disrupt the local economy has motivated the indigenous rural communities outside of the Kaa-Iya Gran Chaco National Park in southeastern Bolivia to organize a multilayered CBC project designed to zone land uses both within and outside the park. The planning process developed by these traditional cultures has enabled them to anticipate and respond to biological, cultural, and economic threats and risks facing the park. At the same time, these indigenous cultures are discovering that the ICDP approach enables them to improve land-use practices, and thus increase incomes in a more ecologically benign manner, while sustaining traditional hunting and wildlife-use practices both inside and outside the park.

A similar movement is developing among the traditional Q'eqchi Maya and Garífuna communities surrounding the Sarstoon Temash National Park in southern Belize. Having been entrusted by the Belize Department of Forests to serve as the local comanagers of the park, these communities organized a steering committee with representatives from each community. This steering committee is now laying the groundwork for a CBC approach that will enable them to generate revenues from visitors to the area, while simultaneously improving and diversifying their land-use practices outside the park to increase incomes, reduce ecological risks, and ensure the integrity of the park's biological systems (Tolisano 1998).

The opportunity to make some money is unquestionably a major factor motivating these communities to participate in ICDPs and buy into the conservation side of the equation. However, both of these examples, and many more worldwide, also show that rural communities will eagerly join forces with the conservation agenda of neighboring national parks when it provides them with an opportunity to have a say in a process that might otherwise become a top-down, dictated policy. The indigenous communities in both Bolivia and Belize recognize that they will have little hand in shaping a changing economy that could overwhelm and ultimately eliminate them unless they step up and take a leadership role in directing the process.

What Works, What Doesn't: A Case Example from the Chocó Forests of Northwestern Ecuador

One of the more ambitious ICDPs in operation is the Sustainable Uses of Biological Resources (SUBIR) project in the Chocó forests of northwestern Ecuador. The project is largely funded through the U.S. Agency for International Development (USAID) and is being implemented by a consortium of international, Ecuadorian, and regional organizations. CARE International, the Wildlife Conservation Society (WCS), and two Ecuadorian NGOs (Ecociencia and Jatun Sacha) represent the lead institutions directing this effort.

The project goal is to protect the unique biological diversity of the Ecuadorian Chocó forests through sustainable natural resource management and use by the rural communities surrounding the 205,000-hectare Cotacachi-Cayapas Ecological Reserve (RECC) (map 13.1). The RECC has been widely recognized

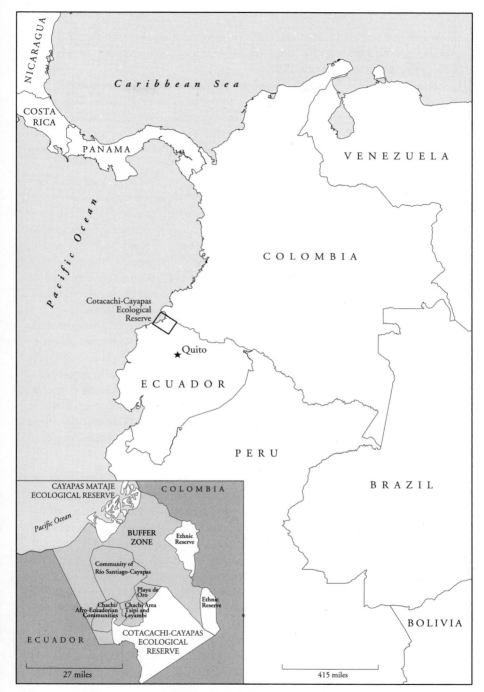

Map 13.1. The Cotacachi-Cayapas Ecological Reserve, Ecuador

as one of the world's most biologically diverse, unique, and threatened natural forest areas, and among the most urgent priorities for biological conservation efforts (Stallings and Hayum 1997).

The project, now in its ninth year of operation, includes five components, each of which is implemented by trained technicians and paratechnicians working at the village level. Many of these paratechnicians carrying out the day-to-day operations of the project are residents of participating villages who have been trained in specific biological, commercial, legal, or related skills, and who are ultimately responsible for achieving project results.

SUBIR has not been without its problems or its critics (Southgate and Clark 1993). The project, now in its eighth year of operation, progressed slowly during its first few years, and accomplishments were often hard to discern (Glick et al. 1994). The project was criticized for trying to reach too many communities and accomplish too ambitious a set of goals for the limited budget it had in hand. There were also arguments that the project's income-generating strategies did not fully reflect local interests or needs, and that its conservation agendas inside the parks and reserves were overshadowing the need to engage surrounding rural communities in the conservation effort (Glick et al. 1994).

However, the SUBIR project has demonstrated a strong response to these mistakes and is now producing significant results that suggest encouraging conservation potentials for this region (Stallings and Hayum 1997; Tolisano 1997). The steady efforts of field technicians and project managers have developed a strong sense of mutual trust and respect between the implementing organizations and RECC buffer-zone communities. This growing trust has enabled the project managers and participating communities to increasingly feel that their long-term goals for the region are compatible. Some recent accomplishments of the SUBIR project include the following:

1. Legal title and land tenure security has been obtained for more than ten communities surrounding the RECC, primarily through the use of trained community paralegals. For example, in the community of Playa de Oro this creative and cutting-edge methodology for conflict resolution resulted in the legalization of more than 10,000 hectares. These combined efforts represent 67 percent of all the land legalized in Ecuador during the four years of the Sixto presidency (1992–1996).

2. An integrated community natural resource management plan combining wildlands protection, forest and agricultural development, nature-based tourism operations, handicrafts marketing, comprehensive biological monitoring programs, and environmental education was completed and implemented by community residents from Playa de Oro and approved by both national government agencies. This is the first such community land-use management plan to be developed and executed in Ecuador. The project is currently assisting ten additional RECC border communities in the preparation of similar integrated land-use plans.

3. More than 130 agroforestry/garden plots were implemented in twenty communities throughout the RECC buffer zone. Forty of these plots are managed by women's groups.

4. Commercialization activities include community-based ecological forestry initiatives assisting more than ten communities outside the RECC to obtain a 60 percent increase in profits from sustainable forestry operations. Ecotourism activities generate income for communities and promote important cross-cultural exchange opportunities for community residents. A sisal pulping facility was constructed and residents of the communities directly outside the RECC now produce and market paper products from this facility. A handmade paper training facility has been constructed in the community of Lita, with ongoing training programs led by local community members instructing residents in the production and marketing of these products.

5. Institutional strengthening strategies designed to ensure the self-sufficiency of participating national and local organizations have caused these organizations to expand their paid staff, increase training opportunities, and raise substantial funds to cover operating costs.

6. Biological monitoring programs have begun discerning the impacts that agricultural and forestland uses are having on biodiversity. These results represent critical information to guide RECC buffer-zone residents and other ICDPs worldwide in the gradual evolution of ecologically responsible land uses.

A less recognized, but equally important, impact of SUBIR has been on local attitudes toward the RECC. Whereas previously local residents saw little need or use for a large protected reserve in their backyards, many residents from surrounding communities now acknowledge the value of the reserve, and in some cases are quite enthusiastic about its presence. They make money from visiting tourists who seek their services as guides, and they have come to recognize the biological and social buffering effect the RECC provides them.

The SUBIR program now appears to represent one of the more successful efforts reflecting most of the key ICDP and CBC project ingredients. It also clearly demonstrates the necessity for extreme patience on the part of funding agencies and participants if these conflictive efforts to support conservation and development are to succeed.

Lessons from the Less Advantaged

Many U.S., Canadian, and European parks are already adopting the lessons of the tropics to solve conflicts with bordering private and public landholders and strengthen the overall conservation potential of the area. The ambitious water management agreements being tested in the Everglades ecosystem of southern

Florida are a prime example of how integrating conservation into the complex and changing economic practices of the lands surrounding a protected area may enable a beleaguered ecological system to survive. Since the early 1980s the focus of management in the Everglades has been on measures that can restore the natural water flows that were severely disrupted by drainage and agricultural development (Gunderson 1997). Years of hydrologic modeling and extensive public consultation have demonstrated that rehabilitating this complex ecosystem will require comprehensive policies that enable water to move throughout the ecosystem in a way that sustains the diverse mosaic of biological communities present without eliminating the business communities surrounding the park. Without these composite social agreements, there is little chance for the Everglades ecosystem to survive the resource demands of the surrounding human population. The actions being taken in southern Florida to protect and restore the Everglades mirror the efforts to balance economic viability and conservation interests that have been employed for decades in developing nations.

The lessons learned through the World Wildlife Fund's worldwide experience with ICDPs, the SUBIR project, and other developing-country investments linking protected areas and rural communities can help form several general guidelines for managers of parks and protected areas in the United States and other developed nations. Some basic principles and ingredients appear to be common to all programs designed to incorporate the needs and conditions of buffer-zone communities into the management strategies for parks and protected areas:

Eliminate land tenure uncertainties. To motivate residents outside protected areas to care about the long-term integrity and security of the reserves, their own security must be guaranteed. Efforts to integrate rural communities into park and protected-area strategies must first begin with efforts to confirm the legal rights of surrounding rural people to inhabit these lands. Anything less will only inspire transitory values. This is not simply a developing-nation concern. For example, many traditional communities in northern New Mexico have voiced conflicting opinions over their rights to use lands that have been designated as public trusts within the last century. It will be essential for the U.S. public and these traditional communities to come to some form of clarity and agreement as to the roles and rights of all users before any meaningful conservation vision can be articulated.

Develop conflict resolution procedures. Conflicts over resource rights and uses are common, especially given the diverse demands and management responsibilities for the ecological values and natural resources both within and outside protected areas. Projects integrating rural community needs into conservation agendas must include clear procedures available to all participants to identify, address, and resolve conflicts that surface. The organizers of such projects must establish clear and culturally respectful *communication* measures, create a stable environment that encourages communication and dialogue, and build the *trust and confidence* among all participants that everyone's interests will be fully respected. Conflict resolution is best carried out through impartial entities agreeing to assist the project efforts. The most successful projects have measures in place to immediately recognize and respond to conflict issues as soon as they arise. Festering wounds left untreated can degrade project efforts very quickly, and must be averted.

Integrate applied field science into development plans. Balancing conservation with a lessened economic burden for surrounding human communities requires the presence of good research, monitoring, and evaluation programs. Management plans should be based on a clear and thorough understanding of existing conditions and trends in terms of biological, physical, social, and economic factors. Any plans that propose to modify these conditions to promote social and economic benefits require the best data available to justify and guide actions. However, this requires that scientific programs be grounded in the real-life needs of people trying to figure out how to live less damaging lifestyles.

Zone land and resource uses based on an integration of gap analysis, social and economic trends, and land-use classifications. Biological and resource conservation objectives must be clearly defined and at the forefront of any efforts to integrate rural communities into park and protected-area management. Landscape- and biological community–level field studies must be carried out and used in the planning process, even if only through rapid assessments, to guide and guarantee this need. Integrating the land uses outside a protected area into the long-term vision for the resources within the reserve requires that comprehensive zoning of acceptable and prohibited uses be developed and agreed upon. Zoning of land uses should include both protected and developed lands, and should incorporate biological, social, economic, and cultural values. The result of this effort should be a demarcation of lands and aquatic or marine systems that should remain minimally disturbed so as to sustain viable populations of resident species, enable dispersal and migratory patterns to continue unimpaired, and protect critical biophysical services such as watershed functions. These minimally disturbed protected areas will likely include lands both within and outside the park or protected area. The demarcation should also then include subdelineations that identify the types and intensity of developed land use that are suitable for other lands and aquatic or marine systems, again within and outside the park. The developed land uses must fit within the constraints of biological, cultural, social, and economic goals and objectives that are mutually agreeable to all participants in the conservation effort.

Abandon top-down, centralized park management plans in place of strategic plan-
ning procedures that incorporate the direct participation of buffer-zone residents into
the determination and implementation of protected-area management objectives,
and that build in the flexibility to change management prescriptions frequently.
Most protected areas rely on comprehensive management plans to document
administrative, infrastructure, human resource, and management decisions and
responsibilities. Typically, these management plans are prepared by park management "experts" using past experiences to define the biological, social, economic, and administrative needs and tasks of the management staff. However,
these plans are often quickly outdated, or too cumbersome for most practi-
cioners to use as working tools. Often they also fail to enable rural community
residents to hear their own voices in the park's management agenda. Strategic
planning enables all affected groups to sit at the table to define the mission,
goals, objectives, and operational procedures for a protected area and its surrounding buffer zones. Strategic plans are revisited on a regular basis (at least
every other year) to enable all stakeholders to make modifications as needed, and
to ensure that the management strategies are fully relevant with ever-changing
social, economic, cultural, or biological realities.

Identify and promote income-earning opportunities for rural residents in adjacent
communities that can generate meaningful levels of income while simultaneously
promoting more ecologically responsible resource uses. It is not possible to encourage residents on the perimeters of protected areas to support the long-term conservation of these areas unless they can first support themselves. Promoting economic development in the vicinity of supposed protected ecosystems certainly
has its risks. However, the opportunity to encourage businesses that may be
more "environmentally friendly" and less damaging to ecosystem structure,
composition, and dynamics should be an integral part of any protected-area
strategy.

Open and develop markets for products that are generated through ecologically
responsible means. Development of income-earning opportunities for buffer-
zone residents must go hand in hand with vigorous marketing of the products
that can emerge from these new ventures. This requires protected-area managers
to broaden their perspectives to include market development for products
related to forestry, agriculture, energy, hunting, fishing, tourism, crafts, and the
like. Vital and dynamic markets are essential if buffer-zone residents are to see
any value and incentive to pursue ecologically benign production, harvest, and
maintenance practices.

Provide training and experiential opportunities for local residents in conservation sci-
ence and planning, ecological monitoring, decision making, and project administra-
tion. Extending the technical skills necessary to plan and carry out field science

programs to participating communities elevates conservation values to equal terms with the development side of the equation. Conservation education and technical training programs must be a central part of any efforts to integrate adjacent communities into protected-area strategies. These programs must ultimately enable rural participants to become the individuals who carry out ecological monitoring efforts, and enforce conservation restrictions that must accompany any carefully planned development measures outside parks and protected areas.

There are no easy formulas for carrying out any of these prescriptions, and incorporating them into existing park and protected-area management practices will require entirely new types of planners, administrators, and park managers. These individuals will be results oriented, creative, willing to solicit and listen to outside input, capable of blending good science with social sensibilities, and highly adaptive. The entire process of planning, implementing, monitoring, and evaluating parks and protected areas will include all the stakeholders concerned with, and affected by, the presence of the park. The lines of communication between all sectors involved—from the donor to the implementing NGOs, and on to the regional and community-based organizations—are kept open and clear, and include thorough conflict resolution measures. All of the players in the project may not agree on philosophical grounds, but they should agree on project and activity objectives, timelines, and results to be achieved.

An increasing number of park managers and conservation activists in the United States and other developed nations are exploring and testing the results from these international efforts, often with promising results. Park managers at Canyon de Chelly NM in Arizona have actively incorporated the participation of surrounding Navajo communities in their strategic plan for the reserve, and Big Bend NP in Texas follows a similar strategic line. In coming years this trend can only be expected to continue. The growing human populations around parks worldwide, combined with the increasing demands for the services parks offer, leave us no alternative. If our wildlands and protected areas are to survive, it will only be because the rural communities surrounding them have agreed that they too want a biologically rich future.

References

Alcorn, Janis B. 1995. Indigenous peoples and conservation. In *Readings from Conservation Biology: The Social Dimension—Ethics, Policy, Law, Management, Development, Economics, and Education,* ed. David Ehrenfeld, 20–24. Cambridge, MA: Blackwell Science.

Alpert, Peter. 1996. Integrated conservation and development projects: Examples from Africa. *BioScience* 46(11): 845–55.

Donovan, Therese M., Frank R. Thompson III, John Faabor, and John R. Probst. 1995. Reproductive success of migratory birds in habitat sources and sinks. *Conservation Biology* 9(6): 1380–95.

Enote, Jim. 1999. Personal communication. Santa Fe, New Mexico.

Glick, Dennis, Constance McCorkle, Alan Patterson, Raymond Victurine, and Joshua Dickenson. 1994. *Sustainable Uses for Biological Resources Project, Phase I Evaluation.* Quito, Ecuador: United States Agency for International Development.

Glick, Dennis, and Michael Wright. 1992. The Wildlands and Human Needs Program: Putting rural development to work for conservation. In *Conservation of Neotropical Forests: Working from Traditional Resource Use,* ed. Kent H. Redford and Christine Padoch, 259–75. New York: Columbia University Press.

Gunderson, Lance H. 1997. The Everglades: Trials in ecosystem management. In *Principles of Conservation Biology,* ed. Gary K. Meffe and C. Ronald Carroll, 451–58. Sunderland, MA: Sinauer Associates.

Heywood, V. H., ed. 1995. *Global Biodiversity Assessment.* Cambridge, England: Cambridge University Press, in association with the United Nations Environment Programme.

Kremen, Claire, Adina M. Merenlender, and Dennis D. Murphy. 1994. Ecological monitoring: A vital need for integrated conservation and development programs in the tropics. *Conservation Biology* 8(2): 388–97.

Larson, Patricia S., Mark Freudenberger, and Barbara Wyckoff-Baird. 1998. *World Wildlife Fund Integrated Conservation and Development Projects: Ten Lessons from the Field 1985–1996.* Washington, DC: World Wildlife Fund.

Mackintosh, Barry. 1991. *The National Parks: Shaping the System.* Washington, DC: U.S. Department of the Interior.

Margolis, Richard, and Nicholas Salafsky. 1999. *Measures of Success: Designing and Monitoring Integrated Conservation and Development Projects.* Covelo, CA: Island Press.

Meffe, Gary K., and C. Ronald Carroll, eds. 1998. *Principles of Conservation Biology.* Sunderland, MA: Sinauer Associates.

Mladenoff, David J., Theodore A. Sickley, Robert G. Haight, and Adrian P. Wydeven. 1995. A regional landscape analysis and prediction of favorable gray wolf habitat in the Northern Great Lakes region. *Conservation Biology* 9(2): 279–94.

Nabhan, Gary P. 1998. *Cultures of Habitat.* New York: Counterpoint Press.

Peres, Carlos, and John W. Terborgh. 1995. Amazonian Nature Reserves: An analysis of the defensibility status of existing conservation units and design criteria for the future. *Conservation Biology* 9(1): 34–46.

Quammen, David. 1996. *The Song of the Dodo: Island Biogeography in an Age of Extinctions.* New York: Scribner's.

Robinson, John G. 1993. The limits of caring: Sustainable living and the loss of biodiversity. *Conservation Biology* 7(1): 20–28.

Soulé, Michael, and John Terborgh, 1999. *Continental Conservation.* Covelo, CA: Island Press.

Southgate, D., and Howard L. Clark. 1993. Can conservation projects save biodiversity in South America? *Ambio* 22: 163–66.

Stallings, Jody R. 1998. Personal communication. Director of SUBIR Project, CARE/Ecuador, Quito, Ecuador.

Stallings, Jody R., and Brian Hayum. 1997. *Sustainable Uses of Biological Resources in Two Biodiversity Hot Spots in Ecuador: Phase III Design.* Quito, Ecuador: CARE/Ecuador.

Tolisano, James A. 1998. *Operations Manual for the Sarstoon Temash National Park Conservation Project.* Rome, Italy: International Fund for Agricultural Development.

————. 1997. An Environmental Assessment of the Sustainable Uses for Biological Resources Project: Phase III. Washington, DC: Biodiversity Support Program.

————. 1994. Culture, conservation, and corridors: Lessons learned from conservation actions in Sri Lanka. In *Conservation Corridors in the Central American Region,* ed. Alberto Vega, 297–314. Gainesville, FL: Tropical Research and Development.

Warshall, Peter. 1989. *Mali: Biological Diversity Assessment.* Washington, DC: U.S. Agency for International Development, Bureau of Africa, Natural Resource Management Support Project.

Wells, Michael, and Katrina Brandon, with Lee Hannah. 1992. *People and Parks: Linking Protected Area Management with Local Communities.* Washington, DC: The World Bank, World Wildlife Fund, and U.S. Agency for International Development.

Western, David, and R. Michael Wright. 1994. *Natural Connections: Perspectives in Community-based Conservation.* Washington, DC: Island Press.

Discussion

The essays in part three are similar in their messages, though they vary on priorities and strategy regarding rural development. All of the authors remind us that current parks are often too small to independently achieve ecological goals of preserving habitat, ecosystem processes, and species. All agree that a landscape-scale approach to conservation and land management, one that extends across institutional boundaries, jurisdictions, and ownership types, is necessary and inevitable. Hence, the authors converge on ecosystem management as a candidate strategy and important opportunity. In addition, each of the essays treats the skills of collaboration as necessary to ecosystem management techniques.

It is in the application of ecosystem management that the essays begin to diverge. Within ecosystem management principles, the authors differ in the level of importance attributed to rural development. Smith argues that development should be a "safe" distance from the park to preserve the park qualities of wilderness and solitude. Tolisano argues for strong conservation of lands, including those outside park boundaries, while conceding that conservation goals may sometimes need to be adapted to meet the development needs of local communities. Both Jarvis and Field expect development around parks, and see the issue as more about how best to manage development rather than how much to allow.

Regardless of development's priority, there is at least one additional convergence among the essays. All the authors consider a strong land ethic—Aldo Leopold's land ethic is reprised in several of the essays—as the foundation of rural development. Practiced by local residents, adhered to by agency officials, and shared with tourists, such a land ethic provides a moral as well as philosophical basis for decision making. As Leopold noted, such a land ethic "enlarges the boundaries" of community and landscape. Such an expanded scale and visionary worldview is critical to understanding the relationship between national parks and rural development.

Conclusion

As stated in the introduction, the central thesis of this book is that national parks and rural development in the United States have been, are, and will continue to be intertwined. The thesis has three main elements. First, national parks play an important role in regional rural development, and a critical role in gateway communities. Second, regional rural development and the growth or change of gateway communities have a powerful influence on national parks—their resources, management, and visitors' experience. Third, this relationship has implications for policy, management, and research relevant to both national park and rural development decision makers, as well as those interested in parks and the citizens of rural areas.

The purpose of this conclusion is to (a) summarize the implications and recommendations of the individual chapters, and (b) propose a modest set of actions to improve the relationship between national parks and rural development. Each of the chapters provided insights with real-world implications for park management and/or rural development. We reviewed the chapters carefully, and summarized the major implications for policy. In some cases, the result is a set of useful insights for improving the relationship between national park management and rural development programs. In other cases, the authors provided specific policy or management recommendations.

Authors' Recommendations

We have organized these contributions as a set of formal statements, and grouped them into several general (and we hope useful) categories. For each, one or more source chapters are identified.

The Role of Tourism in Rural Economies

1. Tourism policy must extend beyond a limited focus on marketing, attraction promotion, and regional "boosterism." There is need for a more integrative approach to rural development planning, one that views tourism within the broader context of community sustainability (chapter 2).
2. Parks create the opportunity to encourage ecotourism and other forms of development consistent with resource preservation. Tourism policy should stimulate such opportunities (chapter 10).
3. Tourism acts as a stimulus to new forms of economic development, but it is not always the dominant form of economic growth for gateway communities and rural regions. This should be reflected in development policies for gateway communities and policies for park management. Rural development initiatives should view tourism as one of many strategies appropriate for local implementation (chapters 2 and 9).
4. Some small rural gateway communities have not always benefited from

tourism as much as other places. This is partly due to terrain, seasonal use of parks, and proximity of larger cities with more developed services. Tourism policy should address these "left-behind" gateway communities (chapter 5).

The Importance of Collaborative Community Planning

5. Recognizing the inherent linkage between parks, rural regions, and gateway communities, mutually supporting strategies for rural development are required. These strategies must include collaborative community planning (chapter 1).
6. Parks often create additional development stresses on the resources they were designed to protect. They often engender unanticipated conflicts among user groups. Creation of regional and local planning bodies with pluralist traditions of participation can ameliorate these effects, and should be encouraged. Institutions devoted to resource preservation, over time, may successfully address continuing problems of development. These institutions should be brought into collaborative planning efforts (chapter 8).

National Park Service (NPS) Responsibilities for Rural Development

7. The NPS should practice integrated planning that embraces four themes: (a) resource protection; (b) resource management and restoration; (c) maintaining habitats for the health of plant, animal, and human populations; and (d) appropriate economic development. These basic principles of sustainable development should be adopted by the NPS (chapter 10).
8. It is critical that the NPS take an active role in ensuring appropriate development in adjacent rural areas and communities. The NPS should take responsibility to influence development in rural areas (chapter 11).
9. Park managers should aggressively seek to maintain the viability of the communities that surround their areas. The key goal of these efforts must be to promote a local sense of community identity that allows people to determine their own destinies. Such communities will be the NPS's strongest allies in efforts to appropriately manage development on adjacent lands (chapter 12).
10. The NPS should enter into collaborative planning with communities to advance diverse regional economic strategies. For example, the NPS should participate with gateway communities in strategic audits and needs assessments, not only of the communities but also of the park itself. This kind of inventory would be especially useful as a basis for collaborative planning (chapter 1).

Regional and Community Responsibilities for Rural Development

11. The long-term sustainability of integrated conservation and development is largely dependent on the effective participation of local people. Citizen participation in community development is critical to develop future leaders and a stronger commitment to community projects (chapters 1 and 13).
12. Each community must devise its own strategy for enhancing its economic future. At the same time, local community leaders must design and implement comprehensive community economic development strategies with an eye to national and regional policies that enhance or constrain community success (chapter 1).
13. Many communities lack development, land-use, or growth management plans. To begin the process of planning for community sustainability, development plans need to be created. These plans should be drafted with a solid understanding of local and regional environmental, economic, and social trends (chapter 9).
14. A wide variety of assistance programs are available to rural regions and gateway communities (see appendix II). Communities should take advantage of current national assistance programs (chapter 1).

Bringing About Change in Rural Development and Tourism Policy

15. Rural economies are integrated into national and global economies. Hence, macrolevel policies to achieve national goals have significant impacts on local rural economies. Rural interests, including national park and tourism interests, need to be systematically considered in the establishment of broader national policies (chapter 1).
16. A national tourism policy that deals only with recreation and focuses only on gateway communities will fail. Any policy focused on a single industry sector will likely become obsolete. Hence, tourism and development policies must be interrelated, broad-ranging, and comprehensive (chapter 1).
17. States, rural regions, and gateway communities need to develop regulatory frameworks bolstered with market incentives and other nonregulatory tools for guiding development, while protecting local and regional assets including national parks (chapter 9).

Necessary Changes to Park Management

18. Park managers need to recognize the interdependence of all forms of natural resource management. To succeed, resource management will have to be considered in an ecosystem context in which resource development, conservation, and protection are considered simultaneously (chapter 10).
19. Park management must involve a continual process of negotiation between stakeholders and should be conceptualized as fluid and dynamic (chapter 7).

20. More effective and inclusive means of coordinating management activities on ecologically interconnected public and private lands need to be developed and implemented (chapter 9).
21. Management of protected areas should be applied to control uses so that relative compatibility of use is maximized (chapter 2).
22. Restoration has been an art and principle practiced by the NPS. The NPS needs to export this experience beyond the boundaries of parks, to assist other public and private entities in incorporating such knowledge into their management practices (chapter 10).
23. NPS planning must recognize and respond to local, regional, and national laws and policies, and international treaties and conventions. Planning should also reflect an understanding of resource-use patterns, social change, and economic forces that are directly or indirectly acting on parks (chapter 13).

Necessary Changes within the National Park Service

24. The NPS must provide support for superintendents and their staffs who aggressively seek regional solutions for development issues that threaten park resources or affect resources outside park boundaries yet are critical to the ecological or historical integrity of park units (chapter 12).
25. Skilled NPS personnel will be essential if the NPS is to engage local community and regional leaders in community/park resource management and rural development planning (chapters 1 and 11).
26. The NPS needs to design and implement a leadership development program for future leaders in the NPS that reflects the role of national parks in rural development. This program should include (a) early identification of employees with leadership capabilities; (b) training that focuses on authorities available for dealing with transboundary issues; (c) training to provide future leaders with skills in negotiation, conflict resolution, communication, and facilitation; and (d) understanding of programs that can aid gateway communities seeking planning and technical assistance (chapter 12).
27. In Alaska, the NPS had little experience in working constructively and continuously with local people. These locals (a) viewed parks as their homeland and as a source of food; (b) believed it was their right (not a legal privilege) to use natural resources within parks as needed; and (c) had a legal basis for continual consumptive uses of park resources. To successfully carry out its subsistence-related mission with local communities, the NPS needs specially recruited and trained employees if ongoing community/agency linkages are to be maintained (chapter 7).
28. The artificial barriers the NPS has erected over past decades separating park staff from technical assistance program staff should be removed, and the two functions blended together in ways that benefit both (chapter 11).

Increasing NPS/Local Cooperation

29. In establishing its policy toward rural development, the NPS must consider that (a) the NPS is an interdependent part of communities and regions; (b) education of and by local communities is required; and (c) while managing for resource preservation and appropriate uses, the NPS must also cooperate with its neighbors on activities that do not compromise the agency's core mission (chapter 11).

30. The challenges of rural development call for effective leadership and collaboration between public land managers and outside partners—including regional residents and national stakeholders. Without proactive, collaborative planning, national parks will most likely become ineffective islands of seminatural habitat surrounded by a sea of development (chapter 9).

31. The NPS must accept the responsibility to reach outside its boundaries and work with adjacent rural communities. The NPS must take its expertise to communities in a cooperative spirit. Unless the NPS steps outside its boundaries, there is little chance that it can influence what goes on there (chapter 11).

32. By working with community leaders, the NPS has an affirmative role to play in preserving the overall character and lifestyle of adjacent rural areas while maintaining opportunities for planned growth to provide good jobs for local residents. Planning must involve the community, and be honored by those authorized to enact the plan through zoning and other governmental actions (chapter 11).

Increasing Collaboration for Decision Making

33. No land-use decision around a national park is exclusively local or national, but always has implications for or effects on both. The NPS should realize its responsibility to actively participate in local land-use decisions, and should similarly be aware of the effects of its own decisions on its neighbors, involving them in the process of decision making (chapter 11).

34. Traditionally, public land resources have not been managed by rural communities, but instead by state and federal officials. Linking the natural resource base of rural regions with sustainable forms of economic development will require greater input from local interests. Hence, managing the natural resource base of parks, protected areas, and other public lands requires greater emphasis on community-based decision making (chapter 2).

35. The common pattern of making decisions behind closed doors and airing policies in public hearings (often acrimonious) is ineffective. Success hinges on the ability of park managers to work with and through local and regional initiatives. Partnerships that originate from outside the park are valuable and should be encouraged (chapter 9).

36. Managers of national parks should be expected to understand not only the

environmental aspects of national parks, but also the social and cultural contexts within which policies and programs are implemented. The current technical and top-down management approach of park professionals needs to be modified (chapter 4).

A Modest Set of Proposals for National Parks and Rural Development

If the relationship between national parks and rural development is to be well understood and wisely managed, concrete actions should take place that enable the policy recommendations of the authors to be put into practice. Hence, we propose a modest set of actions to encourage the integration of national parks and rural development. Some proposals require federal action at the national level others require grassroots support at the local level. We believe these actions could significantly improve the relationship between national parks and the rural regions that surround them, and lead to sound park management and sustainable rural development.

A Policy Summit on National Parks, Tourism, and Rural Development

Many of the policy recommendations made by the authors in this book require action at the national level. These actions would significantly affect state, regional, and local interests. A policy summit on national parks, tourism, and rural development is proposed. This summit would evaluate and propose revisions to existing policy, and propose new policy as needed. It would bring together rural development, national park, and conservation interests. It would include the full range of affected groups—including gateway community, regional, state, tribal, and federal representatives.

The summit would focus on creating complementary policies to stimulate sustainable rural development near parks, engage the tourism industry, and protect park values. It would identify and address conflicting or competing policies that make cooperation and progress unnecessarily difficult. The summit should probably be called by the federal government, but should be organized in collaboration with local communities and other stakeholders. The secretaries of the departments of Interior, Agriculture, and Commerce should take a leadership role in the summit, as well as governors of the affected states. Advance preparation should be intense, inclusive, and participatory. The summit should produce specific recommendations for legislation and policy, identify responsibilities, declare timelines for action, and commit agencies to assessing progress.

Increased Cooperation among Federal Agencies

A critical institutional challenge to improved public land management is the inability of federal agencies to effectively and continually cooperate among themselves. The causes are legion—varying authorities, regulations and policies, different missions and expected outcomes, varying resources (both human and financial), as well as vastly different agency cultures and traditions. Often the basic lack of communication is a source of conflict and inefficiency.

Nevertheless, there must be increased cooperation among federal agencies charged with management of public lands and/or rural development. In some cases, the largest barrier to regional rural development and protected land management is the lack of cooperation among federal agencies. Much can be shared. The U.S. Forest Service, for example, has significant experience in working with local communities, much of it useful to the NPS as it expands its role in rural development. Such cooperation should not only be encouraged, but required.

Various tools for agency cooperation should be engaged. Memorandums of understanding (MOUs) can commit the agencies to cooperative activities. Congressional oversight, including oversight hearings, can inform Congress, focus media attention, and educate the public as to problems and progress. Congress can carefully employ its tradition of line-item appropriations language. Such political strategy can, if effective, direct agency efforts, and if poorly conceived, micromanage the federal agencies and impede progress. Presidential executive orders can provide specific direction and accountability, and unambiguously communicate an administration's intentions with regard to national parks and rural development.

In addition, the leadership of the relevant federal agencies should meet regularly on the topic of rural development, to symbolize and promote cooperation among their agencies. Leaders should include, specifically, the directors of the NPS, Bureau of Land Management, and U.S. Fish and Wildlife Service; the chief of the U.S. Forest Service; and others.

Administrative Innovation to Improve Collaboration

The institutional challenge of innovative collaboration requires additional reforms. In addition to policy revision and increased cooperation among federal agencies, there is a series of more specific federal actions that can empower park managers to engage in the kind of collaborative planning so many of this book's authors cite as the key to successful park management and rural development. These actions—often labeled "reinventing government"—have the potential to significantly reduce institutional barriers, improve working relationships, encourage new forms of shared decision making, increase accountability and public participation, and protect both public resources and private property rights.

Chief among needed reforms is careful revision of the Federal Advisory Committee Act (FACA). FACA's intent was clearly to encourage public participation in federal decision making, by strictly limiting the involvement of public interest groups, restricting the use of advisory councils and other forms of limited public involvement, and ensuring an open and public process to public participation. The results have been disappointing, and there has been a relatively steady call for necessary revisions to FACA that would free agencies to experiment with new forms of collaborative decision making, while protecting public policy from special interest control. Improving FACA would greatly enhance the ability of NPS managers to collaborate in regional planning, include regional and local interests in decision making, and increase the amount and quality of public involvement.

Other innovations are worthy of consideration. Training of NPS managers, focused at the superintendent level, should be increased and expanded to include the skills of collaboration and technical understanding of rural development strategies. Training should not be limited to traditional NPS approaches, but include the training expertise of community development professionals. NPS strategic general management and resource management plans should formally include objectives and performance measures related to the role of national parks in regional and local development.

Creation of an NPS Office of Rural Development

While administrative reforms, increased training, and improved planning can improve the NPS's role in rural development, a specific organizational function is both useful and practical. An NPS Office of Rural Development should be established. Its responsibilities should include (a) technical assistance to rural regions and gateway communities; (b) technical assistance to parks, park clusters (a recent NPS organizational layer), and NPS administrative regions; (c) training of park professionals in rural development and collaboration skills; and (d) assessment of progress in achieving sustainable rural development while protecting park values. The office should also be charged with leveraging other development programs (in both the public and private sector) to achieve NPS objectives. Its staff should include experienced park professionals and experts in rural development.

An NPS Office of Rural Development has several benefits. It focuses NPS efforts, and provides a focal point for contact by the varied range of interested parties concerned and involved with rural development. It brings together existing skills and NPS knowledge, and adds new skills and viewpoints into the NPS hierarchy. It increases NPS involvement in rural development activities, without requiring each park, cluster, or region to reinvent the skills, experience, and assistance capability of a focused office.

Funds and staff for an NPS Office of Rural Development can and should be modest, reflecting the need for careful investment and the use of scarce resources. Only as the office demonstrates its usefulness, and its services are employed to improve park management and rural development, should expansion to the regional level be considered.

Investment in Social Science Research

The rural development literature abounds with information on linkages of communities to agriculture and forestry, and the implications for rural development. In contrast, parks as a centerpiece of rural development are relatively unstudied by the social science community in the United States. The opportunity exists—as well as responsibility—for the NPS and other interested stakeholders to gain a more complete understanding of the relations of parks and neighboring communities. Hence, the NPS should collaborate with other organizations in developing a broad-based research effort on national parks and rural development.

Such an investment would bring to bear the expertise of all the social science disciplines. For example, community economics can be used to examine the economic engines of growth, economic diversity, and community stability. Geographers can examine and describe the influence of parks in the transition of regional landscapes and the impact of rural development on park resources. Sociologists can contribute an understanding of social and demographic change, as well as the importance of a sense of place. Political science can be used to better understand the institutional and structural changes that communities undergo as a tourism economy unfolds.

The research effort should be applied, generating empirical evidence, and providing useable knowledge for park management and rural development. The research must result in improved technical assistance for park managers and community leaders.

An imaginative and creative research effort should be undertaken, in collaboration with federal agencies such as the Economic Research Service, the U.S. Forest Service, and the Environmental Protection Agency. State development and tourism agencies should participate, as the research results have important significance to their work. Land-grant universities, professional societies, community organizations, tribes, foundations, and other organizations should also be involved.

The investment should begin with a research plan, collaboratively developed. The plan should include a proposed research agenda on parks and rural development (see box). It should also include a five-year action plan and budget, and a specific strategy for technology transfer and training. A necessary precursor is a comprehensive assessment of rural development, as well as community, social, and economic change. The plan should also include an inventory of available research programs (including, but not limited to, the NPS Social Science program) that can be called on for assistance.

Collaborative Pilot Projects to Demonstrate Effective Approaches to Rural Development

The NPS, along with other public land management and rural development agencies, should embark on a series of pilot projects in rural development. These projects should be designed to test emerging strategies, provide learning oppor-

Component Activities for the Sustainable Uses of Biological Resources Project, Chocó Forests, Ecuador

INSTITUTIONAL STRENGTHENING AND ORGANIZATIONAL DEVELOPMENT
- Training and technical assistance to NGOs and communities
- Planning and implementation of community natural resource management plans
- Budget support to NGOs
- Community park guard program and forestry policy initiatives
- Development of local administrative and enforcement authority

POLICY AND LEGAL ISSUES
- Training of paralegals in participating communities
- Legal recognition for traditional lands and community organizations
- Facilitation of grassroots and national-level policy changes
- Environmental legal assistance to local authority and communities

SUSTAINABLE LAND-USE MANAGEMENT
- Preparation of regional natural resource management plan
- Preparation of community-level natural resource management plans for traditional lands
- Design, implementation, and monitoring of community-based commercial forestry operations
- Training of paratechnicians in small-animal husbandry, ecological forestry, and agroforestry
- Technical assistance in forest management to local authority
- Development of environmental impact methods for community natural resource management plans

COMMERCIALIZATION AND MARKETING
- Economic and marketing strategies for timber and nontimber products
- Promotion and sales for community businesses
- Budget support for product ecological certification

BIODIVERSITY MONITORING
- Assessment of changes in natural vegetation cover in landscapes in and outside protected reserves
- Assessment of ecological effects from utilization of timber and nontimber forest products
- Assessment of biological change within and outside protected reserves
- Training of community-based parabiologists
- Development of community park guard program
- Publishing and distribution of biodiversity and conservation documents by local participants

Potential Social Science Research Questions

- What are the influences (social, cultural, and economic) of a gateway community located adjacent to a park on the natural/cultural boundary of a park?
- How have parks influenced change in occupational structure, population structure, and other characteristics of gateway communities over time?
- As lands adjacent to parks become more popular as amenity-rich residential locations, what are the implications for park resources, community stability, and change?
- What linkages (both economic and noneconomic) can be established between parks and neighboring communities (i.e., what is the relationship between parks and neighboring communities)?
- How do parks shape—and how are they are shaped by—the regional landscapes of which they are a part?

tunities for NPS managers and local interests, and demonstrate to other parks, regions, and communities what works and what does not.

Such pilot projects might address infrastructure and transportation planning, new forms of collaborative decision making, economic diversification of gateway communities, education and job training, shared resource management, and other rural development efforts. The projects should take place in a varied set of park settings, from the large landscape-level national parks in the western states, to smaller historic sites in the eastern states.

Funding for these projects should be a shared responsibility among the NPS, other federal agencies, and local interests. Locations should be carefully chosen. Regional and gateway community enthusiasm, and NPS and park superintendent support should be the essential criteria for selection. Each project should include a planned and significant evaluation effort, so that the lessons can be systematically learned and communicated.

Such evaluation will require careful consideration of what constitutes success in rural development and park management. Economic prosperity, ecosystem integrity, high-quality visitor experiences, vibrant gateway communities, and fiscal efficiency may all be important factors in defining rural development success. The proposed pilot projects should be evaluated against a comprehensive set of indicators carefully and inclusively established. The weight given to each factor is critical, as is wide involvement in the process of defining successful development.

The Future

This is a critical time of change for the national parks, their gateway communities, and rural America. The new millennium confronts an America very different from that of its historical past. For many national parks the new century hosts a nation vastly different from the one that witnessed their inception. It is an urbanized, suburbanized, and sprawled America, electronically wired and furiously paced. It is an America both hardworking and hedonistic, aging and wistfully young.

In such a nation and such a time, the national parks are likely to be even more precious, especially if they can remain largely "unimpaired for future generations." Yet we as a people cannot, and will not, hold things constant—and this includes the national parks. Growth, development, and change are core to our national culture and our future as a people. The development of the rural regions and gateway communities surrounding the national parks will inevitably continue and intensify.

Hence, the fates of national parks and these rural places, linked by the needs of preservation and rural development, are intertwined. How this relationship is managed over the next decade is likely to determine the future of the national parks. And to the extent that national parks are essential elements of the American experience, the fate of the parks is our own.

Appendix I
National Park Service Acronyms

IHS	International Historic Site
NB	National Battlefield
NBP	National Battlefield Park
NBS	National Battlefield Site
NHP	National Historical Park
NHP & Pres	National Historical Park and Preserve
NHRes	National Historical Reserve
NHS	National Historic Site
NL	National Lakeshore
NM	National Monument
NM & Pres	National Monument and Preserve
NMP	National Military Park
NMem	National Memorial
NP	National Park
NP & Pres	National Park and Preserve
NPres	National Preserve
NR	National River
NRA	National Recreational Area
NRR	National Recreational River
NRRA	National River and Recreational Area
NRES	National Reserve
NS	National Seashore
NSR	National Scenic River/Riverway
NST	National Scenic Trail
PKWY	Parkway
SSO	System Support Office
SRR	Scenic and Recreational River
WR	Wild River
WSR	Wild and Scenic River

Appendix II

A Guide to Federal Programs for Rural Community Conservation and Economic Development Projects

Karen Steer and Nina Chambers

A common theme emphasized throughout this book is that parks must become integrated with their surrounding communities. Conservation of natural resources inside and outside park borders should be planned in coordination with rural development objectives. Presented in this appendix is a guide to federal programs that can support conservation and development projects in gateway communities.

The guide was originally compiled as a resource for gateway community leaders and National Park Service managers to help identify opportunities for funding and technical assistance (*Gateway Opportunities: A Guide to Federal Programs for Rural Gateway Communities;* NPS 1998). The following tables are organized by the various federal agencies mandated to assist community economic development and support national conservation priorities. The tables describe current programs and the types of activities each agency assists. While the programs may change in funding level and availability, the guide represents a fairly comprehensive listing as of 2000.

It should be noted that in addition to these federal programs, states and many nonprofit community organizations have similar technical and financial assistance programs that are not listed.

Programs within the Corporation for National and Community Service

tel: (202) 606-5000, or (800) 942-2677
http://www.cns.gov
1201 New York Avenue, NW
Washington, DC 20575

Agency	Program	Description	Examples of Funded Projects	Contact Information
Corporation for National and Community Service	AmeriCorps	Provides project grants and volunteers for community service projects.	Support for park volunteers in conflict resolution; design and maintenance of nature areas; habitat restoration; other environmental and community service projects	(see above)
	Learn and Serve America School and Community-based Programs	Provides project grants to encourage elementary and secondary schools and community-based agencies to create, develop, and offer service and learning opportunities for school-age youth; coordinates adult volunteers in schools to introduce young people to a broad range of careers and encourage them to pursue further education and training.	Student participation in environmental science and conservation activities; historical restoration projects	
	Volunteers in Service to America (VISTA)	Provides full-time, full-year AmeriCorps/VISTA volunteers to local organizations for defined tasks that address the problems of poverty. Volunteer projects improve the community's ability to solve its own problems.	Volunteer support for community-based initiatives	

Programs within the Department of Agriculture

http://www.usda.gov
1400 Independence Avenue, SW
Washington, DC 20250

Agency	Program	Description	Examples of Funded Projects	Contact Information
Farm Service	Conservation Reserve Program	Offers long-term rental payments and cost-share assistance to establish long-term resource conservation on sensitive cropland or marginal pastureland. This includes measures to reduce soil erosion, improve water quality, and enhance and restore wildlife habitat.	Conservation of sensitive farmland; soil, water, and wildlife protection	tel: (202) 720-5295 http://www.fsa.usda.gov
Forest Service	Heritage Resources Program	Provides assistance to protect and restore heritage resources that are available for the education and use of current and future generations; to increase visitor satisfaction through awareness and participation in inventory, restoration, and protection from vandalism.	Inventory, restoration, and protection of cultural resources	tel: (202) 205-1389 http://www.fs.gov
	National Forest–dependent Rural Communities Program	Provides assistance to communities located in or near national forests, and economically dependent on forest resources, which are faced with acute economic problems associated with federal or private-sector resource management decisions and policies. Financial aid is extended to these communities to help them develop strategic plans to	Development of nonfarm small businesses; recreation and tourism development; farmers' market establishment; timber stand improvement planning; marketing activities; planning for value-added production; environmental restoration jobs for unemployed farmers and loggers	

(continues)

283

Programs within the Department of Agriculture (*Continued*)

Agency	Program	Description	Examples of Funded Projects	Contact Information
		diversify the economic base and to improve the economic, social, and environmental well-being of rural areas. This program is available only to counties within 100 miles of U.S. Forest Service lands that are at least 15% dependent on natural resources, and in towns with populations no greater than 10,000.		
	Rural Community Assistance Program	Provides technical and financial assistance to foster sustainable rural economic development and resource management through wise use of forest resources.	Broad-based assistance to help communities capitalize on their potential to diversify and expand their economies through natural resource conservation within three program areas: rural development, economic recovery, and economic diversification	
	Rural Development Grants	Provides economic development planning grants, technical assistance, and information to help communities address long-term economic problems.	Development of new technologies and alternative forest product industries; sustainability and marketing assistance for special forest products (such as herbs, mushrooms, moss, and pine needles); value-added development of such industries as furniture manufacturing	
General Jurisdiction	Rural Community Advancement Program	Provides support for statewide strategic planning, coordination, and development activities, and collaborative efforts by state and local communities.	Consolidated funding for direct and guaranteed water and waste disposal loans and grants; solid waste management grants; community facility land and grants	tel: (202) 720-2847

Natural Resources Conservation Service	Conservation Operations Program	Provides technical assistance to land users, communities, and government agencies in planning and implementing conservation activities.	Assistance in developing community-based conservation and management plans; technical assistance to improve conservation practices	tel: (202) 720-1845 http://www.ncg.nrcs.usda.gov
	Environmental Quality Incentives Program	Provides technical, financial, and educational assistance for environmental enhancement to participating farmers and ranchers facing serious threats to soil, water, and related natural resources.	Soil, water, and natural resource conservation on farmlands	
	Farmland Protection Program	Provides funds to purchase conservation easements in order to limit nonagricultural uses of productive farmland.	Conservation easements on threatened farmlands	tel: (202) 720-2847 http://www.ncg.nrcs.usda.gov
	Forestry Incentives Program	Technical and financial assistance is given to plant trees on private, nonindustrial lands, and to establish timber industry improvements.	Tree planting	
	Resource Conservation and Development Program	Initiated in 1962, this grassroots, multiagency collaboration provides technical assistance and small grants to plan, develop, and implement projects that meet the environmental, economic, and social needs of an area. An RC&D council is formed by local volunteers with a coordinator assigned to them. The following four areas are emphasized: (1) natural resource conservation; (2) resource development; (3) community/economic/business development; and (4) environmental education. There are currently 315 RC&D areas.	Assistance to cooperatively owned businesses; development of a revolving loan fund for community projects; workshops in nonprofit management, grant management, land-use planning; community center development; wetlands protection; tourism conferences and planning events; and stream habitat restoration	

(continues)

Programs within the Department of Agriculture (*Continued*)

Agency	Program	Description	Examples of Funded Projects	Contact Information
	Small Watershed and Flood Prevention Program	Provides cost-sharing grants and technical assistance to protect, manage, improve, and develop water and related land resources of a watershed.	Wetlands creation and restoration; protection of water and fish habitat; watershed survey and management	tel: (202) 720-3527 http://www.ncg.nrcs. usda.gov
	Watershed Surveys and Planning	Provides technical and financial assistance to federal, state, and local agencies for coordinating water programs. These include programs that help solve problems of upstream rural community flooding, water quality related to agricultural nonpoint sources, wetlands preservation, and drought management for agricultural and rural communities.	Watershed surveys; watershed protection management plans	
	Wetlands Reserve Program	Voluntary program to restore wetlands, improve habitat, and protect waterfowl. Landowners establish conservation easements and receive the agricultural value of land.	Conservation easements to restore wetlands on private lands; wetlands restoration and conservation	
	Wildlife Habitat Incentives Program (WHIP)	Voluntary program to develop and improve wildlife habitat on private land through technical assistance and cost-sharing grants. NRCS offers financial incentives for landowners to develop habitat for fish and wildlife.	Restoration and conservation of wildlife habitat on private lands	
Research Education and Economics; Cooperative State Research,	Communities in Economic Transition	Targeted to increase jobs in rural communities, this program offers strategic planning for economic development, and technical assistance for enterprise development and management.	Planning and assistance for tourism development, home-based businesses, value-added forestry, youth employment, and small businesses	tel: (202) 720-2810 http://www.reeusda.gov http://www.econ.ag.gov

Education and Extension Service (CSREES)	Cooperative Extension Service	Provides grants to land-grant institutions to conduct scientific investigations on issues critical to the economic, agricultural, societal, health/safety, and environmental progress of rural areas.	Use of local land-grant universities to conduct economic, agricultural, environmental, and health and safety analyses for communities	
	Fund for Rural America	Provides extension services through land-grant universities and extension offices, natural and social science research, and technical assistance	Research-based technical assistance (both natural and social science research)	
	Rural, Economic and Social Development	Works through land-grant universities to apply social science research to issues and problems prominent in rural areas.	Applied social science research	
Rural Community Facilities Development Division: Rural Housing Service	Community Facilities Loans	Provides loans to construct, enlarge, extend, or improve community facilities that provide essential services.	Construction of municipal buildings and schools, social and cultural facilities, and other public infrastructure	tel: (202) 720-1490 http://www.rurdev.usda.gov/rhs
Rural Development: Office of Community Development	Empowerment Zone/Enterprise Community	The EZ/EC Program is a community-based sustainable development initiative for economic revitalization that provides competitive community block grants for comprehensive strategic plans. Plans include economic, physical, environmental, community, and human development projects. There are currently 30 ECs and 3 EZs in rural areas. EZ/EC designation entitles the community to millions of dollars in funding, as well as the authorization to apply for benefits from other department programs.	Venture capital fund to invest in businesses located within EZs; development of home-based businesses; construction of fire stations; expansion of local library and increased telecommunications capacity; promotion of community beautification through recycling programs; establishment of youth recreation centers; leadership classes; training of community outreach organizers; development of rural transportation systems; job training workshops	tel: (202) 619-7981, or (800) 645-4712, or (800) 851-3403 http://www.ezec.gov

(continues)

Programs within the Department of Agriculture (*Continued*)

Agency	Program	Description	Examples of Funded Projects	Contact Information
Rural Development: Rural Business Cooperative Service	Business and Industrial Loans	Provides guaranteed bank loans for public, private, or cooperative organizations, Indian tribes, and individuals in rural areas for improvement of economic and environmental characteristics of the rural community.	Catfish farming; agribusiness expansion; development of radio stations; tourism infrastructure development; conservation-based microenterprise development	tel: (202) 690-4730 http://www.rurdev.gov
	Rural Business Enterprise Grants	Provides investment in human and physical resources of the community to develop land, create assistance programs, encourage business growth, and create jobs.	Eco-industrial park development; small-business development; construction of recycling operations; conservation-based microenterprise development	
	Rural Cooperative Development Grants	Provides grants that improve economic conditions in rural areas by promoting the development and commercialization of new services and products that can be produced or provided in rural areas. Grants can be used for technical assistance and training for small businesses, and for analyzing business opportunities.	Microenterprise development and technical assistance; identification and feasibility studies for business opportunities	
	Rural Economic Development Loans and Grants	Provides loans and grants to projects that promote rural economic development and job creation, including funding for project feasibility studies and start-up costs.	Water and sewage treatment plants; income-generation projects	
Rural Development: Rural Utilities Service	Technical Assistance and Training Grants	Provides project grants to identify and evaluate solutions to water and wastewater disposal problems.	Assistance and training for water and waste disposal problems	tel: (202) 720-9637 http://www.usda.gov/rus
	Water and Waste Disposal Systems for Rural Communities	Provides direct and guaranteed loans for the installation, repair, improvement, or expansion of rural water facilities.	Water and waste disposal facilities	

Programs within the Department of Commerce

http://www.doc.gov
1400 Constitution Avenue, NW
Washington, DC 20230

Agency	Program	Description	Examples of Funded Projects	Contact Information
Economic Development Administration	Local Technical Assistance Program	Provides project grants to enlist the resources of designated university centers in promoting economic development; support demonstration projects; and disseminate information on economic development issues of national significance.	Use of local university resources to research economic opportunities in the community, and to develop feasibility studies on innovative projects	tel: (202) 482-2127 http://www.doc.gov/eda
	Planning Program for Economic Development Districts, Indian Tribes, and Redevelopment Areas	Provides grants to conduct economic development planning and implementation of programs designed to create or retain full-time permanent jobs and income for the unemployed and underemployed in areas of economic distress.	Establishment of vocational-technical facilities and skill centers for training; development of new businesses; economic diversification; assistance for planning activities through hired personnel and technical support	
	Public Works and Facilities Development Program	Grants are provided to help distressed communities attract new industry, encourage business expansion, diversify local economies, and generate long-term, private-sector jobs.	Construction of water and sewage facilities and other public infrastructure; construction of social and cultural facilities; renovation of historic buildings; construction of tourism facilities and vocational training centers	
National Telecommunications and Information Administration	Public Telecommunications Facilities Program	Provides matching grants to nonprofit organizations to improve the quality of, and public access to, education, health care, public safety, and other community-based services.	Improvement of rural community access to education, health care, public safety, and other community services	tel: (202) 482-2048 http://www.ntia.doc.gov

289

Programs within the Department of Education

tel: (202) 205-8270, or (800) USA-LEARN, or (800) 872-5327
http://www.ed.gov
600 Independence Avenue, SW
Washington, DC 20202-7320

Agency	Program	Description	Examples of Funded Projects	Contact Information
Office of Vocational and Adult Education	Adult Education State Grant Program	Provides grants to develop teacher-training programs and small business demonstration projects.	Development of teacher-training and special demonstration projects	(see above)

Programs within the Department of Housing and Urban Development

tel: (202) 708-2290
http://www.hud.gov
451 Seventh Street, SW
Washington, DC 20410

Agency	Program	Description	Examples of Funded Projects	Contact Information
Community Planning and Development	Community Development Block Grants (CDBG)/ Economic Development Initiative	Provides project grants, workshops, and training to help administer local community block grant programs.	Housing, infrastructure, and business loans; grants, workshops, and training to help administer local community block grants	(see above)
	Youthbuild Program	Provides grants to economically disadvantaged young adults to obtain education, employment skills, and meaningful on-site construction work experience. Preference is given to EZ/EC-designated areas.	Youth training for construction	

290

Programs within the Department of the Interior

http://www.doi.gov
1849 C Street, NW
Washington, DC 20240

Agency	Program	Description	Examples of Funded Projects	Contact Information
Bureau of Land Management	Recreation and Cultural Resource Management	Provides project grants, facilities, equipment, and training to manage and preserve recreation and cultural resource values of public lands and to increase public awareness and appreciation of these values. This program is applicable only to lands administered by the BLM.	Leave-no-trace program; fishing, travel, and tourism activities; cooperative interagency visitor services; funding for archaeological training and research; interpretive signs for cultural sites	tel: (202) 452-5134 http://www.blm.gov
Fish and Wildlife Service	Coastal Wetlands Conservation Grants Program	Provides matching grants to coastal states for the acquisition, restoration, or enhancement of coastal wetlands, which must be administered for long-term conservation benefits.	Coastal wetlands restoration and conservation	tel: (703) 358-2201 http://www.fws.gov/cep/cwgcover.html
	Cooperative Endangered Species Conservation Fund	Provides grants to state agencies to develop programs for endangered and threatened species conservation. This includes land acquisition, protection, and public education. State agencies are required to have a cooperative agreement with the DOI to participate.	Program development for species and habitat protection; land acquisition for endangered species protection	tel: (703) 358-2171 http://www.fws.gov/r9endspp/endspp.html
	North American Wetlands Conservation Grants	Provides matching funds for federal, state, local, and private projects focusing on wetlands acquisition, restoration, and enhancement.	Wetlands restoration and conservation	tel: (703) 358-1784 http://www.fws.gov/r9nawwo/index.html

(continues)

Programs within the Department of the Interior (*Continued*)

Agency	Program	Description	Examples of Funded Projects	Contact Information
	Partners for Fish and Wildlife	Provides partial funding and technical assistance to private landowners through cooperative agreements to restore wetlands, grasslands, riparian areas, and other habitats; to conserve fish and wildlife and provide opportunities for public enjoyment through nonconsumptive activities; and to establish partnerships with other agencies.	Habitat restoration and conservation; development of wildlife-related recreation opportunities	tel: (703) 358-2201 http://www.fws.gov/r9 dchpfw/index.html
	Sport Fish Restoration (Wallop-Breaux Program)	Provides funds to acquire and improve sport fish habitat, conduct aquatic education, and develop boat ramps, fishing piers, pumpout facilities, and other fisheries-related recreational facilities.	Sport fish habitat conservation and fishing recreation facilities	tel: (703) 358-2156 http://fa.r9.fws.gov/
	Wildlife Restoration (Pittman-Robertson Program)	Provides grants to restore or manage wildlife populations and the provision of public use of these resources. This includes land acquisition and research. Grants must be administered through state fish and wildlife agencies.	Wildlife restoration; land acquisition for wildlife populations and recreational use	
National Park Service	Challenge Cost-Share Program	Established to broaden opportunities for nonfederal involvement in NPS activities. This program provides matching grants for projects on park lands or in support of NPS programs outside park lands.	Historic and archeological site restoration; scientific research; park trail maintenance; interpretive exhibits; summer youth employment	tel: (202) 343-9577 http://www.nps.gov
	Historic Preservation Fund Grants-in-Aid	Provides matching grants to states for the identification, evaluation, and protection of historic properties. This includes surveying, preservation planning, improvement of local	GIS cultural resource layer (Pacific Northwest); historic rehabilitation tax credit program; videotape production; historic building restoration	tel: (202) 343-8167

Program	Description	Contact
	historic preservation ordinances, support for technical or professional administrative assistance, nomination of properties to the National Register of Historic Places, and education.	tel: (202) 565-1200 http://www.cr.nps.gov/rtca/flp/flphome.html
National Park Service Federal Lands-to-Parks Program	Provides assistance to public agencies to acquire federal land for public park and recreation use.	Purchase of federal lands for recreation and park facilities, including interpretive centers, picnic areas, and community gardens
Outdoor Recreation Acquisition, Development and Planning (Land and Water Conservation Fund Grants)	Provides financial assistance to states and political subdivisions for the preparation of statewide comprehensive outdoor recreation plans (SCORP) that identify needs for conservation and development of outdoor recreation resources and objectives (state program), as well as the acquisition and development of outdoor recreation areas and facilities (federal program). Facilities must be open to the general public. *Note: The state component is not currently funded.*	Acquisition of federal land for development of outdoor recreation areas and facilities; construction of picnic areas, campgrounds, and bike trails; other recreation projects	tel: (202) 565-1133 http://www.cr.nps.gov/lwcf/lwcf.htm
Park and Recreational Area Programs	Coordinates with other agencies to inventory and study public park, parkway, and recreational area programs not under the jurisdiction of USDA.	Interagency planning for recreation programs	tel: (202) 565-1200
Rivers, Trails and Conservation Assistance Program	Provides staff assistance to support government and citizen partnerships to increase the number of rivers, trails, and landscapes protected. Programs include: (1) Rails-to-Trails Program, which converts old railway beds to recreation trails; (2) Heritage Partnership Program, in	Provision of technical and some financial assistance to communities to construct trails and other recreation areas	tel: (202) 565-1200 http://www.cr.nps.gov/rtca

(continues)

293

Programs within the Department of the Interior (*Continued*)

Agency	Program	Description	Examples of Funded Projects	Contact Information
		which communities designated as Heritage Partners receive technical support for project planning and implementation; (3) American Heritage Rivers Initiatives, which support community-led efforts relating to rivers that spur economic revitalization, protect natural resources, and preserve historic and cultural heritage; and (4) other RTCA programs that support river corridors management, technical assistance to watershed associations, river greenways development, and wild and scenic rivers.		
United States Geological Survey	State Partnerships	Provides project grants to develop partnerships with state agencies and institutions to gather, analyze, and distribute biological science information needed for natural resource management decision making.	Development of partnerships with state agencies and other institutions to gather and distribute science information for natural resource decision making	tel: (703) 648–4260 http://www.usgs.gov

Programs within the Department of Transportation

tel: (202) 366-0660
http://www.dot.gov
400 Seventh Street, SW
Washington, DC 20590

Agency	Program	Description	Examples of Funded Projects	Contact Information
Federal Highway Administration	Federal-Aid Highway Program	Provides grants to improve public roads, restore roadside beauty, facilitate wetland mitigation, and ensure habitat protection.	Roadside beautification; wetlands protection	(see above)

Federal Highway Administrative Funds	Provides funds to develop and maintain recreational trails, restore areas damaged by recreation impacts, develop trailside and trailhead facilities, provide features that facilitate the access and use of trails by people with disabilities, acquire easements for trails or trail corridors, and construct new trails crossing federal lands.	Trail construction, special access trails, trailside and trailhead facilities
Federal Lands Highway Program	Provides access to and within national forests, national parks, and Indian lands.	Facilities for pedestrians and bicyclists; trail construction and maintenance
Recreational Trail Program	Provides funds to state agencies for provision and maintenance of recreational trails. Trails and trail-related projects must be identified in, or further a specific goal of, the Statewide Comprehensive Outdoor Recreation Plan (SCORP), required by the Land and Water Conservation Fund Act. This program will soon be part of the Federal-Aid Highway Program.	Acquisition of land for trails
Scenic Byways Program	Provides funds for pedestrian and bicycle trails along highways.	Construction of scenic byways; pedestrian and bicycle trail facilities
Surface Transportation Program, Transportation Enhancement Activities	Provides funds to state and local governments for water-related projects, wetland mitigation, landscaping, trails, historic preservation, and other projects.	Scenic beautification; pedestrian and bicyclist facilities; trail maintenance; acquisition of scenic easements and historic sites; restoration of historic transportation buildings, structures, and facilities; archaeological planning and research

Programs within the Environmental Protection Agency

tel: (202) 260-2090
http://www.epa.gov
401 M Street, SW
Washington, DC 20460

Agency	Program	Description	Examples of Funded Projects	Contact Information
Office of Air and Radiation	Sustainable Development Challenge Grants	Provides project grants to help catalyze community-based and regional projects that promote sustainable development to improve environmental quality and economic prosperity. An objective of this program is to build partnerships that increase a community's long-term capacity to protect the environment through sustainable development.	Sustainable forestry; SmartWood certification program; other projects that link environmental sustainability and economic prosperity	tel: (202) 260-6226, or (202) 260-6812 http://www.epa.gov/oar
Office of Environmental Education	Environmental Education Grants Program	Provides grants for projects which design, demonstrate, or disseminate environmental education practices, methods, or techniques.	Education and training program development with environmental curricula; design of field methods, practices, and techniques; assessment of specific environmental issues or problems	tel: (202) 260-4965
Office of Wastewater Management	State Revolving Loan Fund Program	Provides funding for a variety of water quality programs.	A variety of both point-source and nonpoint-source water quality projects, including water treatment facilities, watershed protection, estuary habitat preservation, excavation and removal of contaminated soil, soil erosion control, and streambed restoration	tel: (202) 260-7359

Office of Water	Capitalization Grants for Clean Water State Revolving Funds	Provides revolving loans to state agencies for water quality activities, such as wastewater treatment and riparian buffer protection.	Wastewater treatment loans; riparian buffer protection	tel: (202) 260-2036
	Hardship Grants Program for Rural Communities	Provides grants and technical assistance linked to Clean Water State Revolving Fund loans to fund wastewater treatment for small rural communities.	Wastewater treatment and rural sanitation	
Office of Wetlands, Oceans, and Watersheds	Five-Star Restoration Challenge Grants	This grants program is an outgrowth of President Clinton's Clean Water Action Plan. It provides modest financial assistance to support community-based wetlands and riparian restoration projects, to build diverse partnerships, and to foster local natural resource stewardship.	On-the-ground habitat restoration; education, outreach, and community stewardship	tel: (800) 832-7828
	Wetlands Protection Development Grants	Provides financial assistance to support wetlands development or enhance existing programs.	Wetlands restoration and protection	tel: (202) 260-5084

Programs within the National Endowment for the Arts

tel: (202) 682-5400
http://arts.endow.gov
1100 Pennsylvania Avenue, NW
Washington, DC 20506-0001

Agency	Program	Description	Examples of Funded Projects	Contact Information
National Foundation on the Arts and the Humanities	Promotion of the Arts Grants to Organizations and Individuals	Provides project grants to support the arts through heritage preservation, education, youth cultural education, among others.	Preservation of New Mexico's historic adobe churches; preservation of Alabama's musical tradition; mentor program to teach youth about traditional culture	(see above)

Programs within the Small Business Administration

Agency	Program	Description	Examples of Funded Projects	Contact Information
Small Business Administration		tel: (800) U-ASK-SBA, or (800) 827-5722 http://www.sbaonline.sba.gov 409 Third Street, SW Washington, DC 20416		
	Loans for Small Businesses	Provides direct loans and counseling for small businesses.	Establishment and maintenance of small businesses	(see above)
	Service Corps of Retired Executives (SCORE)	A nonprofit organization funded by SBA that provides technical assistance to small businesses through free counseling and workshops.	Business counseling and technical assistance for small businesses	
	Small Business Development Center Program (SBDC)	Provides management assistance to current and prospective small business owners by offering one-stop assistance in designated centers. There is an SBDC in every state, with a network of nearly 1,000 service locations.	Business counseling, feasibility and market studies, other business research	

About the Contributors

FRANCIS T. ACHANA is completing a Ph.D. in the Department of Forestry and Natural Resources at Purdue University and holds an M.S. in resource recreation and tourism from the University of Idaho. He is originally from Ghana. He attended the University of Ghana at Legon, where he studied modern languages (Spanish and French), and the Polytechnic University of Madrid in Spain, where he studied tourism and hotel management.

BEN ALEXANDER is the director of the Working Landscapes Program at the Sonoran Institute and works out of the Institute's Bozeman, Montana, office. Prior to working for the Sonoran Institute, Mr. Alexander worked at The Wilderness Society as a research associate. He holds a B.A. in history from Tufts University and a M.A. and M.Phil. in American studies from Yale University. His most recent publication, with Ray Rasker, is *The New Challenge: People, Commerce, and the Environment in the Yellowstone to Yukon Region.*

NINA CHAMBERS is a research associate for the National Park Service Social Science Program. She has worked for the conservation of protected areas and protected species in the United States, Latin America, and the Caribbean. Her work has included conservation and rural development planning and the involvement of local communities in natural resource management. Ms. Chambers was a contributing author to *Conservation of Biodiversity and the New Regional Planning* (1995).

DONALD R. FIELD is professor in the Departments of Forest Ecology and Management and Rural Sociology at the University of Wisconsin. Dr. Field previously served as associate dean, College of Agricultural and Life Sciences; associate director, Wisconsin Agriculture Experiment Station; and director, School of Natural Resources at Wisconsin. He served for nineteen years in the National

Park Service as research sociologist, senior scientist, chief scientist, and associate director of science in the Pacific Northwest region of the National Park Service. His current research interests focus on the relationship of national parks to adjacent social cultural landscapes.

GEORGE B. FRISVOLD is an associate extension specialist in the Department of Agricultural and Resource Economics at the University of Arizona and coeditor of the *Journal of Agricultural and Resource Economics.* He has been a visiting scholar at India's National Institute of Rural Development, a lecturer in the Department of Geography and Environmental Engineering at the Johns Hopkins University, and chief of the Resource and Environmental Policy Branch of the USDA's Economic Research Service. Dr. Frisvold served on the senior staff of the President's Council of Economic Advisers in 1995 and 1996, with responsibility for agricultural, natural resource, and international trade issues. His recent publications include *Global Environmental Change and Agriculture: Assessing the Impacts,* a collected volume edited with Betsey Kuhn.

DENNIS GLICK is the Stewardship Program director for the Greater Yellowstone Coalition. He previously directed that organization's Greater Yellowstone Tomorrow Project, which developed a long-range vision and blueprint for the 18-million-acre Greater Yellowstone Ecosystem. Mr. Glick has worked extensively on wildland protection and rural development projects both in the United States and internationally. He was the former codirector of the Wildlands and Human Needs Program of the World Wildlife Fund and the regional conservation officer for the Wildland Management Unit of CATIE in Turrialba, Costa Rica. He has published numerous articles and book chapters on issues related to ecosystem protection, community-based conservation, and national park management. He holds a B.S. from the School of Forestry of Oregon State University and an M.S. from the School of Natural Resources of the University of Michigan.

GARY PAUL GREEN is professor of rural sociology at the University of Wisconsin–Madison-Extension. His teaching, research, and outreach activities focus on community and regional development. His current research is examining the organization of local economic development in rural communities and the role of community-based organizations in job training. Dr. Green is the author of *Finance Capital and Uneven Development* (1987) and numerous journal articles.

T. DESTRY JARVIS is senior advisor to the assistant secretary, Fish and Wildlife and Parks. An appointee of President Clinton, he is responsible for advising the assistant secretary on a broad range of matters of National Park Service policy, including the fee program, Alaska lands issues, wilderness, concessions management, and others. From 1993 to 1998, he served in the Clinton administration as assistant director of the National Park Service, responsible for external affairs. He supervised the Office of Congressional and Legislative Affairs, the Office of Communications, and the Office of Tourism. In addition, he also advised the director on policy and communicated with external organizations. He served from 1989 to 1993 as the executive vice president of the Student Conservation Association Inc.; from 1972 to 1988 as vice president for policy with the National Parks Conservation Association; and from 1969 to 1972 in the U.S. Army, attaining the rank of captain, with service in Vietnam. He is a 1969 graduate in biology from the College of William and Mary.

DARRYLL R. JOHNSON is a research sociologist at the USGS, Biological Research Division, Cascadia Field Station at the College of Forest Resources, University of Washington. He has extensive research experience focusing on conventional visitors to units of the National Park System and rural residents in and around Alaska National Parks. He is coeditor of two books: *Ecosystem Management for Parks and Wilderness* (with J. K. Agee), and *Human Ecology and Climate Change: People and Resources in the Far North* (with D. L. Peterson). Mr. Johnson is the author or coauthor of over sixty technical reports dealing with human dimensions of national parks in the United States.

WILLIAM KORNBLUM is chairman of the Center for Urban Research and professor of sociology at the Graduate School of the City University of New York (C.U.N.Y.). A specialist in urban social ecology, Dr. Kornblum is currently working with the Lila Wallace Foundation and the Urban Institute on their Urban Parks Initiative. He has conducted research on national parks in metropolitan regions, including Gateway NRA, Fire Island NS, and Cape Cod NS, and is currently helping the Central Park Conservancy develop its restoration and management plans for New York's Central Park. He is the author of numerous books and monographs, including, with Terry Williams, *Uptown Kids: Struggle and Hope in the Projects* (1994), *Blue Collar Community* (1974), and *Sociology in a Changing World* (2000).

JULIE LEONES, an extension economist in the Department of Agricultural and Resource Economics at the University of Arizona, died of breast cancer on March 2, 1999. She was forty years old. During her nine years at the University of Arizona, Dr. Leones's research interests included regional impact analysis and the role of recreation and tourism in rural economies. She had been actively involved in statewide community tourism development programs and was named Arizona Cooperative Extension Faculty of the Year in 1992. Previously, Dr. Leones spent six years in the Philippines as a Peace Corps volunteer, a Fulbright-Hays scholar, and an affiliate fellow at the International Rice Research

Institute. She authored over seventy publications including journal articles, book chapters, extension publications, and the *Community Development Issues Newsletter.*

GARY E. MACHLIS is the visiting chief social scientist for the National Park Service. He is also associate vice president for research and professor of forest resources and sociology at the University of Idaho. He has been a visiting professor at Nanjing Technological College in China and at Yale University and is currently adjunct professor of public policy and urban affairs at Southern University and A&M College at Baton Rouge, Louisiana. He has written numerous articles and several books on issues of conservation, including *The State of the World's Parks* (1985), the first systematic study of threats to protected areas around the world, and, with Don Field, *On Interpretation: Sociology for Interpreters of Natural and Cultural History* (1992).

DAVE MARCOUILLER is an associate professor of urban and regional planning at the University of Wisconsin-Madison and a resource economist with the University of Wisconsin-Extension. His work focuses on the linkages between natural resources and rural economic development, with a particular interest in the mechanisms behind income generation and distribution to rural households. His recent work has been published in *Land Economics, Economic Development Quarterly,* the *Journal of Planning Literature, Tourism Economics, Forest Science,* the *Canadian Journal of Forest Research,* and the *Northern Journal of Applied Forestry.*

JOHN C. MILES is director of the Center for Geography and Environmental Social Sciences at Huxley College of Environmental Studies, Western Washington University. A former Dean of the College, Dr. Miles is the author or editor of five books, including *Guardians of the Parks: A History of the National Parks and Conservation Association.*

JOSEPH T. O'LEARY is a professor of outdoor recreation and tourism in the Department of Forestry and Natural Resources at Purdue University. His professional interests include the social behavior and travel patterns of domestic and international recreation consumers and the social impacts of recreation resource development. He has over 200 research articles and publications in a variety of journals, including *Journal of Forestry, Journal of Leisure Research, Leisure Sciences, Tourism Management,* and *Journal of Travel Research.*

HAL K. ROTHMAN is professor of history at the University of Nevada-Las Vegas, where he edits *Environmental History.* He is the author of *Devil's Bargains: Tourism in the Twentieth Century American West* (1998), which received the 1999

Western Writers of America Spur Award for Contemporary Nonfiction; *Saving the Planet: The American Response to the Environment in the Twentieth Century* (2000); *The Greening of a Nation? Environmentalism in the U.S. Since 1945* (1997); and *Preserving Different Pasts: The American National Monuments* (1989), as well as the editor of *Reopening the American West* (1998), coeditor with Mike Davis of the *Grit Beneath the Glitter: Tales from the Real Las Vegas* (2000), and with Char Miller, *Out of the Woods: Essays in Environmental History* (1997).

RICHARD B. SMITH is a former National Park Service employee. During his thirty-year career with the NPS, he served in Yellowstone NP, Yosemite NP, Grand Canyon NP, Carlsbad Caverns NM, in the NPS Washington, DC, headquarters, and in two of its regional offices in Philadelphia and Santa Fe. His last assignment with the NPS was as the associate regional director for Natural and Cultural Resources in the Southwest regional office, Santa Fe, New Mexico. Prior to joining the NPS, Smith was a U.S. Peace Corps volunteer in the National University in Asunción, Paraguay. Since his retirement in 1994, Mr. Smith has provided conservation consulting services in Latin America for the World Bank, the InterAmerican Development Bank, the U.S. Peace Corps, the United States Information Agency, the United Nations, and several private consulting firms. He has authored numerous magazine and journal articles on conservation issues in the developing world.

KAREN STEER currently works for Sustainable Northwest, in Portland, Oregon. She was an intern for the National Park Service Social Science Program as a graduate student at the Yale School of Forestry and Environmental Studies. Prior to graduate school, Karen was a U.S. Peace Corps volunteer in Honduras, where she served as a protected areas consultant and worked with communities located in the buffer zones of national parks. She was contributing author to *Collaborative Planning Beyond Park Boundaries: An Evaluation of the Gateway Community Initiative.*

GENE F. SUMMERS, a professor emeritus in the Department of Rural Sociology, University of Wisconsin-Madison, is a past president of the Rural Sociological Society and chair of that group's Task Force on Persistent Rural Poverty. He currently serves as program manager of the North American Program of the Land Tenure Center at the University of Wisconsin-Madison. His research and writing have focused on ways of reducing rural poverty, including community economic development, rural labor markets, and rural industrialization. Dr. Summers is the author or editor of fourteen books, including *Working Together for a Change: Creating Pathways from Poverty* (1997), as well as over 100 articles and chapters in books.

JAMES TOLISANO is program director for the Institute for Conservation Studies and associate professor of conservation science at the College of Santa Fe. He has worked over the last twenty years for the World Bank, United Nations, U.S. Agency for International Development, World Wildlife Fund, the Wildlife Conservation Society, and other international, national, local, and tribal organizations in more than thirty countries. Since 1994, he has been actively involved in the design, implementation, institutional development, and monitoring of the Sustainable Uses of Biological Resources Project in Ecuador. Mr. Tolisano has authored numerous articles and reports; edited *Protecting Water Quality in the National Forests* (1989), *Strategies for Quantifying In-Stream Flows: A Practical Handbook* (1990), and *Silviculture for Southwestern Forests: A Practical Handbook* (1990); and authored chapters in several books, including *Conservation Corridors in the Central American Region* (1993) and *Biodiversity and Management in the Madrean Evergreen Ecosystem* (1994).

Index